FACE
OF
NORTH
AMERICA

FACE OF

NORTH AMERICA

THE NATURAL HISTORY

OF A CONTINENT

BY Peter Farb

Illustrations by Jerome Connolly

HARPER COLOPHON BOOKS
Harper & Row, Publishers
New York and Evanston

For Oriole

First HARPER COLOPHON edition published 1968 by Harper & Row, Publishers.

Library of Congress Catalog Card Number: 62-14598

Contents

Illustrations

DRAWINGS (*Continued*)

PHOTOGRAPHS

PHOTOGRAPHS (*Continued*)

Introduction

Here is our continent: the land we live in, the country we fly over or drive through; the forests and fields and streams that we so often unthinkingly take for granted. Peter Farb has been exploring this land for many years. He has talked with all sorts of experts; studied its geology, biology, and history; looked at its surface—and at its animal and plant inhabitants—with his own clear eyes; and now he has reported on what he has found. I think that anyone, reading his account, will come out with new insights and new understandings because he has pieced together background information from many fields of knowledge. But the result is not patchwork: it is a picture of the nature of our continent, made with much love, and with attention both to detail and to the grand design.

We all know, of course, that our land is remarkably varied and often spectacular. We know about the Grand Canyon and Niagara Falls, the California redwoods, the Everglades, the Painted Desert. But often we do not know about the fascinating bits of the landscape that have been preserved in our own home regions through the expanding state and national park systems. Peter Farb has cited these different parks as examples all through his text; at the back of his book he gives a state-by-state and province-by-province list of them and the continent's other outstanding natural areas, with notes on their characteristics. As I read his account, I kept wanting to get my car out and go see for myself.

From now on, I'll keep a copy in the glove compartment of that car; there should be, it seems to me, a copy carried in every car.

We need Peter Farb to counteract the monotony of those superhighways that allow us to drive so rapidly from hither to yon. Even though the landscapes we pass are in large part the consequence of human action, the background of nature is always there. Surely we can get more enjoyment out of living if we learn to understand and appreciate the forces that formed this world we live in: the action of glaciers and rivers and mountain uplift; the way climates and soils govern natural vegetation and still channel man's use of the land. Peter Farb has sketched in this background admirably.

But often we want to get off the superhighways and look at the countryside more closely. As we have got more and more involved in our cities and suburbs, our highways and airways, it seems to me that we have come more and more to realize the need for escaping at times from the man-altered landscape that ordinarily surrounds us. Our forebears did a pretty thorough job of modifying the vegetation and animal life of the land, but here and there bits and pieces have been left for us to contemplate. This book will help us see them more clearly and with greater understanding.

This is the natural America—what is left of it. It is our heritage. Treasure it we should; but we can gain most if we also try to understand it.

MARSTON BATES

University of Michigan
Ann Arbor, Michigan

Preface

Scenery graces the American land in a way that seems haphazard. But this is not really true. Spanish moss festooning cypresses is an unmistakable earmark of the southern lowlands. The tortured outline of black spruce, molded by wind and the bite of frost, suggests the north woods, and no other place. Likewise, the silhouette of a saguaro cactus, its branches held aloft like candelabra, is the emblem of southwestern deserts. Each landscape is the result of the complex interplay of many forces throughout the long history of the continent.

The true impact of landscape upon the beholder is not the present scene alone. Rather, understanding lies in knowledge of the many forces —climate, vegetation, soil, geologic change—that have molded the scene. A swamp I know, a place of brooding, lonely beauty, attracts many people simply because of the sensory impression it offers. But there are other people who can read this landscape. They see in the surrounding ridges and the soil that this swamp is a legacy of the last ice sheet, some ten thousand years ago. They see, too, unmistakable signs of the swamp's future: that it is destined to become dry land, which in its own way will nurture yet another community of living things.

This book is about the remarkable diversity of landscapes on the North American continent and the forces that produced them. (North America, in this book, has been limited to what biogeographers label the

Nearctic realm—roughly, all the land in the western hemisphere north of the Tropic of Cancer, which passes through northern Mexico.) I have tried to avoid racing pellmell across the continent in the manner of the sightseeing guide who directs the reader's hurried attention to the right and then the left. I have concentrated on the basic forces that have sculptured and etched the land—and then tried to illustrate each of these by means of particular scenes. It is my hope that the reader's actual visits to these landscapes will be enriched, and also that the same basic principles can be applied to understanding still other similar landscapes.

Running through all the discussions is the theme of a shifting equilibrium: between land and water, between the forces of mountain-building and erosion, between the various plant and animal communities. The first section outlines geological processes that shaped the continent. The second is concerned with the seacoasts—the rim of the land which is the scene of unending assaults by waves, currents, and tides. The third section deals with water falling upon the land and with the transitory nature of lakes, rivers, and bogs. The fourth, on mountains, is an account of how even the mightiest land forms are subdued by water, in the form of glaciers, streams, frost, and rainfall. Forests, the product of an abundance of water, are discussed in the fifth section; the concluding section concerns the drylands, a domain in which water is in short supply.

I have designed this book in the hope of serving a dual purpose. It can be read at home to summon up recollections of places the reader has visited, thereby perhaps giving new insights into things already seen. It can also be used as a traveler's guide, both for learning of areas worth visiting and for answering questions about scenes encountered en route. For that reason, the index is particularly detailed, and the appendix lists natural areas that demonstrate the major themes in earth history, wildlife, and vegetation.

A project of this sort could not have been undertaken without the generous help and enthusiasm of many people. I have visited nearly all of the places mentioned in this book; everywhere my questions were answered in detail, especially by those dedicated custodians of the landscape—the employees of the National Park Service, Forest Service, and National Wildlife Refuge System, and by their Canadian counterparts. I wish to offer my appreciation to all of these people, through whose eyes I was able to see the truly significant forces that molded the landscape, and whose interpretations make even the unspectacular landscapes dramatically alive.

Many persons have made useful suggestions about what to cover in the text (and likewise about what to omit, in order to keep the book to a manageable length). I am grateful in particular to the following for their assistance, encouragement, and many courtesies:

Paul Errington, Iowa State University; E. H. Graham, Soil Conservation Service, Washington, D. C.; Daniel B. Beard, National Park Service, Washington, D. C.; James B. Craig, American Forestry Association, Washington, D. C.; Robert Porter Allen, National Audubon Society, Tavernier, Florida; Robert A. Wells, Fish and Wildlife Service, Washington, D. C.; M. N. Taylor, Trees for Tomorrow, Merrill, Wisconsin; Gilbert F. White, University of Chicago; J. M. Aikman, Iowa State University; Frank Egler, Aton Forest, Norfolk, Connecticut; and C. W. Mattison, Forest Service, Washington, D. C.

Three knowledgeable readers of the North American landscape, who offered many helpful ideas during the early stages of this book, did not live to see its completion—Frederick C. Lincoln, Fish and Wildlife Service; Hugh H. Bennett, Soil Conservation Service; and James Cullinane, National Park Service.

The lucid drawings illustrating the text are the work of Jerome Connolly, a young artist who has brought exceptional devotion as well as skill to the execution of his task. Especially helpful in obtaining the photographs were Harper Simms and F. Glennon Lloyd of the Soil Conservation Service, Robert A. Wells of the Fish and Wildlife Service, and Carlos Whiting and M. Woodbridge Williams of the National Park Service.

Lastly, for their infinite patience and sympathy I wish to thank my editors at Harper & Row, Richard McAdoo and John Macrae.

PETER FARB

PICTURE CREDITS: National Park Service, U.S. Department of the Interior: 23, 57, 101, 107, 108, 113, 141, 145, 153, 162, 163, 167, 181, 198, 199, 223, 228, 231, 232, 242, 246; Rex Gary Schmidt, U.S. Fish and Wildlife Service: 44, 55; U.S. Forest Service: 67, 82, 93, 140, 159, 196, 257; U.S. Soil Conservation Service: 151, 217, 253, 258; U.S. Geological Survey: 230; Frank Dufresne, U.S. Fish and Wildlife Service: 103; U.S. Army Corps of Engineers: 80; Oregon State Highway Department: 64, 70; New Hampshire Planning and Development Commission: 121, 123. The vegetation map of North America on page 175 is from *Textbook of Botany* by E. N. Transeau, H. C. Sampson and L. H. Tiffany, Harper & Brothers, 1953.

I

THE SHAPING
OF A CONTINENT

1 : The Sculptured Land

THE LANDSCAPE OF NORTH AMERICA one sees today is only a fragmentary scene in the long history of the continent. Man's knowledge of the continent's beginnings is sketchy; ideas of the land's future are even less certain. Today's beholder of stretches of prairie, soaring mountains, margins of seacoast can see but one stage in North America's natural history. The shapes and forms that the land has taken appear to lie at random upon the continent. The variety of their shapes is almost infinite; yet as one examines the continent, its landscapes are seen to stem from a few basic themes and are the logical developments of prodigious changes in climate and other natural forces during the continent's several billion-year history. Familiar scenes appear to possess a permanence that is not theirs. In the short span that is human life, mountains may seem formidable, but they too vanish as surely as does a seaside castle made of sand.

The surface of the North American continent is like a bowl: a rim of mountains slopes down to a broad, flattened interior. The northern rim is formed by the Innuitian and East Greenland ranges of the Arctic. The Appalachians are on the east, the Ouchita Mountains on the south. The western edge has a double rim formed by the complex of Pacific coast ranges and the Rocky Mountains. This continental bowl was wrought by forces of nature—caldrons of volcanoes, crushing pressure of sediments, ice sheets thousands of feet thick, the uplift of whole mountain chains hundreds of miles long—that make man's unlocking of the atom seem puny by comparison. The sculpturing of the bowl and the finer etching of its surface have been going on for so many hundreds of millions of years as to stagger man's everyday sense of time.

Time and powerful tools have produced a scenery remarkable for its diversity. The North American continent contains both humid rain forests and glaciers, both moss-draped southern swamps and frozen tundra. An hour's drive toward the summit of a western mountain may begin in a sun-baked desert and end in a bleak alpine wilderness. The continent is made up of many bits and pieces that are legacies from past eras in the earth's history. Much of eastern and central Canada consists of a core of rocks that has stood above the sea for more than half a billion years. The Appalachians have a long history of periods as towering mountains alternating with inundations by the sea; their northern portion has been etched by glaciers as recently as 10,000 years ago. The vast central heartland of the continent has periodically been the bottom of a shallow sea. The Rocky Mountains are a comparatively youthful chain; the Cascades are the product of still more recent lava flows and volcanic eruptions. The mountains that fringe the Pacific Ocean are still rising in many places, and the shores of the Gulf of Mexico are at present steadily encroaching upon the water. What is meadow today might have been sawtoothed peak a few million years ago; a few million years in the future it may be sawtoothed peak once more. The brief span of human history has witnessed no more than a tiny segment of the cycle of the rise and fall of the land.

North America is a low platform rising above the sea. Beyond the outlines shown in atlases, large portions of the continent slope out to sea under shallow waters. On the Atlantic coast, this drowned continental shelf extends seaward as much as a hundred miles, where it suddenly plunges into abysmal ocean depths. The famous fishing banks of the North Atlantic—such as Georges Bank off Cape Cod and the Grand Banks of Newfoundland—are merely higher parts of the continental shelf. The continental land mass is made up largely of granite—a rock originally produced by the cooling and solidifying of hot liquid rock, known as magma, at a great depth below the earth's surface. The upper layers of rock are mainly composed of sediments, which may have originated in any of several ways but in most places are derived from the weathering of previously exposed granite. Wherever the granite itself is exposed, it usually means that the layers of sedimentary rock that covered the surface at the time the granite was formed have since been eroded away.

These granite and granite-derived rocks of the continent float upon a bed of heavier rocks, the dense basalts that form the crust of the earth beneath the seas. Both the granite of the continental mass and the basalt of the sea floor rest upon a base called the Moho. The continent puts down roots to an estimated depth of twenty miles into the Moho, whereas beneath the sea floor, the Moho lies at a depth of only about four miles.

The shaping of this continental mass has resulted from the pull and give of so many forces that only the bold outlines of the story can be traced; the full details probably never will be known. The beginnings of the continent are lost in the shadowy past. Many theories to explain the origin of the continents have been put forth, but none that is agreeable to all scientists. One of the most intriguing of these theories is that of the "floating continents." This theory suggests that originally there was a single giant continent called Pangaea, composed of lightweight granite floating like an iceberg on a sea of denser basalt. Then, according to the theory, this blob of granite broke into a number of large pieces, which drifted apart. As the Americas drifted westward, the great mountain ranges of the Pacific coastal region were hurled skyward, in much the same way that the prow of a ship hurls up waves.

This theory captures the imagination for several reasons. A glance at a globe seems to verify that the continents fit together like the pieces of an immense jigsaw puzzle. The convex bulge of eastern South America, for example, appears to be a companion to the concave hollow of western Africa. Similarly, the jagged east coast of North America fits into place reasonably well with that of western Europe. Antarctica and Australia fill the gap between east Africa and southeast Asia. There are numerous objections to this theory as a complete explanation; but there is also recent evidence that the continents have drifted slightly. Among numerous other theories, one suggests a segregation, during the youth of the planet, of the lighter rocks into the continental masses and the heavier rocks into the ocean floor. Another theory postulates that the continents are the portions of the molten globe that solidified first while the planet was being formed.

No one is quite certain, either, how long the continents have existed; but there is general agreement that they were formed when the earth was young, four to five billion years ago. If it were possible to produce a motion picture that had just one frame for every five years of the long period since the continent was formed, the film would still require nearly one year to be shown. In such a film, several thousand years of earth history would flit across the screen in a few moments; the imperceptible year-to-year changes in the earth would be speeded up and made visible.

At first, the film would reveal a study in rocks and water, a colorless gray world without the least sign of life. Every few minutes or hours, the seas would part and volcanoes would rise, spewing forth lava and blotting out the scene with their clouds of ash. The earth would shudder as whole blocks of the crust were lifted, tilted, slid over other rocks. These higher blocks, attacked by wind and water, would be molded temporarily into jagged mountains, and then quickly ground down to a monotonous uniformity. But even while these peaks were being subdued, others on the continent would be rising.

The film would show the sea alternately wash across the face of the continent and then withdraw. With each advance it would create sedimentary rocks. Everyone knows that if a jar of muddy water is allowed to stand for a few days, the mud particles soon separate from the clear water and filter to the bottom. That is what happens under the seas that inundate the continent, only on a much greater scale. The sediments carried in the seas filter to the bottom and become compressed into rocks. Such rocks are named according to the kinds of sediments that compose them: sandstone is made up of sand particles, shale of mud, limestone of the compacted skeletons of marine organisms, conglomerate of a mixture of materials. When the land rises again, causing the sea to withdraw, the sedimentary rocks are hurled upward, crumpled and contorted by pressure. This higher land is attacked anew by the forces of erosion, which break it down into new sediments, out of which new rocks are formed.

As the film droned on month after month, one would see the same story told over and over again. Only toward the end of the picture, when events of the past half billion years or so were depicted, would the New World take on a barely recognizable shape. At that time, the western hemisphere probably consisted of one large land mass that included the present North America and some of the continental shelf, the land now under the Gulf of Mexico, the islands of the West Indies, and South America. The next 150 million years saw the forces of destruction working to undo this continental rise. Once again North America was ground back toward its basaltic foundations. The Atlantic Ocean swept over the northeastern parts of Canada and the United States, and the Gulf of Mexico again flooded the heartland of the continent.

A reminder of this ancient interior sea exists today in the numerous salt basins found in New York, Ontario, Ohio, and Michigan. Individual salt beds in Michigan are upwards of 500 feet in thickness, and the total depth of some of the basins is close to half a mile. Additional evidence for the periodic advance of the seas upon the continent exists in the fossils of sea creatures found atop peaks in the Rockies and Appalachians, as much as a thousand miles from the nearest ocean today. Once, these mountaintops themselves lay under the sea. Year after year, the shells of countless sea creatures rained down to the bottom, where, after more ages, their limy substance became compacted into the rock known as limestone. Later, a shift in the crust buckled this layer, and it rose as a mountain range whose peaks contained the fossils preserved in the limestone.

Some 350 million years ago, the flooded center of the continent was hemmed in by mountainous borders. The eastern shore was a land which geologists have named Appalachia; it consisted of mountains lying east of the present Appalachians and extending out into what is now the Atlantic Ocean. In the west, currents from the inland sea washed against the shores of Cascadia, a domain composed of the present far western states and provinces, as well as of some land now under the Pacific Ocean. To the south was a third land mass—Llanoria—made up of Mexico, Texas, and other land now lying under the Gulf of Mexico.

Swamps developed along the edges of this shallow sea. The climate was mild and uniform, an eternal springtime in which thick jungles of vegetation flourished. There thrived plants which are familiar today as humble growths but which then dominated the plant kingdom. Great thickets of horsetails grew luxuriantly along the edges of the swamps; ferns grew to the size of trees more than 40 feet high. Some club mosses, forerunners of what are commonly called "ground pines" today, soared to more than 125 feet and had trunks about five feet in diameter.

The borders of the inland sea were not constant. Every time the water level rose, the sea buried extensive forests under the sediments it carried. When the sea retreated, new forests were born, and these inevitably met the same fate. All this dead vegetation, as layer after layer was buried and compressed, became consolidated into the fossil fuel known today as coal. To produce a layer of coal one foot in thickness, about twenty feet of original plant material had to be compacted. The extent of these buried forests can be gauged by the fact that one Nova Scotia coal bed has more than 75 seams, one atop the other, each representing a buried forest. The thickness of some of the Pennsylvania coal beds is about 250 feet.

The coal forests endured for perhaps 85 million years, and they gave their name to the period in the history of the continent known as the Carboniferous. This was followed, about 225 million years ago, by another period of upheaval—the uplift of mountains, violent volcanic eruptions, the spread of deserts and of glacial ice. Thus was ushered in

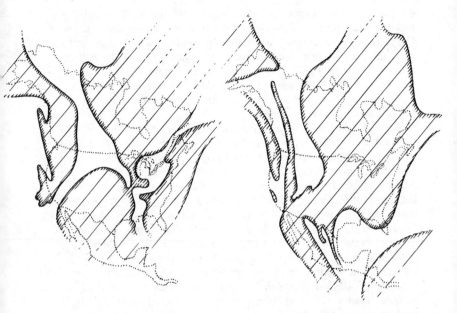

the age of reptiles, which lasted for roughly 125 million years, during which time the continental mass again emerged from the sea. About 60 million years ago, when the dinosaurs became extinct and the mammals rose to mastery of life, the western mountain ramparts were uplifted and the continent assumed roughly its present outline—except for Florida, which emerged later.

Although there have been additional incursions by the sea during the last 60 million years, never again did water inundate more than a scant five per cent of the continent at any single time. The seas occasionally spilled over the borders of the south Atlantic and Gulf coasts, and flooded small portions of what now comprises northern California, Oregon, Washington, and British Columbia. During this time, the Great Plains were formed, largely of sediments washed down from the Rockies. The land around the Colorado River was uplifted as a plateau; as it rose, the river cut down through the rocks, creating the abyss of Grand Canyon. About a million years ago the present shoreline of the Gulf of Mexico was established when an obscure island became joined to the mainland, thus forming the peninsula of Florida. Volcanoes were exceptionally active in the west; lava flows formed the extensive Columbia

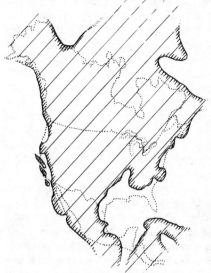

MAPS OF NORTH AMERICA 375 million, 150 million, and 50 million years ago reveal the constant changes in the borders between land (hatched) and sea.

Plateau in the Pacific northwest. Periodically Alaska was linked with Siberia by a wide land bridge that allowed many species of animals and plants to migrate in both directions.

The detailed etching of the northern part of the continent began about one million years ago. At that time the climate became so cold that snow, instead of melting during the summer, remained the year round and formed immense glaciers. The ice sheets did not form at the North Pole and sweep southward, as many people believe. In North America there were two centers from which the ice spread. One was centered in the vicinity of Hudson Bay, the Laurentide sheet; in the western part of the continent, ice formed in the mountains and merged into a single vast sheet, known as the Cordilleran. The eastern sheet reached southward for some 1600 miles into the Mississippi Valley and the northern plains. At its greatest extent it probably covered some five million square miles, approximately the present area of the Antarctic ice sheet. The western focus of ice was in the mountains of Canada; from it, valley glaciers extended southward down the Rockies and Cascade-Sierra ranges. At its maximum the main western sheet was about 1200 miles long and 400 miles wide; in addition, some 70 isolated glacial areas extended as far south as what is now New Mexico. All of this vast area of the continent was covered by ice at one time or another in the past million years, although not all of it was covered at any one time.

There were periods of general advance and retreat by the ice, but they were not uniform. Lobes moved forward in one place, remained stationary at another, or retreated in still another. For example, the ice began a major retreat about 25,000 years ago. But then, some 18,000 years ago, it reversed direction and began its final important surge southward, penetrating nearly to the Ohio River. For about 5000 years after that, the ice generally melted, uncovering portions of what are now the Great Lakes. Then, 12,000 years ago and just before the onset of the big melt, it spread southward again, covering Lake Michigan. Although portions of it endured in the vicinity of the Great Lakes and northern plains until about 6000 years ago, the ice sheet has never returned.

The margins of the greatest southward penetration of the glaciers can be traced in part by bands of low hills that extend westward from New York City to the Ohio River. The southern borders of the sheet were roughly the present course of the Ohio and Missouri rivers. Much of the Ohio River system was created when small streams that once flowed northward to Lake Erie were blocked by the ice. They took new routes just south of the edge of the glaciers, probing for any weak spots in the terrain and eventually developing a channel that was to become the Ohio River. Similarly, the Missouri River, which rises in the Rockies, once flowed northward. When that route was blocked, the water followed the southern edge of the glaciers; and thus, after traveling 1500 miles, the Missouri found a link with the Mississippi. Following the melt of the ice, the Missouri and Ohio both kept to approximately the new routes.

The million years of the ice age produced four successive sheets with intervening periods of warming, during which the ice retreated northward. The present time is probably another period of interglacial warming, a pause before the advance of yet another ice sheet. Parts of the last ice sheet are still very much present. Many small glaciers still remain in the Rockies and the Cascades, and many large ones exist in Canada and Alaska. Greenland is almost completely covered by ice, two miles deep in places. Even at its edges, the Greenland sheet looms nearly 2000 feet above the North Atlantic, and it periodically sends huge icebergs drifting into the sea lanes.

Although temperatures plummeted during the glacial epochs, extraordinary cold is not necessary for the formation of a glacier. All that is required is that more snow fall during the winter than is melted during

THE GLACIERS at their farthest penetration covered most of Canada, much of the northern United States and of the western mountains. In the east the ice sheets radiated from two points around Hudson Bay, leaving a driftless area between in Wisconsin and Illinois. In the west, valley glaciers merged to form the Cordilleran ice sheet. Remnants of these glaciers exist throughout this area.

the summer. Seen under a microscope, a fresh snowflake has a delicate six-pointed shape. At first the flakes collect in fluffy masses, separated from each other by their points. But as the water of which they are composed evaporates, these points are lost. The flakes become rounded and thus fit together more closely, in the same way that marbles fit more closely into a jar than do jagged pieces of rock. As additional snow falls, the flakes become packed together. The flakes begin to merge, first into clusters, then into chunks, until under the weight of additional snow they are all compressed into ice.

Thus year by year, inch by inch, a towering mound of ice several miles high was built up. Eventually, a time came at which the mound began to spread outward, flowing in much the same way as a thick batter dropped on a griddle. Under its own massive weight, the ice mound behaved rather more in the manner of a liquid than of a solid. As the ice kept accumulating, the mound went on spreading outward; it radiated over North America.

The moving wall of ice, which at times pushed forward at the speed of a foot a day, altered everything in its path. It ripped out immense boulders and used them as sandpaper to scrape off the thin veneer of soil. The glacier was like a monumental plow upon the land, scooping out depressions in the earth and grinding boulders down to pebbles. As it swept down over New England, it plucked rocks out of even the highest mountains. The craggy outlines of the Old Man of the Mountain in New Hampshire were etched by moving ice. Often huge boulders were picked up by the ice, moved for several miles, and then dropped in awkward positions. These erratics, as they are called, can be seen throughout the glaciated regions: a boulder precariously balanced on top of another, similarly precarious boulder, or a huge rock dropped in the midst of a pasture where there is not another rock within sight. So mighty was the transporting power of the glaciers that near Conway, New Hampshire, a huge block of granite—80 feet long, 40 feet wide, and weighing nearly 5000 tons—was moved at least two miles. Many erratics were carried considerably greater distances, some as much as a thousand miles. More often, a boulder was shattered and the pieces were dropped by the ice as it moved forward, to form the nearly straight lines of rock fragments known as boulder trains.

Some of the ice was always melting, even during its period of advance. Gradually, a balance was reached between the rate of melt and the rate of advance. Whenever that happened, the ice stood still. Great quantities of boulders and rock particles were dropped at the melting edge, forming a ridge or moraine. As the ice continued to melt, the immense amounts of material thus swept forward were spread out over the land like a sheet. This till sheet, as it is called, overlies the greater part of the area covered by the glaciers. It is thinnest in New England, increases in thickness in western New York, and in the north-central states deepens to several hundred feet. The reason for the variation is that the western rocks were softer and furnished more grist to the grindstone of the glaciers. Also, owing to the flatness of the land in the western glaciated areas, less of the till was washed away by water currents when the ice melted.

The glaciers created two kinds of landscapes: those from which they took material and those to which they brought it. The New England mountains, from which rocks were plucked and soil stripped, are largely an area of denudation. Some of the dislodged materials were later deposited in Connecticut and other places, thus creating good farmlands at the expense of the region from which the soil was taken. With the good soil came the boulders that Connecticut farmers have had to harvest as an annual crop, continually gathering them as they are exposed and piling them into stone fences. The sediments produced by the grinding down of the peaks also went into the building of many of the coastal features of New England—Cape Cod, Martha's Vineyard, Nantucket, Long Island. Similarly, the successive advances and retreats of the ice performed a bulldozing operation in the vicinity of the Great Lakes, widening and deepening these former river valleys into huge lake basins. The melt distributed this quarried material over wide areas of the midwest.

Anyone who drives through back roads in New England, southern Michigan, or Minnesota will occasionally see long winding ridges that look at first glance like abandoned railroad beds. These serpentine ridges, which are usually about 60 feet high, are also products of the glaciers. They are known as eskers, a name derived from a Gaelic word that means path; these formations are common in Ireland, where they often serve as footpaths across bogs. Eskers were formed during the retreat of the ice. As streams of meltwater flowed under the sheet or through cracks in it, the debris they carried was laid down to form the beds of these streams, whose banks were the ice sheet itself. The banks eventually melted, leaving only the debris that formed the streambed— a long, winding ridge higher than the surrounding countryside. It is not often possible to obtain a clear view of these gracefully curving ridges, since they are frequently masked by vegetation; some of the most perfect examples, however, can be seen around Bangor, Maine.

The glaciers swept before them not only the inert stuff of the continent, but living things as well. Animals, being mobile, were able to retreat southward, although undoubtedly hordes of them perished. Many great beasts that are extinct today—mammoth, mastodons, ground sloths —as well as other kinds that survived, migrated ahead of the advancing wall of ice. The luxuriant forest that had prospered even within the Arctic Circle was overwhelmed. As the ice pushed southward, the doomed trees in its path continued to scatter seeds. Those blown to the north perished, but those carried southward grew into new forests. Canadian plants, such as spruce and fir, were pushed into what is now the United States and flourished there. Along the backbone of the Appalachian Mountains, even the little tundra plants found locations which were unfavorable for the growth of other kinds of plants but where they could prosper without competition. Four times the land was scraped clear of life by the ice sheet; four times, in the wake of the retreating glaciers, the denuded land was reclaimed by the forests. So vigorously has been their spread northward that in the approximately 10,000 years since the last glacier, the hardwood forest has reclaimed more than half of New England.

Ice sculptured the face of the northern part of the continent, but since the last retreat other influences have also been at work. Volcanoes have been active, particularly in the Pacific Northwest, where they extend in a sweeping arc to the Aleutian Islands of Alaska. After being warped under the tremendous burden of the ice sheets, many areas around the Great Lakes and in New England and Canada are springing back to their former height. The release of huge volumes of water from the melting glaciers has drowned shorelines and rearranged the drainage patterns of lakes and rivers. The scenery is still being altered by monumental shifts of the earth's crust along fracture lines or faults. The present-day scenery of the continent has thus been formed largely by destructive forces at work. It is astonishing to realize how much of the grandeur of the North American landscape is a by-product of upheavals and destruction. The awesome Grand Canyon, for example, is due simply to a river that eroded its bed.

The Rocky Mountains are today thousands of feet lower than when they were first uplifted. Their mantle has been stripped away, carried down the flanks of the mountains by torrential streams. All rocks eroded from the heights make a passage toward the sea. Their movement and rate of progress are irregular; eventually, they are crushed and decomposed and spread as an even film over the lower plains of the continent. But even there the particles are not at rest; they are carried into the streams of the Missouri and Mississippi river basins. Finally, the mud— upwards of a million tons of it a day—reaches the mouth of the Mississippi, where the delta thus created is steadily encroaching upon the Gulf of Mexico. Thus, the same basic raw material has contributed to the making of strikingly different landscapes: soaring peaks, luxuriant grassland, a meandering river, a delta.

Landslides are sudden and dramatic examples of the leveling down of mountains, but there are other, less spectacular earth movements that accomplish the same result over longer periods of time. One of these is creep. Anyone who has climbed even a low hill will have noticed that the soil is deep at the foot, thinner on the slopes, and quite thin at the summit. Soil is constantly being created at the summit by the disintegration and decomposition of rocks, but there is a continual loss to the lower slopes. This downward movement of the soil is virtually invisible to the casual eye, but its effects are often clear enough. Several years ago, after some homeowners near Los Angeles had built on one of the mountain slopes, the whole face of the cliff began imperceptibly creeping downward. At first the shift caused slight cracks in the foundations of the houses. Later warping became evident, pipes were bent, and finally many of the houses became uninhabitable.

Some of the most striking scenery on the continent has been produced not by destruction alone but by the unequal resistance of rocks to the forces of destruction. When one kind of rock disintegrates more rapidly than a neighboring kind, the result may be such a phenomenon as the badlands of South Dakota, or the Great Falls of Yellowstone, or the limestone caves of Virginia and Kentucky. In the southwest, unequal resistance has produced some of the most bizarre of American landscapes: pinnacles and spires, natural bridges and arches.

So great are the destructive forces acting upon the continent that in an estimated 25 million years America would be leveled to a monotonous plain, were it not for the compensating force of uplift. Uplift is the continual rejuvenator of the continental mass. Even today, the Pacific shore in many places is rising in relation to the level of the sea. The area around Hudson Bay similarly is being uplifted; fish traps constructed along the bay shore several hundred years ago are now at a considerable distance inland. In the recent past, vulcanism has created many high places, among them the peaks of the Cascades in Washington, Oregon, and northern California, as well as mountain areas in southern Colorado, northern New Mexico, and Arizona. Although only 33 active volcanoes exist in North America at the present time, there is little doubt that volcanoes will continue to build the landscape in the future.

Today much of the continent has emerged from the sea; mountains tower above the plains; climatic belts are sharply defined. The history of the continent is a reminder that this sort of diversity does not long endure. For the present, North America is blessed with a remarkably varied landscape and comparative stability of its shoreline, mountains, and plains. But in the endless revolving of the geologic cycle, this may be merely the pause before a new series of upheavals.

II

THE WATERY RIM

Rocks, trees, and white water are the primary elements of the sea-scape of the North Atlantic shore. To visit the coastal area of Maine, for example, is to be in the constant presence of rocks. They are a rampart against the sea; they provide foundations for the gnarled fingers of tree roots that seem to grasp at them. The rocks of the New England shore impressed early explorers like Captain John Smith, who wrote of what is now Maine: "This coast is mountainous and Iles of huge Rockes, but overgrowne for most part with most sorts of excellent good woods." Smith found it remarkable that "such great Trees could grow upon so hard foundations."

Almost everywhere the rocky coast is one of sharp irregularity—islands, jutting headlands, deep bays, numerous peninsulas. If every curve and twist of the shoreline were followed, the distance between Portland, Maine, and the Canadian border would be 2500 miles, whereas the straight-line distance is a mere 200 miles. A jagged shore of this sort indicates a seacoast produced by submergence. The myriad offshore islands on the Maine coast are the summits of hills drowned by the advance of the ocean upon the land. The islands are not arranged at random. In some places they appear as long, straight rows marching down into the sea, moving into deeper and deeper water until finally the vanguard disappears under the breakers. If one stands at the shore and turns from the marching islands to look toward the hills, it becomes clear that the islands are actually a continuation of the same chains of hills, which have been partly covered by a rise in the level of the sea.

At one time the rocky shore of New England and Canada was probably a gentle coastal plain dipping gradually toward the water's edge, as the New Jersey coast does today. Its outer edge extended some 100 miles farther seaward than the present coast of Maine. The higher parts of this plain today form underwater shoals like the Georges, Quereau, and Grand fishing banks. In preglacial times some of the islands that now loom out of the ocean, such as Monhegan, must have been mountains that soared above the plain. Soundings taken in the Gulf of Maine have revealed the courses of stream valleys that cut through the plain before it was inundated. The long, narrow mouths of today's rivers—the Kennebec, Penobscot, and Damariscotta, among others—at one time were fertile valleys opening into the sea. Wherever the level of the ocean rose, the waters could easily pour inland and penetrate between the hills. Most of the valleys in Maine and New Brunswick were flooded in this way. In other places, such as the southern half of Nova Scotia, the ridges were parallel to the shore and the sea could not reach the valleys; as a result, there are few deep indentations on these coasts.

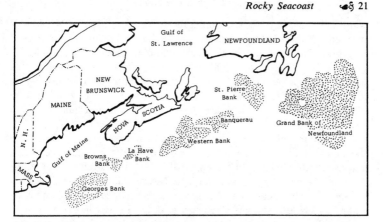

FISHING BANKS of New England and the Maritime Provinces are higher parts of the continental shelf that have been covered by the ocean since the glacial melt.

One obvious cause of the submergence of the shoreline is the melt of the glaciers. It has been calculated that the glaciers at their maximum held some nine million cubic miles of water in their icy grip. More than three-fourths of this ice has now melted, and the level of the sea has risen accordingly. But the immense weight of the glaciers themselves probably accounted for the major part of the submergence. Geologists have determined that the greatest submergence took place at about the time this land was crushed beneath the ice sheets. It is clear that then the Atlantic washed even farther inland than today, for marine deposits have been found 80 miles from the shore and nearly 500 feet above the present sea level. The land has since rebounded somewhat, but it is still about 1200 feet lower than at the beginning of the glacial age.

The rugged shore extends northward from Massachusetts with few interruptions. The desolation of bare rock and gray sea suggests a throwback to an earlier chapter in earth history. Little vegetation clothes these granite headlands, but along the ledges they are dotted with close-packed colonies of sea birds. When Jacques Cartier approached the Bird Rocks of Newfoundland in 1534, he was amazed at the fantastic numbers of these birds. "All the ships of France might load a cargo of them without once perceiving that any had been removed," he declared. When Audubon visited the rocks in 1833 he found them so crowded with birds that the nests almost touched each other. Many kinds of birds are nearly as abundant today. Among the most attractive bird inhabitants of the rocky shore are the gannets, found from the St. Lawrence northward, although they are best seen at the Avalon Peninsula of Newfoundland and at Bonaventure Island off the Gaspé Peninsula. On jagged ledges shrouded in fog and drizzle, these magnificent birds—whose plumage is gleaming white, their backs tinged with gold, and which have a wingspread of six feet—precariously raise their young. From the ledges they flap out to sea, spending hours on the wing in order to reach feeding grounds which are sometimes more than a hundred miles away.

There is, for all their desolation, an air of newness about these rocky shores, for it was only a geological yesterday that the glaciers retreated and the conifers reclaimed the denuded land. Great stretches bordering the shore, especially in Labrador and Newfoundland, are still barren of trees. Newfoundland's fauna is still impoverished: out of approximately 790 North American bird species only 121 nest in that province. There were no moose until they were introduced half a century ago. Even that symbol of the north, the mallard duck, is absent.

So desolate did the Newfoundland coast seem to Cartier that he speculated whether this might be "the land God gave to Cain." The ruggedness of the rocky coast is due mostly to its youth and not to the attack of the waves, for the granite rocks have been largely resistant to carving. There are, however, some very striking pillars, arches, and sea caves. The carving of the shore by waves is particularly noticeable in New Brunswick and northern Nova Scotia, where the waves break directly against less resistant sedimentary rocks. In these places the shore is being cut back at a rate of from one-half to one foot a year, leaving the more resistant rocks as headlands thrusting into the surf.

Among the places where the effect of the battering of the waves can be seen, one of the most notable is the unsheltered island of Monhegan, Maine, whose steep cliffs are directly in the path of storm waves. During heavy seas the crest of White Head, about a hundred feet above sea level, is drenched with spray. Another wave-battered spot is Percé Rock at Gaspé—a long, narrow island which has been pierced by an opening large enough for small boats to sail through. Here the cliffs, rising sheer 300 feet above the

GANNETS

whitecaps, have been carved into the shape of a tall chimney that faces out to sea.

Mount Desert Island, Maine, contains no view that is unique. Elsewhere in New England there are mountains more rugged, valleys more impressive, seacoasts more strikingly wave-cut. But nowhere else is all this rockbound scenery combined in so small an area. It was the French navigator Samuel Champlain who, steering a course among the Maine

EBB TIDE at Acadia National Park, Maine, reveals a wave-cut cave and numerous crannies in which shore animals are protected from the drying sun and wind.

islands, first came upon a rocky mass rearing out of the surf. From the sea it appeared nearly destitute of trees, so he named it *Isle des Monts Deserts*—"Island of the Barren Mountains." Mount Desert is the largest of the myriad islands that dot the Gulf of Maine, and it holds the highest point of land, 1532 feet above sea level, on the entire Atlantic seaboard north of Rio de Janiero.

At the beginning of the ice age Mount Desert consisted of a high east-west ridge which had resisted the erosion that wore down the rest of the island into low hills and valleys. As the ice moving in a southeasterly direction ground inexorably down from Canada, it excavated eleven parallel notches in this ridge, thus dividing it into a series of separate mountains. The deepest of the notches, gouged out to a depth below sea level, was invaded by the ocean to form Somes Sound, which nearly cuts the island in half; most of the other notches now contain lakes. Other reminders of the glaciers are everywhere on the island. On the rocks scratches and grooves made by the moving ice reach all the way to the tideline. As the ice moved slowly over the mountains, it smoothed their northern faces but plucked out huge blocks of granite from the southern, giving that face a rugged, notched appearance. The final chiselings of the rock masterpiece of Mount Desert Island are the work of the battering waves, which have cut sea cliffs and undermined blocks of granite, toppling them from their foundations.

Along the rocky coast are small areas of sand and gravel beach, some formed from glacial debris, others built up by the action of storm waves. In sheltered places on the shore, waves and currents deposit huge quantities of sand, gravel, and small boulders. These are added to the materials cut from the weaker rocks along the headlands, and in this way the narrow beaches that fringe the cliffs are formed. Cliffs and fringe beaches—these are characteristics of a youthful shore. As the shoreline matures, the waves continue to deposit material in the many coves and bays; at the same time, rivers fill in many of these places by bringing down particles of rock from the land. At several places in northern New England, the jagged coast has been evened by the wearing back of the headland cliffs and the filling in of bays. When this stage is reached, the rocky shore has matured.

During the maturing process many of the islands lose their individuality and become tied to the mainland by sandbars; New Englanders usually refer to these sandbars as "necks." One of the best examples is at Marblehead, Massachusetts. At one time, there was a large, rocky island offshore; but as waves and currents set about grinding it down, pebbles were chipped off and added to the debris brought by the cura broad, sloping terrace. This terrace or beach eventually grows so broad that waves must travel over considerable distances of shallow bottom before they reach the shore. Thus friction is increased, and the force of the waves steadily declines. Ultimately, the waves expend so much of their force in overcoming friction upon the shallow bottom that they no longer reach the cliffs. When this happens, erosion of the cliffs ceases, and the shoreline is stabilized. The coast now enters a period of settled old age, in which it remains undisturbed until at some future time the land sinks or the ocean rises.

Most waves are the result of wind acting upon water. A wave may develop only a short distance offshore, or it may be caused by a storm in mid-Atlantic, a thousand miles away. Imagine the surface of the ocean as calm and almost sheetlike before a storm. As the winds grow and push shoreward, the sheet becomes wrinkled into a series of parallel furrows. The top of each furrow is the crest, and the valleys between crests are known as the troughs. As the force of the winds increases, the crests of the waves become increasingly high.

Contrary to belief, the individual drops of water in each wave do not move shoreward. Rather, each wave is shaped like an endlessly revolving tube, with the individual drops following a circular path from crest to trough and back to crest again. The energy of this revolving motion can be transferred from one wave to the next, and so on endlessly until the wave motion eventually reaches the shore. Offshore, the waves are arranged in long parallel swells. As the water grows shallower, however, the bottom of the revolving tube scrapes against the ocean floor and is slowed down by friction. The crest of the wave, on the other hand, meets no obstacle; it continues advancing faster than the lower part, until finally it reaches the mathematical limit at which its height can be supported. Then the crest topples in a rush of white froth.

The tides—those unceasing forces of erosion and the depositing of the eroded materials—have had much more effect in sculpturing the shoreline than the sudden, overwhelming force of storm waves. At work night and day, at all seasons, in times of calm and of storm as well, the tides have produced much of the scenery of the rocky coast. Everyone has observed the rhythm of the tides, for it is one of the most striking features of the shore. In most places on the rocky coast, two high tides and two low tides occur in each tidal day, a period lasting 24 hours and 50 minutes. The heights reached by the tides vary markedly from place to place. The island of Nantucket, 30 miles south of Cape Cod, Massachusetts, has a very small tidal range—but the Cape itself often is subject to ten-foot tides. Northward from Cape Cod, the range of the tides continues to increase. It is twenty feet at Eastport, Maine, and twenty-two feet at Calais, Maine. The highest tides of all are at the head of the Bay of Fundy, between Nova Scotia and New Bruns-wick. There, the difference between high and low tide varies as much as 50 feet, producing the greatest tidal range in the world. The volume of water moved by the tides is enormous. Every day, four billion tons of water pour into Passamaquoddy Bay in Maine, and the Bay of Fundy receives about 200 billion tons a day.

Tides are caused by the gravitational pull of the moon, and to a lesser extent of the sun and the planets, upon the waters of the world. Anyone who has visited the shore has probably noticed that just as the moon rises 50 minutes later each day, the tides also lag about 50 minutes from day to day. A particularly observant visitor will also have noticed that the highest tides—called the spring tides—occur twice each month, when the moon is full and again when it is new. At these times, the posi-tions of the sun, moon, and earth form a straight line, and the augmented pull of sun and moon hurls the waters high against the shore. Twice each month, also, at the quarter moons, the tides are at their lowest; they are then called the neap tides. At that time the sun and moon are at right angles in relation to the earth, and the pull of each partly coun-teracts that of the other.

Between the shoreline covered by high and low tide is a restless zone crowded with forms of life that have managed to adapt to this difficult environment. When the waters of the tide sweep in and the spray glistens upon the rocks, what had appeared to be a barren world comes to life. Special hardiness is required to survive the onrushing of the waters. Most inhabitants of the rocky shore adapt to it by clinging. Limpets hold fast by suction; barnacles cement their shells to the rocks; mussels anchor themselves with clusters of taut threads. Starfishes cling to the rocks by the suction of their innumerable tube feet, so tightly that the animal cannot be forcibly removed without damaging it.

One of the most striking features of the life of the rocky shore is its zonation into narrow bands, which range from the perennially wet forms of life below the low-water mark to those pioneers that receive only the spray brought to them at high tide. As an animal or plant lives progres-sively higher on the beach, the hazards—exposure to wind and surf, the drying-out effect of sun and air—markedly increase. Those animals and plants that live in the perpetual wetness beyond the low-water mark do not have to endure these hazards. But they have sacrificed sunlight and the competitive advantage of colonizing the new domain of the shore. Land organisms are believed to have served their apprenticeship on the testing ground of the beach. Such familiar intertidal animals as snails, crabs, and sandhoppers have relatives that have already graduated to life on dry land.

During the retreat of the tide, the zones of life are displayed with textbook clearness. As the glistening rocks emerge from the water, the numerous snails slowly make their way over them and pasture on the slippery films of minute algae that adhere to them. Uncovered also are vast numbers of mussels, which bind themselves to the rocks with shining filaments secreted by a gland on the single large foot. A few of the strands snap with each assault of the waves, but the rest hold. The mollusk so arranges the filaments that the thin edge of its shell is pointed into the breakers, thus meeting the shock of the waves in the manner of a ship's prow.

At the threshold of the sea, in the uppermost tidal zone—the most precarious zone of all, beyond the reach of all but the highest tides— live the barnacles. They are protected from the surf by the shape of their low and conelike shells, over which the water rolls harmlessly; attached to the rocks with cement, the cones do not wash away despite the tremendous force exerted by the waves. Barnacles are among the most successful shore inhabitants, so numerous that they encrust the upper zones with a flinty layer of white. They are able to colonize exposed rocks which are buffeted by such heavy surfs that often not even seaweeds can gain a hold on them. Their tenacity appears even more remarkable when one realizes that these barnacles attach themselves to the rocks as naked young, before they are equipped with protective shells.

The young barnacle, which in this stage resembles its relative the shrimp, is carried by the waves to these exposed positions and somehow manages to obtain a hold. It cements itself to the rock and promptly secretes a fortress, a limy shell composed of six plates that fit with great precision over its delicate body. Inside the fortress the young barnacle changes into the adult form, and there lying upside down, with its six pairs of plumelike appendages pointing towards the roof of the shell, it spends the rest of its life. When the tide is in, two doors of the shell open and the barnacle, unfurling its plumes, sweeps in the microscopic food that has been brought to it by the sea.

Closer to the water grow the various seaweeds, themselves rigidly zoned into locations on the beach corresponding to their ability to endure being dried out. Seaweeds thrive on rocky shores, and in their profusion are symbols of these wave-beaten coasts. Their abundance is due in part to the secure anchorage a rocky coast offers, compared with the shifting underpinnings of a sand or gravel beach. Living highest on the beach is the orange-red spiral wrack. When the tide is out, it lies prostrate and seemingly lifeless on the rocks. With the return of the waters, its fronds gracefully lift to create an underwater forest. Between tides the wrack hoards its store of moisture under its rubbery fronds. Apparently delicate like a fern, it can endure the surf because it yields to it, rolling with the force of the sea. The bladder wrack has evolved its

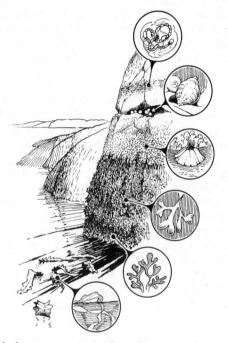

LOW TIDE reveals the zones on a rocky shore. The topmost band, above the high-tide line, is a black zone formed by algae. Immediately beneath it is a zone where periwinkles find shelter in rock crevices. The white masses of barnacles usually mark the high-tide line. Below them are the seaweed zones of rockweed and Irish moss. The lowest zone, that of the ribbonlike kelps, is revealed only by the lowest monthly tides, at which time the fronds lie draped on the glistening rocks.

own method of keeping itself erect when the tide is in: it is buoyed up by bladders filled with gases it secretes.

The wracks and many other seaweeds put out from one end of their ribbons what appear to be roots, but these are actually structures for holding fast to the rocks. So efficient are these holdfasts that few of the seaweeds break loose, and those only as a result of abrasion by wave-tossed debris or unusually heavy storms. Nearer the water, below the zone of the wracks, grows the red Irish moss; nearer still, and revealed only by the lowest tides, are the kelps with their long ribbonlike fronds. Each of the seaweeds nurtures its own community of living things—sea squirts, starfishes, mussels, worms—which are protected under the wet coverings of the weeds while the tide is out.

During storms, despite the efficiency of their clinging organs, some of the little shore animals inevitably become detached and are carried by the waters out of their habitual zones. But when calm is restored the animals sort themselves out, returning as if by magic to their accustomed places. Notable examples are the periwinkles; a number of species of these snails live along the rocky coast, each species inhabiting its own particular zone. Scientists who analyzed the behavior of periwinkles on the beach discovered that the animals find their way back by means of a complex interplay of gravity, light, and relative wetness or dryness. For example, one kind of periwinkle, which inhabits the uppermost part of the shore, displays a greater tendency to move up the beach against the force of gravity than do those of its near relations that inhabit lower portions of the beach. It is safeguarded from traveling too far up the beach by yet another response. When it dries out beyond a certain point, its gravity-overcoming response ceases to function. The result is that it stops, precisely in its accustomed place. Similarly, certain periwinkles respond negatively to light. One species, which lives sheltered among the seaweeds of the lower beach, begins to move when it is exposed to light; sooner or later, it again reaches the shelter of a seaweed and its travels cease. The end result of these and other responses is that each species is impelled toward a particular zone suited to the habits of its kind.

HOLDFAST ADAPTATIONS of the inhabitants of the rocky shore are typi-fied by the multitude of tube feet on the starfish's underside (bottom left). At the extreme right is a close-up view of the holdfast of a kelp, which somewhat resembles the root system of a tree; hordes of mussels find shelter within its branches. The three seaweeds in the center are, left to right, the winged kelp, the sea colander, and the horsetail kelp.

Along the rocky coast are stretches of sandy beach and tidal marsh that interrupt the barricade of rocks. Each of these environments possesses its own animals and plants, each with modifications that enable it to live there. South of Portland, Maine, sandy beaches are increasingly abundant; in the vicinity of Boston Harbor, the coast is lined with them. The land bordering Boston Harbor has a history of submergence similar to that of the Maine coast, but its rocks have been less resistant to the battering of waves.

When Boston Harbor was covered by the ice sheets, mud and gravel were deposited in mounds or hills known as drumlins. As seen from a low-flying airplane, a drumlin has the shape of an egg lying on its side and half submerged; it is usually 50 to 100 feet high and often more than half a mile long. Drumlins originated from little knobs in the landscape that protruded into the underside of an ice sheet. The knobs were composed of clay, which adheres to clay more readily than it does to ice; as successive stages of the ice moved over the knobs, the clay particles carried by the glaciers were captured, along with large amounts of sand and gravel which were mixed with them.

When the Boston Harbor area was submerged after the retreat of the glaciers, many drumlins were covered by water, while numerous others kept their tops above sea level, thus forming the many small islands that dot the bay. At some places the drumlin islands are so close together that they touch, producing formations such as Spectacle Island, which derives its name from the fact that the two drumlins composing it are so nearly identical as to form an almost perfect eyeglass shape. These islands are under continual attack by waves and currents; many of them have already been broken down and now survive only as shoals. Some have disappeared within historic times: one, which was about twelve acres in extent only a little more than three centuries ago, has now been reduced to a jumble of boulders. Drumlins are common features of the landscape almost everywhere throughout the glaciated region of the continent, but swarms of them exist in eastern Massachusetts (Bunker and Breed's hills are drumlins) and in Connecticut, New York, and Wisconsin. It has been estimated that there are upwards of 10,000 drumlins in New York and more than 5000 in southeastern Wisconsin alone.

The best known of the sandy beaches that interrupt the rocky shore is Cape Cod. Its bent elbow, thrusting far out into the ocean, presents an obstacle to the mixing of warm tropical water from the south with the cold northern currents. It is also a barrier to the movement of sea animals: the kinds of life that exist on the north and south shores, sometimes only a few thousand yards apart, are often quite different. The cape is also a dividing line for the geologist, since south of it the long, sandy beaches become increasingly more common.

Cape Cod is an outstanding example of the sea's power to create new landscapes. It owes its existence entirely to raw materials provided by the glaciers and to the force of tides and currents. The advancing front of the last glacier pushed down to what are now Cape Cod, Buzzards Bay, and Long Island. There it remained nearly stationary for several thousand years; then, as it melted, it deposited countless millions of tons

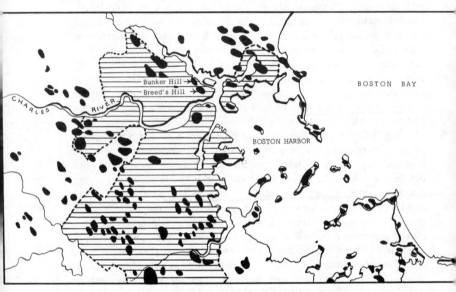

DRUMLINS are numerous in the vicinity of Boston.

of rock and gravel which it had borne with it. That debris formed a long ridge or moraine, which now makes up the hillier parts of Cape Cod, Rhode Island, and Long Island. During the subsequent melting of the ice, streams flowed over this ridge, depositing lighter materials immediately to the south in the form of sandy beaches, known to geologists as outwash plains.

The glaciers began the building of Cape Cod, but the ocean currents completed it. Once a wave breaks, it loses its power to carry sediment; at that point it drops most of the load it has been carrying. As a result, the ocean floor at the point where the waves break is gradually built up to form a sandbar. If one end of the sandbar touches land, it creates what is known as a spit, which continues to grow at its unattached end. This is exactly what has happened at Cape Cod. The land originally deposited by the glacier forms the upper arm and elbow of the cape. To this the ocean currents have attached, almost at a right angle, a long spit which makes up the forearm of the cape. The growing end of the spit, however, has been deflected by currents trying to make their way around it, and as a result the sandbar has now curved westward at the wrist. The illusion of a whole arm is completed by a number of small finger-shaped spits radiating from the wrist near Provincetown.

Such has been the construction of Cape Cod, but all the while destructive forces have also been at work. Ocean waves pounding upon the exposed portions of the eastern shore have gnawed away at it, leaving sea cliffs which in places rise 120 feet above the tides. The different degrees of resistance offered by a rocky shore and a sandy shore can be detected by the ear. Where rocks dominate the scene, one cannot fail to hear the waves grinding away, wrenching at the boulders, and then making use of the particles as grindstones for further breaking down of the rocks. The sound of the destructive forces at work is memorable—a nervous, low rumbling, like the bass section of an orchestra. The sound of the sea at Cape Cod is different; the tones of the swells are clear and rhythmic as they roll without obstacle onto the beaches.

Any irregularities that may have existed originally in Cape Cod's shoreline have by now been smoothed out, and the famed beaches stretch for miles in nearly straight lines. But the future of the cape is bleak. In some places the shore is receding by as much as three feet a year, although the average rate is much slower. Perhaps another 5000 years will see the waves triumphant over the shoreline, leaving only a submerged bank to mark the former position of the cape. And then again, in the endless turning of the wheel of destruction and rebuilding, there may be a change in the level of the sea or a shifting of the earth's crust; when that happens, the bank will rise again above the tides and begin the growth of land once more.

At Cape Cod the sea dominates everything, and even the vegetation has had to accommodate itself to survival amidst the salt-laden winds and spray. As one explores the hills forming the central ridge of the cape, it appears as though some gigantic scythe had swept over the trees, mowing them to a uniform height. The cape is one of the windiest places on the Atlantic coast, and the gusts have a cutting edge which shears off the tops of any trees that attempt to poke above the general level. The wind not only prunes back the tops; it also deprives the trees of life-giving substances. It dries out the leaves and the soil itself, leaving the trees with a perpetual thirst.

The result is a forest of pygmy trees, true-to-scale miniatures, produced in the same way as the bonsai trees grown by Japanese gardeners. On Cape Cod one can step over whole bonsai forests at a single stride. There are gnarled oaks that reach only to a man's belt. Thousands of pines, a whole forest of them, are twisted out of shape as they crouch toward the protection of the land; they may grow no higher than one's knee. Saw down one of these miniature trees and count its annual growth rings; it will be seen that it is not a youngster, but numbers its age in decades. Everything is reduced in size; even the cells of a pygmy tree are smaller than those of the same kind of tree growing in a more protected site.

The same forces that created Cape Cod have molded many other places on the coast southward to New York City. Lying off the southern shore of the cape are Martha's Vineyard, Nantucket, and the Elizabeth Islands. The shape of most of these islands is roughly that of a triangle with the long base at the south. The glacier created the ridges that form the apex and sides of the triangles; between the sides are sandy outwash plains that slope gently to the sea. Most of the islands have jagged southern shores that resulted from the rise of the sea after the melt of the glaciers.

Long Island, New York, resembles a giant fish with a sweeping forked tail, its head pointed toward New York City. This fantastic shape had its origin in the glacial moraine that stretches along the hilly northern portion of Long Island to form the fish's backbone. All the land south of the moraine is a flat, sloping outwash plain. Toward the eastern end the moraine divides, one spur forming the upper fin of the tail, Orient Point, the other the lower fin, terminating with Montauk Point. The two peninsulas are the result of a minor retreat by the glacier. First the ice advanced as far south as Montauk, where it remained stationary for several thousand years, creating the southern spur of the moraine. Then the ice began to melt, only to become stabilized again a few miles to the north, producing the upper fin.

The moraine continues westward from Long Island to Staten Island and thence into New Jersey. It is breached by a channel called The Narrows, which forms the entrance from the Atlantic Ocean into New York Harbor. If it had not been for the power of the Hudson River in breaching the moraine and keeping The Narrows open, the metropolis of New York would not have grown up around this protected harbor.

From Staten Island the moraine follows a generally westward direction. It marks the most southerly influence of the ice sheets upon the Atlantic coast. The contrast is striking as one passes from the narrow boulder-strewn beaches of New England to the wide, sandy ones of New Jersey. And with the change from rock to sand, from pounding surf to rhythmic breakers, there is a marked alteration in the forms of life that have accommodated themselves to existence along the shore.

3 : Sand Beaches

BULLS ISLAND, near Charleston, South Carolina, presents a vivid contrast to the Maine islands. Unlike the rocky coast, where the conifers seem to clutch at the rocks for support, the terrain of Bulls Island is gently rolling and covered with a luxuriant vegetation of oaks, magnolias, pines, and palmettos. Its broad beach stretches in a straight line, and the landward side of the island tapers off gently into tidal marshes. Wherever one looks there is a peaceful landscape of sea islands, salt marshes, sandy beaches. In contrast to the newness of the Maine coast, this shore gives the viewer an impression of great antiquity. The lines of the landscape are graceful curves, all jagged edges having been erased by time. The conflict between sea and land does not seem so urgent here, for the shoreline has been established by numerous compromises between land and sea over immense stretches of time.

The symbol of these ancient shores is the grain of sand which is the very stuff of their construction. Each grain is the end product of earth processes that date back to the continent's beginnings. Sand grains are mineral particles that range in diameter from about two-thousandths to eighty-thousandths of an inch. They are derived from the weathering of rocks: limestone, feldspar, and any of a dozen others, but especially quartz.

A typical grain may arrive at the beach from a distance of several hundred miles inland, where perhaps a boulder has been torn loose from a mountainside. During the journey of that boulder down the mountainside, it has been fractured and then splintered. Many of the particles, after being ground to a fine powder by a swift river have been dropped during the passage to the sea. The grains that complete the trip may arrive at the beach in no more than a few days, or they may travel for several years. The sea does the final sorting of the grains, according to their weight: the lighter ones are carried away by the waves and deposited elsewhere, the heavier ones are flung back upon the upper beach.

The sands differ from place to place according to the nature of rock from which they were derived. The sand beaches from New Jersey northward owe their origin largely to a mixture of minerals carried shoreward by the glaciers. Farther south, the proportion of limestone in the sand increases; along the North Carolina coast as much as a tenth of the sand may be composed of particles of broken shells. Southward from North Carolina, the sands again are of mineral origin, derived from the weathering of rocks on the eastern slope of the Appalachians. On a number of Florida beaches, the ocean currents have tossed up quantities of quartz. These beaches are famed for their glistening whiteness and uniformity, and also for their hardness; the packed sands of Daytona Beach, on which many automobile records have been set, are virtually pure quartz. The composition of the beach sand changes once again in southern Florida, where quartz becomes mingled with shell and coral fragments. On the Gulf coast, the sands usually contain a large proportion of mud and decayed plants.

A grain of sand is virtually immortal. It is the end product of the wearing down of rocks, the smallest fragment of matter to survive the destruction of a boulder. Each grain at the beach is cushioned against further abrasion by being surrounded with a film of water, whose volume is approximately equal to the volume of the grain. Along the wet lower beach the grains appear to be closely packed, but in fact they never touch. The large grains above the high-tide line, on the other hand, are dry; as they rub against one another they produce the familiar "singing" of the sands.

These inert bits of mineral matter seem inhospitable as a setting for life. In contrast to a rocky coast, the uncovering of the sandy beach at ebb tide reveals a world apparently barren. Instead of the crowded life that fills the rock pools and crevices, the sandy beach at low tide reveals only the marks of the waves and the flotsam they have carried shoreward. The shifting sands of the beach afford no surface to which either the seaweeds or the little animals they shelter under their moist fronds might attach themselves. Nor does a sandy beach provide the crevices and boulder-shaded pools that protect the animals along rocky coasts from drying sun and winds during the time between tides. But a sandy beach does offer one advantage: except for the topmost layer, which dries out between tides, it is constantly moist.

Everywhere the observant visitor can see subtle evidence of the abundant life underfoot. The beach is peppered with the tiny holes of ghost shrimp. There are delicate traceries on the sand not caused by wind or tide. Sometimes sand tubes protrude from the surface, little turrets with obvious signs of animal craftsmanship. Some animals of the sandy beach survive dryness and escape from enemies by burrowing into the constant moisture just beneath the surface. Such an animal, in addition to the ability to dig, must possess a mechanism for breathing and feeding above the surface of the sands while the rest of its body is buried.

Many species have developed ways to tap sustenance from the sea without deserting their sanctuaries below the sands. A common method is that of certain tube-building worms, which collect shreds of plant and animal life from the debris that rains upon the surface of the sand. These worms usually inhabit the lowest parts of the beach, where they are uncovered for only a short time each day by the retreat of the waters. Each worm secretes a mucus which it uses as a cement to construct a tube of sand grains. Although the tube usually projects less than an inch above the surface, it is often at least a foot long; ten inches of that length are occupied by the animal, and the additional space at the bottom serves as a retreat while the tide is out. When the tide is in, the worm climbs toward the turret and exposes its gills for breathing; its threadlike tentacles gracefully wave through the water, seining in food. If

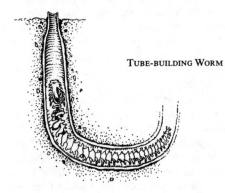

TUBE-BUILDING WORM

it is threatened, it retreats in a blur of haste into the bottom of its tube. The little animal can rush up and down with ease because it is equipped with bristles and hooks that give its body purchase on the slippery sides of the tube.

A more elaborate builder is the ghost shrimp. Its little burrows, often no more than an eighth of an inch in diameter, riddle the beach. They are entranceways to a maze of chambers and passages that descend to depths of several feet, then lead again to the surface at another place. The body of this shrimp is long and slender, a counterpart of the passageways. Many of its appendages are modified to the shape of paddles that beat untiringly when the tide is in, pumping a current of water through the burrow. The ghost shrimp feeds by rising to the mouth of its burrow and sifting the sand grains in search of minute sea animals and decaying plants. As frequently happens in the crowded world of the sands, the shrimp is not the sole inhabitant of its apartment. It also has a lodger, a little crab which nets food from the currents of water pumped through the burrow by the shrimp.

The marine animals most perfectly adapted for life within the sands are the two-shelled mollusks or bivalves, such as the clams. Some bivalves, for example the oysters and mussels, inhabit rocky coasts, but many kinds possess the ability to burrow deeply and with incredible speed into sand; some can even burrow into wood and soft rock. All burrowing bivalves possess a long breathing tube or siphon that reaches above the surface of the sand and carries oxygen and food to the animal as it lies hidden below. Their shells are smooth and flattened, with the result that the sand offers little resistance to their burrowing. Some clams have shells flattened almost to a razor's edge, and can slice through the yielding sands to great depths.

The sandy beaches are the homes of many kinds of burrowers that wait for the sea to bring them sustenance. If one looks carefully, one may sometimes see sand grains arranged in the pattern of a star, evidence that a burrowing starfish lies just beneath the surface. Starfishes are the most voracious carnivores of the beach. The undersides of their arms carry a multitude of tube feet—powerful organs which in the starfishes that inhabit rocky coasts are used to exert suction, but which in the sand-dwelling species are pointed and adapted for digging. A starfish in the process of burrowing appears to sink directly into the sands. It also moves with remarkable speed under the surface of the sand, where it feeds upon whatever living animals it finds: mollusks, crustaceans, and worms.

Among the hosts of small creatures buried in the sand are crabs that expose only their feathery antennae to the water when the tide is in, netting prey. Gliding over the sands at ebb tide are the snaillike whelks in search of buried prey. They are able to distinguish between the jets of water expelled by the breathing tube of a hidden crab and the surrounding water. When prey is found, its shell is either enfolded by the whelk's muscular foot and pried open, or banged by the whelk's own shell until it breaks. Certain sea snails are able, using their feet as a drill, to bore neatly through the shell of a clam, and then to feed through the opening. The whelk itself may become the prey of other sand dwellers, particularly some crabs whose massive pincers can crush its shell.

GHOST SHRIMP

Although a visitor to the beach seldom notices a crab buried only a few inches from his feet, numerous shore birds—sanderlings, plovers, terns, gulls, and others—are adept at locating this prey. A shore bird appears to be playing a kind of game with the waves as it rushes up the beach just ahead of the advancing foam, then wheels as though in pursuit of the retreating water. Actually, the bird is attempting to catch one of the hosts of little crabs or other shore animals before it burrows completely out of sight. Often a gull which has captured a prey with a hard shell will carry it aloft and then drop it on a paved road or pier so as to shatter it. Birds are not the only outsiders that come to prey on the inhabitants of the beach community. With each advance of the sea upon the beach, fishes also follow the waves in search of small shore animals.

There are other enemies of a more complex sort. On certain Atlantic shores, for example, the animal population was greatly reduced a few decades ago by a microbe. Its immediate victim was eelgrass, which once grew densely on protected shores, but which during the 1930's was nearly eradicated. A change in the salinity and temperature of the water, which encouraged the growth of a parasitic mold, was the cause of one

of the most rapid epidemics in botanical history. The mats of eight-foot-
long eelgrass had formed an underwater jungle in which a profusion of
life—starfishes, clams, worms, jellyfishes, snails, numerous small fishes
—took shelter, found food, and reproduced. With the disappearance of
the eelgrass, the whole superstructure of lives dependent on it went also.
To take the most striking example, the brant, a small goose, lost its feeding grounds and in a few years declined to a mere fifth of its former
abundance. Not only did the living things that had depended on the
eelgrass disappear, but the sea began to wash away beaches formerly
stabilized by its roots. In a number of places, beds of eelgrass have now
recovered from the epidemic and are becoming the center once again of
a complex of associated life.

The beach is littered with the flotsam of past generations—clam
shells bored through by predatory univalves, crabs' pincers, shattered
snail shells—all laced together by strands of seaweeds and shore plants.
Also trapped in the strands may be remnants of lives from other beaches
and deeper water, carried to the shore by currents. Among these are the
spiral shells of the ramshorn, a relative of the squid, and the papery
"shell" (actually the egg case) of the paper nautilus, a relative of the
octopus. Sometimes found also are the strange balloon-like sails of the
Portuguese man-of-war, blown off course from the Gulf Stream.

The most abundant drift at the beach consists of the shells of uni-
valve and bivalve mollusks. So durable are these shells that they outlast
those of all other sea creatures; as they gradually disintegrate their fragments mingle with the particles of quartz and other minerals to become
part of the sand itself. Nearly every shore has its own particular collection of shells that distinguishes it from other shores. A Maine beach
yields the shells of barnacles, mussels, and periwinkles and, in some
places, scallops. Whelks, moon snails, and clams are particularly common from New Jersey to Virginia. On the Florida beaches are found a
great number of different kinds of shells, mostly the various ark or pen
shells.

Owing to a combination of tides and local currents, several little
islands off southwestern Florida have been heaped with greater quantities of shells than can be found anywhere else on the continent. On
Sanibel, Captiva, and Marco they litter the beaches in such countless
millions that dozens shatter underfoot with every step. They range from
the little angelwings, as fragile as the foam, to ponderous univalves such
as the conches. In the interior of these islands, out of reach of the
waters, are other huge mounds of shells, refuse heaps left by the Indians who for generations feasted on the mollusks carried to the islands

by the tides. Some of these mounds of discarded shells are believed to have reached the height of a five-story building, but the mounds have now largely been leveled by shell-collectors.

The shell of a mollusk is secreted by a thin organ, called the mantle; the basic raw material of the shell is calcium carbonate derived from minerals in the animal's food supply. The mantle also secretes the pearly material that lines the interior of the shells of some species and the pigments which are responsible for their color. The shapes and patterns that distinguish each kind of shell are the result of the rhythmic use of the pigment and shell materials by the mollusks. Some mollusks add calcium carbonate at a steady rate, building a shell that has a symmetrical pattern of ribs, ridges, and spirals. Other mollusks grow in spurts, and thus their shells have numerous spines and knobs, often in fantastic shapes. Still other factors influence the form of the shell. A mollusk with a smooth mantle produces a smooth shell, but one having a ruffled mantle produces a shell that is correspondingly ruffled. When some mollusks

SHELLS of whelk and clam; moon snail egg case; shell of moon snail

slow down their growth, a thickened lip is formed at the edge of the shell; as growth accelerates once more, the lip is left behind as a ridge or series of spines.

In contrast to the moist and populous sands between the tides, the sand beyond the reach of the water is usually dry and easily blown by shore breezes. Dry sand and wind are two of the components for the creation of dunes, but a third is no less necessary. This is an obstruction: driftwood, a rock, even a tuft of beach grass, which will slow the wind and cause it to drop its cargo of sand grains. After a mound of sand has been built up, rain is necessary to prevent further blowing and to allow one of the quick-growing beach plants to put out roots.

There are many plants that can anchor a mound of sand and begin the creation of a dune. One of these is beach heather; another is dusty miller, a relative of the sagebrush of the western deserts. Dune grass, however, is the most efficient anchor on the dunes of the Atlantic coast. A single plant rapidly develops horizontal stems that creep along the mound, producing every few inches a new tuft of leaves and roots. Soon the mound is laced with a network of roots which bind it. The anchored mound now forms a greater obstacle to the wind than did the original obstruction; it catches increasingly large amounts of sand which build the mound still higher. Once again it is stabilized by a new layer of dune grass; and in no more than a few years, if conditions are right, a dune five or ten feet high may be built up, each grass-stabilized layer overlapping the previous one like the skins of an onion.

Some dunes on the Atlantic coast reach heights of 30 or 40 feet, but mostly they are only passing features of the landscape. Some dunes are destroyed by the sudden accumulation of too much fresh sand, which smothers the stabilizing grass. Sometimes a probing finger of the wind finds a weak place, which is enlarged until the dune is destroyed. These blowouts sometimes begin with the death of an inconspicuous little plant, which may hold no more than a square foot of sand in the grasp of its roots and the shelter of its leaves. But its death is a temporary breach in the dune's defenses against the wind. The breach is repaired if another quick-growing plant takes its place; but once the wind begins to enlarge the breach, the dune's destruction is certain. As the wind whips through the vulnerable opening, it can outflank the dune and reach the landward side. There it dislodges the sand grains held by the roots of plants near the breach. Soon one plant topples, then another. What started as an insignificant opening soon becomes a full-scale blowout. Now trees, shrubs, and grass are undercut at a faster rate; the loosened sand is piled up until it smothers the vegetation on other dunes near by, thus killing their protective armor. The destruction continues until the dunes have been leveled, or until there is a lull in the winds sufficiently long for plants once again to stabilize any mounds that remain.

Although dunes frequently occur in areas of high rainfall, the conditions for life on a dune approximate those in a desert. The dunes retain little moisture, and the summer sun may heat the sands to temperatures above 150 degrees. Yet, just as in other hostile environments, life has adapted itself to an existence on the dunes. Only a few kinds of animals can survive in such an environment. Predominant among these are mice, which escape the heat by leading nocturnal lives, and insects, which can escape the burning sands simply by taking flight or by spending the hottest part of the day in deep burrows. Many of the perennial plants of the dunes probe for water by means of taproots, which often descend fifteen feet and sometimes twice that distance. Other plants hoard their moisture under the protection of a waxy coating, just as do many of the cacti and succulents of the desert. The leaves of dusty miller are covered with white hairs which reflect the sunlight and also provide insulation. A number of kinds of plants grow their leaves at such an angle that the sun strikes only the thin edges.

Dunes exist not only along the ocean shore, but also inland wherever both abundant sand and strong winds are present. At Great Dunes National Monument in Colorado there are dunes nearly 700 feet high; gypsum dunes covering about 500 square miles are found at White Sands, New Mexico. Surrounding the Great Lakes are numerous knolls which have the shape of dunes but are completely covered by what appears to be an established community of trees and shrubs. These are in fact ancient dunes, formed about the time of the melting of the last glacier, when the debris that covered much of the land was swept by the winds into towering mounds.

Even today, wherever the prevailing winds blow inland around the Great Lakes, dunes are still being formed. These dunes are a meeting place of northern and southern vegetation. Side by side grow cacti from the southwestern deserts and pines from Canada. Although the ancestral homes of these plants are thousands of miles apart, they have a common bond: their adaptations to a world where water is scarce. In the north the pine must survive the lack of available moisture in the frozen soil;

SHIFTING SANDS of a dune, only partially stabilized by grass, advance inland.

accordingly, its leaves are thick-skinned and have few breathing pores through which water might be lost. The cactus of the desert copes with prolonged drought by virtually dispensing with leaves; those it does possess have been reduced to spines, while the thick, fleshy parts of the plant are actually stems. Because of their similar adaptations, pine and cactus live as neighbors on the dunes, together enduring the drying winds and blazing sun.

Most of the finest dunes on the Atlantic coast have been bulldozed out of existence to make way for ocean-front buildings. Similarly the barrier islands, another typical formation of the sandy shore, have been invaded by developers. Barrier beaches form only along sandy coasts that slope gently down to shallow water. Where the ocean remains shallow for great distances offshore, the waves break long before they reach the mainland. As a wave breaks, it scoops up sand and hurls it in front of itself, forming a ridge. At first the ridge is submerged, but it eventually grows into a thin barrier island.

Many noted beach resorts—Miami, Daytona, Hatteras, and Atlantic City, among others—are situated on barrier beaches. Cape Hatteras is formed by a series of barrier islands, as much as 25 miles from the mainland, that shelter Pamlico and Albemarle sounds. The island is so narrow that at some places only a few hundred yards of sand lie between Pamlico Sound and the Atlantic Ocean, although at one point the width of the island is about three miles. Hatteras is the meeting place of the cold ocean currents that pour down from the north and the warm, northward-flowing Gulf Stream, which lies a dozen miles offshore. The meeting of these two currents produces almost unending fog and sudden storms, and has resulted in the formation of the treacherous Diamond Shoals.

Between the wave-built barriers and the mainland are salt marshes or lagoons of quiet water. With the passage of time, these are filling in, joining bar with bar and the bars with the mainland. Roanoke Island, which lies behind the barrier island of Hatteras, was the scene of the first English attempt to establish a colony in the New World. Now the inlet through which the ships entered the sound no longer exists; it was closed off by the constant growth of the barriers. The filling in of the lagoon is caused by the action of storms, during which the waves overtop the barrier and hurl sand behind it. Filling in takes place on the land side also, as streams carry sediments into the lagoon. Ultimately, barrier island and mainland are joined; the lagoon disappears, replaced first by temporary swamps and eventually by dry land.

Most of the Atlantic and the Gulf coasts are protected by strings of

offshore sand barriers. The lagoons they shelter are the route of the
Intracoastal Waterway, which offers protected sailing almost without
interruption from New Jersey to Mexico. The vigorous shore currents
that sweep the eastern coast of Florida have built a series of barriers extending from the Sea Islands of Georgia southward to Miami. One continuous lagoon, known as the Indian River, is about 130 miles long.

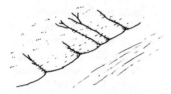

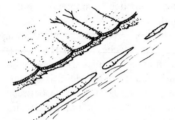

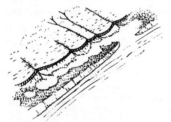

DEVELOPMENT OF A SANDY COAST begins with a youthful coastal plain and
shallow water offshore. In the center diagram, sandbars and a lagoon have begun
to form. As the shore matures (bottom
diagram), the lagoon fills, linking the
bar to the shore and creating dry land.

Cape Kennedy is on one of these barriers, which lies twenty miles from
the mainland. Padre Island, off the southeastern coast of Texas, is about
140 miles long. The water between Padre and the mainland is a complex of ponds, islands, and mudflats, providing a diverse habitat for a
startling variety of birds. In just one day, a bird-watcher here tallied 204
different species; and more than 500 different kinds have been seen at
one town on the lagoon. The birds that attract the most attention are
the long-legged waders. In the estuaries and offshore islands are seen

three species of egrets and four kinds of herons, in addition to wood storks, the spindle-legged birds known as stilts, and roseate spoonbills.

The Blackjack Peninsula, which juts into the lagoon at the southern end of Padre Island, is the wintering ground of what is possibly the best-known bird on the continent, the whooping crane. The entire world population of wild whoopers, some 40 at this writing, winter at the Aransas Refuge on the peninsula, and in the spring fly to their breeding grounds in northern Canada. Whoopers are huge white birds with black wingtips and carmine heads; their wingspread is greater than the height of a tall man. Their call, which resembles an Indian war whoop and carries for miles, is produced from a five-foot-long windpipe coiled like a French horn. Whoopers are among the rarest birds in the world; only two decades ago they tottered on the brink of extinction. Now, due to the cooperation of thousands of sportsmen and bird-watchers along their migration route, they are safe from wanton shooting. They have made a long flight back from near extinction, and in recent years there has been a steady increase in their numbers.

The mainland behind the offshore barriers is incredibly complex, particularly in the region between New Jersey and North Carolina. As can be seen on a map, the little islands, peninsulas, and plumelike systems of inlets bear a superficial resemblance to those of the Maine coast. They owe their configurations primarily to the work not of the sea but of the rivers. The courses of the rivers that flow into the Atlantic along this section of the coast once formed a tree-like pattern, with many intricate branches leading to a main trunk. When the sea advanced upon the land after the melting of the last glacier, it moved far up the main branches,

filling from hill to hill the valleys the rivers had formed, and thus creating a ragged shoreline.

The drowning of the lower reaches of a river is nowhere better seen than at Chesapeake Bay. Once the mouth of the Susquehanna River, the bay was flooded by the rising sea for a distance of about 175 miles upstream. The Potomac, the Rappahanock, and other rivers that today flow di-

WHOOPING CRANE

rectly into the bay were at one time mere tributaries of the Susquehanna. Because these rivers ran through low-lying land, only a slight rise in sea level was sufficient to inundate them above their confluence with the Susquehanna.

Chesapeake Bay, although it has a surface area of more than 3000 square miles, is quite shallow. The shallowness has created numerous areas along its shores that are not land and not bay either. These marshes are the scene of a quiet but ceaseless struggle between the plants, which attempt to stabilize the shore, and the tides, which disrupt them. Twice each day, at high tide, the bay sends long fingers deep into the marshes, uprooting the reeds and cattails; as the tide retreats, it carries away with it a few clumps of plants and soil. The land, on the other hand, seeks to extend its domain by sending a rain of seeds upon the sandbars. Practically all of the seeds are doomed to perish, but occasionally a few bars do become anchored by growing plants and begin the formation of an island. Most such islands are soon destroyed by storm waves, which beat them down into sandbars once again. There is forever an uneasy balance between sea and land. For each advance made by the land in choking off a stream channel with sediment and plants, the land suffers a loss elsewhere as waves cut a channel that did not previously exist.

The marshes of the Chesapeake are linked with those on the entire Atlantic coast through an invisible highway traveled by numerous kinds of birds on their migrations. In 1935 the late Frederick C. Lincoln, of the U.S. Fish and Wildlife Service, completed a painstaking analysis of thousands of records of banded waterfowl. By linking on his map the places where metal bands had first been attached to the birds' legs with the places where the birds had later been recaptured, he was able to show the existence of ancestral routes taken by the birds on their flight over the continent each spring and fall. The most easterly of these routes follows the coastline and is known as the Atlantic flyway; other major routes follow the Appalachian ridges, the Mississippi basin, the marshes of the Great Plains, the valleys of the Rocky Mountains, and the Pacific shore.

The Atlantic flyway is shaped like a vast funnel, its wide end spreading over the eastern half of Canada and New England. The funnel narrows at the Chesapeake marshes, then follows a slender path down the coastline to southern Florida. Many birds drop off to their wintering grounds along the way, but some of them follow the stepping-stones of the Caribbean islands—Cuba, Hispaniola, Puerto Rico, and the Lesser Antilles—to South America. Chesapeake Bay is an important focal

FOUR PRIMARY BIRD FLYWAYS of North America are the Atlantic (black circles), Mississippi (crosses), Central (white circles), and Pacific (dots).

point for the Atlantic routes, and indeed many birds travel no farther. Huge concentrations of waterfowl can be seen at the mouth of the Susquehanna River and at many other places in the Chesapeake, as well as at Back Bay in Virginia, and at Pea Island and Currituck and Pamlico sounds in North Carolina.

Submergence and emergence are two major forces that have molded the coastal landscape of the Atlantic. The submerged valleys of New England, the drowned rivers of the middle Atlantic states—both are evidence of the rise of the sea in recent times. Similar signs can be seen along the coast of Florida and the arc of the Gulf of Mexico. Tampa Bay, Mobile Bay, and many shallow inlets on the Texas coast are drowned estuaries. But for every drowning of a shore, there has also been a compensating uplift. It was shown several decades ago that a series of seven terraces extends inland from the present coastlines of the Atlantic and Gulf. They march from the shore to the interior and appear as broad steps, the highest of which is 270 feet above present sea level. Each of these terraces bears the mark of what must once have been sandbars, beaches, or wave-cut cliffs, evidence that in times past the seas that lapped against the land came much farther inland than at present.

The uncovering of one of these terraces has resulted in the formation of the Great Dismal Swamp of the coast of Virginia and North Carolina. The swamp covers an area of approximately 1500 square miles, in the middle of which is Lake Drummond, so called although it is only a few feet deep. The terraces have been traced down the east coast of Florida as far as Lake Okeechobee, south of which the surface of Florida forms one large terrace. At the tip of Florida, however, a major change occurs in the coastline—the Keys, created not by wind and waves, not by emergence and submergence, but largely by the work of living things.

4 : Corals and Deltas

I N ALL OF NORTH AMERICA, there is no other place like the string of
Keys that trail from the tip of Florida into the Caribbean. Hosts of
living things have created land by transmuting the substance of the sea
into rock. These coral islands—one portion of the numerous coral reefs
that are found throughout the Bahamas and the Caribbean—stretch
southward from Miami for 200 miles, slicing directly across the warm
waters of the Gulf Stream.

Although corals are found on other shores of the North American
continent, the conditions required by the reef-building kinds are met
only at the southern tip of Florida. These little coral animals have rigid
temperature demands: they grow only in shallow seas where the temperature stays above 70 degrees, and are thus restricted to the waters washed
by the Gulf Stream. Also, they require currents strong enough to bring
them a constant supply of food.

A glance at a map reveals that the Keys are divided into two groups,
an upper and lower. The upper Keys begin at Biscayne Bay, just south
of Miami, and are strung in a long line down to Loggerhead Key. This is
the most ancient portion of the Keys, built by coral animals during a
warm period before the last ice age. During this interglacial period the
seas stood higher than they do today. The little soft-bodied animals, each
of which secreted a protective cup of lime, grew abundantly, forming
immense colonies. Gradually the colonies merged, to become the founda-

tions of the reef, and new colonies grew atop the older ones. Then, as the glacial ice built up in the north, the level of the ocean dropped. Finally the water level fell so low that the reef was exposed to the air, which killed the coral animals instantly. Recent research indicates that this interglacial reef was largely destroyed, to be formed anew during the postgiacial melt, and finally uncovered once more. Whatever the exact dates of its formation may have been, the reef-building days of the upper Keys are over. What must have been a magnificent spectacle of living corals and their associated plants and animals has now been reduced to a lifeless mass of rock.

The lower Keys were formed in another way. Mingled with the sediments that collected in the protected waters to the west of the coral reef were the remains of numerous sea creatures; eventually this mixture was compacted into the white, fine-grained rock known as limestone. The limestone was uplifted, whereupon it began to be attacked by currents and tidal rips, which gradually carved it into islands. The difference in the origin of the two groups of Keys is apparent when the life they support is examined. The upper Keys are clothed with West Indian hardwoods; there are no pines, whereas on the lower Keys pines abound. On the lower Keys are also found the last surviving Key deer, now numbering probably more than two hundred. These deer, dwarf relatives of the whitetail, weigh less than 50 pounds, or about one-sixth as much as a normal white-tailed buck.

Offshore from the Keys the right conditions still exist for the creation of reefs, and under the indigo waters a new living wall of coral is being built. This reef can be inspected by chartering a glass-bottomed boat or, better, by donning a mask and snorkel tube to view the underwater garden at close hand. The impression that one gains from specimens of coral found upon the beach is a poor substitute for the luxuriance of a flourishing reef. At first glance, from the surface, the reef is a tapestry of muted colors. But as the skindiver descends, a world of fantastic shapes is revealed: some corals grow numerous branches and resemble saguaro cacti; staghorn corals look like antlers adorning the reef; brain corals resemble specimens in a medical display case; and still others resemble shrubs, fans, and stars.

The corals form the foundation upon which the complex life of the reef is built. Practically every cranny and crevice holds some strange tropical fish, and shadows dance across the corals as whole schools of fishes pass overhead. Sponges grow on the corals and rival them in diversity of color and shape; brilliantly colored worms, adorned with gills that resemble feather dusters, glide over the sponges. Into this pasture

come the harvesters. Sleek barracudas, armed with razor teeth, slice
through the waters. Sharks prowl the reef, convoyed by pilot fishes. What
appear to be delicate undersea blossoms are in reality the stinging tentacles of sea anemones, relatives of the corals. And some of the corals

CORAL COLONIES, each composed of numerous individual polyps, assume a multitude of strange shapes. At left, front to back, are brain coral, ivory bush, and
horny coral. At right are a sea fan and a staghorn coral.

themselves are likewise equipped with minute stinging cells that produce a burning rash on human skin.

The little coral polyp looks deceptively simple, like a frayed piece of
string. The string is actually a hollow tube, and the frayed end a circle of
tentacles surrounding the mouth. The cells on the inside of the tube
digest the food brought in by the tentacles; the cells on the outside take
lime out of the sea and convert it into the animal's external skeleton,

thus contributing to the building of the reef. Mollusks possess a similar ability to form external skeletons, but only the corals exist in sufficient numbers to produce reefs. All of the individuals in a colony spring from a single egg which hatches into a polyp. That polyp in turn produces buds which form new polyps, and each of these new polyps also reproduces by budding. Thus, each colony is a pure culture of a particular species, one that has its own pattern of growth. A single colony may reach a diameter of ten feet, although only the corals growing on the outside are alive.

CORAL POLYP

Each coral has an unseen partner, without which it could not manage to live in the crowded conditions of a colony. Its tissues contain multitudes of microscopic algae; together, the animal and the plants carry on their life processes with greater efficiency than either could alone. The algae obtain their minerals and carbon dioxide from the polyp; in return, the polyp receives oxygen and probably certain carbohydrates from the algae.

Corals grow on the wave-swept side of the Keys facing the Atlantic. On the Gulf side a different form of life, the mangrove tree, carries on the work of creating land out of water. In the protected waters of Florida Bay, mangroves have constructed their own wilderness by building thousands of islands, some only a few dozen square feet in area, which are separated by a crazy-quilt pattern of bays, figure-eights, and lagoons.

The mangrove is remarkable in that it can be nourished by salt water, which is lethal to most land plants. The seedling of a mangrove begins life on a branch of the parent tree, growing as if it were a twig until it reaches a length of about ten inches. Then it drops from the branch and drifts with the current. This twig, tinged with the green of future promise, is already a complete plant. The tube is the future trunk; the pointed tip is the beginning of a root system; the soft green other end is the first branch. The seedling's potential growth is husbanded, sometimes for months, while it floats at the whim of currents and waves. Sooner or later it reaches a sandbar or a mudflat yielding enough to allow the pointed end to become imbedded, but firm enough to hold it in place against the waves. When it has gained a foothold, the seedling sends out arching roots that cling to the ridge of land. Soon a maze of prop roots has grown out of the trunk and clutches at the ridge.

These roots form a strainer that collects the debris of the sea: frag-

CONTORTED ROOTS of a mangrove mark the boundary between sea and land.

ments of shells and corals, driftwood, seaweeds, sediments. As the debris is trapped among the roots, an island, at first no more than a few feet square, is born. Swirling currents or a hurricane may uproot the mangrove before it matures, but if it survives, the pioneer tree is festooned with seedlings hanging from its branches. Many seedlings are carried away by the currents to colonize sandbars and mudflats elsewhere; others become imbedded in the debris strained out of the sea by the parent tree. There they sprout and grow, putting out more arching roots, which collect more debris. Several decades after the pioneer seedling arrived at the bare ridge, a flourishing island has been created that can stand against the waves.

The mangrove forest of southwestern Florida, extending from Key West to north of the Ten Thousand Islands, ranks as one of the major areas of its kind in the world. While mangroves in the Keys usually are low-growing, those along the Shark River estuary rise to some 80 feet, with trunks nearly seven feet in circumference. As they march into the waters, they beat down and tame the tides, expanding the perimeters of their own islands and linking island with island.

Other living things are quickly drawn to the new world which the mangroves have created. Other trees take root in the train of the sea-ward-marching red mangroves. Directly behind them are the slightly less adventurous black mangroves; lacking the stiltlike roots of the red man-grove, they are equipped instead with numerous breathing roots that project from the mud like bristles. Following the black mangroves out to sea are buttonwoods, cedars, and palms. Air plants perch in the tree branches, decorating the mangrove forest with blossoms that do not belong to the trees.

The arching roots of the mangroves are encrusted with the white shells of oysters that have become adapted to a life out of water at low tide; swarms of crabs scuttle through the maze of branches; there are even ant nests, their locations on the roots marking the highest reaches of the tide. Terns, pelicans, wood storks, egrets, spoonbills, and herons populate these tiny islands in enormous numbers, protected alike from the blasts of wind and from the hand of man. So many birds with white plumage roost in these trees that from a distance the islands appear speckled as though with huge snowflakes.

With conditions so favorable in Florida Bay for the growth of man-groves, one might ask why this whole area has not already been con-verted to dry land. One reason is that hurricanes periodically visit these shores, stripping leaves from the trees and even blowing off the bark in sheets, leaving their trunks naked and bleached by the sun. There is another check, also, on the spread of the mangroves. The life they har-bor eventually brings about the destruction of the trees themselves. The thousands of birds attracted to each island excrete a guano which in its undiluted state can destroy even the hardy tissues of the mangroves. Year after year, the mangroves are scorched by the ceaseless rain of guano. What was once a luxuriant forest becomes a stark graveyard, exposing the island to wind and waves. The soil washes back into the sea, until only a sandbar remains to mark the site of what had been a tree-clad island. But in the endless cycle of land against sea and sea against land, a new seedling will eventually arrive at the desolate sand-bar, to begin once more the process of building an island.

Along much of the Gulf coast from northern Florida to Texas, land is created in a different way, by numerous rivers that spew immense amounts of silt directly into the gulf, thereby extending the boundaries of the land. The Mississippi River, for example, carries so much silt from the interior of the continent that it is pushing the coast into the gulf at an average rate of 300 feet a year. Much can be learned about the Gulf coast simply by looking at a map. First, notice how the shoreline bulges at those places where the rivers reach the gulf. These bulges on the coast are built of the sediments carried down by the rivers—the Mississippi, the Rio Grande, the Brazos, the Colorado of Texas, the Chattahoochee, the Apalachicola, and still others. Second, the map shows that many of these river systems flow almost directly from north to south, thus reaching deep into the interior of the continent where they tap a continual supply of eroded soil. Third, notice that the Gulf of Mexico is almost completely ringed by land, with only a few gaps on the eastern

A FORLORN MANGROVE in the Florida Keys is the first step toward the birth of a new island. A brown pelican has already taken possession of the treetops.

edge between the islands of the Antilles. Thus the gulf is virtually an enclosed sea; one characteristic of such a sea is that the currents along its shores are comparatively weak.

The weakness of the currents, which are unable to carry away the immense loads of sediment, allows huge deposits to be formed at the river mouths. The rivers of the Atlantic coast do not generally form such bulges; they carry less sediment, and the powerful ocean currents wash much of what they do carry out to sea. The sluggish waters of the gulf have the effect of an immovable wall upon a moving river; as the river bumps against this wall, it drops its load. An underwater embankment is formed, which is further enlarged by additional loads. The result of this piling up of sediment is the creation of an expanse of new land that is approximately triangular in shape, with the apex pointing upstream, thus resembling the shape of the Greek letter *delta*.

The Mississippi River has created one of the major deltas of the world. Each year it brings to its mouth more than 400 million tons of sediment. To visualize this amount of mud and sand, imagine it as equivalent to enough material to cover 250 square miles, or a fifth of the land area of Rhode Island, to a depth of a foot. Some of these sediments are carried out into the gulf, but most remain to block the Mississippi, forcing its mouth to divide into several channels, each of which is constantly forming deltas of its own. These deltas occasionally surround portions of the gulf and thus create lakes; that is how enormous Lake Pontchartrain, near New Orleans, was formed.

The delta of the Mississippi has a surface area of some 12,000 square miles, but hidden from view is the much vaster underwater foundation upon which the delta is built. In places this pile of soil stripped from the heartland of America is several miles thick. The weight of these accumulated sediments is causing the underlying rock layers to sink, thus pulling down the level of the coastlines adjoining the delta as well, and allowing the gulf to encroach upon the land of Louisiana and Mississippi.

The delta is the scene of an unequal contest between land and water, in which the land is clearly the victor. The Mississippi, called the Father of Waters, might also be called the Mother of Lands. Virtually all of the state of Louisiana and much of the state of Mississippi have been created by the river. The land-building forces are aided by plants, which quickly take hold on mudflats and protect them from the storm waves. The waterways in many places are clogged from bank to bank, almost as if they were solid land, with growths of one of the most beautiful pests to grow on the continent—the water hyacinth.

There were no water hyacinths in North America until about 75 years ago, when they were introduced from the tropical streams of Brazil by people unaware of the dangers that lurked in their exquisite orchidlike blossoms. At first they were planted in water gardens, but they soon escaped and grew with extraordinary vigor in nearby swamps. They multiplied so rapidly that within fifteen years they had become serious pests. In only three weeks they can double the area of water covered by their shiny leaves. In one place in Florida, a mere twenty clumps of plants increased in a few years to a total of a million and a half plants. Since they shut out all sunlight from the water, they create a biological desert under their leaves; wherever they grow, they kill fish and cover the winter feeding grounds of waterfowl. They have so blocked the navigable waterways in many parts of Florida and the Gulf coast that even boats with powerful motors are often unable to grind their way through the floating mass.

The delta of the Mississippi is the land of the bayous, a name derived from the Choctaw Indian word meaning "a sluggish stream." Bayous are waterways so nearly without motion that they seem to ooze out of the swamps. Looping and twisting, narrowing to ditches and widening into little lakes and pools, they branch and rebranch, until finally they lead

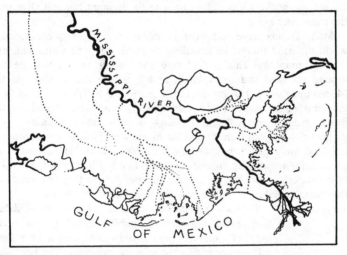

THE DELTA of the Mississippi River has been built up by the accumulation of sediment. Dotted lines indicate channels previously used by the river.

to the gulf or, sometimes, back to the Mississippi itself. Many of the bayous no longer have a connection with the Mississippi, having been first cut off and then completely isolated by the shifting mud of the delta. Mud is everywhere, in the streams and marshes, on the shore and on the leaves of plants. The clogging environment of mud creates many difficulties for life, but it offers an abundance of decaying plant matter that is attractive to vast populations of worms, bivalves, crustaceans, and the larger forms of life that feed on them.

The wilderness of the bayous is a patchwork of habitats—aquatic and marsh communities, dark cypress swamps, towering hardwood forests—whose composition is directly related to the water level. Perhaps the most fascinating of all the habitats is the cattail marsh, the home of many

striding, long-necked birds. The cattail has found its own way of surviving on the mudflats. When the seeds that emerge from the tight brown
cylinders atop its waving spikes have sprouted, they do not reach toward
the light as do seedlings of most plants. Instead, they plow through the
mud, branching and rebranching into a mesh of underground stems. The
stems of most plants would soon rot in such continual contact with
water, but those of the cattail are protected by a waterproof covering.
In addition, they contain a food hoard which can tide over the plant if
the marsh should dry up, allowing it to lie dormant but still alive until
the water rises again.

Many factors have conspired to make the bayous a concentrated
world of living things: its isolation, its fertile soil, the warm sun, and
the high humidity. This land of mud and waterways is a vast meeting
ground for land and water birds, and it is also the terminus of the
Mississippi flyway. During the fall migration, this flyway is used by a
greater number and variety of birds than any other. They funnel into the
flyway from many different habitats—forests, lakes, meadows, and
mountains—of both Canada and the midwestern United States. Most of
the land birds pause only temporarily at the delta before continuing
south to their wintering grounds in Central or South America. For most
of the waterfowl the journey ends at the gulf, where they fan out along
the coastal marshes, banqueting on the luxuriant water weeds.

Protruding from the marshes are mounds of debris
that resemble overgrown anthills. Each of these is the
lodge of a muskrat family, and nowhere on the continent
do these animals exist in such profusion. The Louisiana
race of muskrats, inhabiting the coastal marshes from
southern Texas to western Alabama, outnumbers the
common muskrats found elsewhere throughout the continent, even though the latter occur wherever there are
undisturbed rivers, lakes, or salt marshes. A muskrat
looks like a large meadow mouse with webbed hind feet
and a flattened tail—its adaptations for swimming. Its
lodge is constructed of clumps of matted vegetation—
giant reeds, canes, and cattails—built in shallow water
to a height of four feet. It uses the cattail stalks not only

MUSKRAT

as food but also in the construction of a floating raft, on which the animal rests while feeding, as well as to camouflage resting holes in its territory.

The muskrats and the cattails inhabit a borderline land between salt water and fresh water, between land and sea. In their ability to accommodate themselves to these conditions, they are but variations on the constant theme of the irrepressibility of life along the shore.

5 : The Western Boundary

A NYONE WHO HAS VISITED both the Atlantic and Pacific shores cannot fail to have been conscious of the differences between them. Never does even the bold Maine coast approach the ruggedness of the Pacific shore, particularly that from northern California to Alaska. Here are steep, nearly vertical cliffs and imposing headlands; here are islets of resistant rock, known as sea stacks, jutting out of the ocean offshore.

The western boundary of the continent is a land fashioned by waves, whose work can be seen with a clarity that is scarcely equaled elsewhere in the world. Wherever the visitor turns his gaze, the outcome of the ceaseless battle between waves and rocks is evident. The battering ram of the sea possesses a force which during storms may amount to a ton per square foot of rock—an impact greater than that of a tank smashing into a stone wall at full speed. At Point Reyes, north of San Francisco, cliffs some 600 feet high breast the waves like the prows of a fleet of giant sailing ships. Along the shore are grottoes pounded out by the waves, some of them hundreds of feet long. Nowhere is there an extensive coastal plain; currents have built sand spits and barrier beaches at only a few places on the Pacific shore. Unlike the drowned coast of Maine, the Pacific shore is largely one that has risen, and is still rising, above the sea.

At many places along the shore are cliffs set well back from the water. Their tops are flattened, smoothly leveled by the bulldozer action of waves when the land was much lower in relation to the sea than it is today. Many of the terraces are so broad and level that one might suppose a land developer had been at work. Occasionally, the surface may be broken by a small hillock or two, remnants of sea stacks not completely ground down before the land rose beyond the reach of the waves. Behind some of these terraces the land rises abruptly again, into cliffs left by yet another higher and more ancient sea. In the Coos Bay section of Oregon, for example, these terraces rise like a flight of broad flat steps to a height well over a thousand feet above the present sea level.

Compared with the jagged estuaries of the Atlantic shore, the Pacific coast seems almost uniformly straight. Puget Sound, San Francisco Bay, and Monterey Bay are among its few irregularities. The reason for this evenness can be seen by standing on one of the terraces or cliffs which commands a wide view of the shore. The waves roll in unbroken until they reach the sea islands and promontories. There they pile up, and their full force is concentrated against the projecting rocks. By the time the waves reach the little coves between the headlands, their force is broken and scattered. Thus, the waves exert their greatest force against the headlands that disrupt the regularity of the shoreline. The very formations least able to withstand the waves—the coves, which are composed mainly of weaker rocks and sand—are also those against which the waves strike with the least force. The result is a balance between the erosion of headlands and coves that prevents the formation of deep irregularities.

It seems nearly impossible that any living thing could survive amidst such a surf; yet living on the lower rocks and meeting the full force of the waves are a profusion of starfishes. Along the northern Pacific shore, these animals are noted for their number, diversity, and magnificent coloration. Here can be found not only giants several feet in diameter such as one would expect, but very small and fragile species as well. Starfishes survive the waves by lying spreadeagled on a rock, taking advantage of the very weight and power of the waves to keep themselves pressed into place. In addition, they are equipped with a system of hydraulic pumps on the undersides of their arms that create suction. But among the inhabitants of the world of waves not even the starfish has the endurance and strength of the abalone, a large sea snail prized for its mother-of-pearl shell. The abalone possesses a muscular foot like other mollusks, but the mucus it secretes gives it a power of suction equaled by few other marine invertebrates.

Few seacoasts of the world have the sheer grandeur of British Co-

WAVE-BATTERED Oregon shore, showing sea cliffs and island remnant of wave erosion. Eventually the headlands will be cut back and the island will disappear.

lumbia and Alaska. Between Seattle, Washington, and Skagway, Alaska, is a thousand-mile inland waterway—"The Road that Walks," the Indians called it. This Inland Passage is hemmed in by lofty mountains that rise out of the water, and broken here and there by fjords of awesome beauty. The present passage was once a long valley lying parallel to the ocean between two mountain chains. When this land was covered by the glaciers, it sank and was flooded by the seas; the valley was transformed into a long waterway. Each of the myriad islands that rears above the gray waters of the passage is actually the summit of a mountain that has been submerged. The fjords are the mouths of former rivers that emptied into this valley; they were deepened and widened by the glaciers and finally submerged.

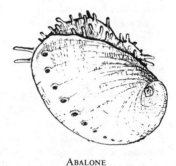

ABALONE

The tides in the passage are much more complex than the simple advance and retreat of the waters on many Atlantic shores. The tides on the Pacific coast not only move east and west as they ebb and flow upon the beach; they also sweep from south to north. If San Diego, California, has high tide at 5:00 A.M., for example, it will not be high tide at Vancouver until three hours later, or until six hours later halfway up the coast of Alaska. The Inland Passage is actually much like a series of connected basins of water, the more southerly of which are filled by the tide while those to the north are still empty. As the water runs downhill from the filled to the empty basins it creates a current that sometimes attains a speed of more than ten miles an hour and forces even steamers to drop anchor.

The farther north up the passage that one penetrates, the more numerous the glaciers become. The waterway's northern terminus is Glacier Bay; here, signs of the ice age are everywhere—in the glacial debris with which the entrance to the bay is littered, and in the many small icebergs drifting on the waters. As one travels the 50 miles up the bay, the meaning of the surrounding formations becomes increasingly evident: they are the moraines and outwash plains left by the glaciers. More than twenty tremendous glaciers and many lesser ones have their origin in the peaks with their covering of perpetual snow. Some of these are thousands of feet thick in places; flowing down the mountain valleys to the ocean, they terminate in towering cliffs that break up into huge blocks of floating ice. Muir Glacier, the largest of these, is nearly two miles wide, with a sheer face that rises 265 feet above the water. Most glaciers travel only a few inches a day, but this giant river of ice moves as much as 30 feet in a single day.

Some 300 years ago the entire bay was covered by an icecap estimated to have been 3000 feet high. Since then the ice has been retreating. Between 1899 and 1946, for example, Muir Glacier melted back thirteen miles, leaving the cabin that John Muir had built close to its terminus far from it. As one travels up the bay one can see the remains of forests that flourished in the warm interglacial periods, were later buried by new advances of the ice, and have recently been uncovered again.

Between the glaciers and the entrance to the bay, one can see how plants reclaim lost dominions in the wake of the retreating ice. At the mouth of the bay is a mature forest of spruce and hemlock, draped with moss and populated by bears, martens, mink, wolverines, and Sitka blacktail deer. Approaching the glaciers one passes through a younger coniferous forest, then through clumps of cottonwood and alder, and finally through dwarf willows. The trees merge gradually with the more humble pioneers that grow within the shadow of the glaciers: horsetails, fireweed, and numerous alpine flowers. Beyond them on the bare rocks are those outposts of plant life, the hardy lichens and mosses. Soon even these disappear, and there is no plant concealing the nakedness of the recently uncovered moraine.

The farthest southward penetration of the ice sheet on the Pacific coast was into the vicinity of Puget Sound. To the north, where the earth sank groaning under the weight of the ice, much of the shorescape was sculptured by the glaciers. To the south, where the land has risen from the sea, is a region shaped largely by the power of water. Lying athwart this transition zone is the Olympic Peninsula whose geologic history is one of uplift and wearing down of great mountains, of perpetual advance and withdrawal of the sea. During the past million years its gradual emergence from the sea has been counterbalanced by the continual erosion of its summits. The present shore of the Olympic Peninsula is a wild land of precipitous cliffs, some plunging 300 feet to the breakers.

The sea at work upon the rocks resembles a quarrying operation. As the waves smash against the cliffs, the air within the cracks in the rocks is compressed. In this way a tremendous pressure is built up which may eventually lift a whole section of rock out of the cliff. The sea is an unchained force relentlessly clawing at the land. First it gets a finger into an opening, then a hand, and finally a powerful arm. A small crack may eventually lead to the downfall of a whole cliff.

MUDDY MORAINE at Glacier Bay, Alaska, is the end of a river of ice born in the whiteness of a mountain snowfield thousands of feet above it.

At first the crack is merely widened; then the waters probe the excavation, digging out the less resistant material. A cave is formed, which may go on deepening until it penetrates the promontory, perhaps forming a tunnel. Such a tunnel is continually being widened around its circumference until all that remains is an arch, one of the most magnificent features of the Pacific shore. Finally, the piers upon which the arch rests grow so thin that it collapses into the sea. All that remain are the pillars, formations known as sea stacks, surrounded by a jumble of boulders. These fragments are eventually deposited at the base of the cliffs, where they are splintered, turned, and polished. Because of the variety of the rocks that compose these cliffs, the beach pebbles of the Pacific are often remarkable for their colors as well as for their smoothness.

Southward from the Olympic Peninsula, the shore is a series of variations on the theme of rocky cliffs and creamy surf. In some places sea arches dominate the scene; elsewhere, submerged rocks create islands of foam on the surface of the water. At a few places, for example north of Cape Arago, Oregon, there are stretches of broad beach and sand dunes. But beaches such as these are only a minor interruption of the basic theme of rocks. South of Puget Sound, the largest break in the Pacific coastline is the Golden Gate of San Francisco, an unimpressive cleft in the rocks which turns out to be a passage into a succession of large bays. Here the complex rise and fall of the land has created one of the great protected harbors of the world. Along the ocean-fronting land a series of terraces give evidence of gradual emergence, whereas the bay and the gateway itself are revealed to have been partially submerged.

At San Diego, in southern California, a bay of a different sort has been formed by shore currents that have swept sand and gravel northward. The result has been a curved bar or hook extending nearly to the bold headlands of Point Loma. Year by year, the outlet of the bay formed behind the hook tends to grow narrower. In fact, had no dredging or engineering works been undertaken to counteract the currents, they probably would have closed the outlet and converted San Diego Bay into a lagoon. That has happened already at other places, notably around Oceanside, California, where gravel deposits have blocked the outlets of several streams. Similarly, the Santa Clara River no longer even meets the ocean; throughout its lower reaches it enters and gradually merges with a swampy lagoon.

One of the most arresting places on the entire Pacific shore is the Monterey Peninsula. Few miles of the American continent have been trod so thoroughly by naturalists as this point of land, not only because the beauty of its clear blue waters is unsullied by sediment but also because of the incomparable views of the sea birds and animals it affords. In the same way that Cape Cod forms a biological dividing line on the Atlantic shore, Monterey is the meeting place of the sea animals of the north and those of the south.

Typical of the southern fauna is the California sea lion—the trained "seal" of the circus—an intelligent and agreeable creature whose most northerly breeding area lies a little south of Monterey. Few mammals are so perfectly adapted to life in the water. Sea lions are exceedingly agile swimmers. Using their front flippers as paddles and their rear ones as rudders or brakes, they can swim almost equally well on their backs, their bellies, or their sides. Although clumsy on land, they can cover ground at a lumbering gallop. They climb rock bluffs that would be difficult going for a human being, and leap fifteen feet from a ledge to a rocky beach with no apparent harm.

Sea lions are mammals that have abandoned life on land and returned to salt water, as whales did before them. But sea lions still have links with the land: their young must be born there, and moreover they must learn to swim. To cross the evolutionary boundary between land and sea, certain modifications in their bodies were necessary. Their feet were altered into swimming flippers, and between the skin and body there developed a layer of spongy tissue, impregnated with oil, which acts as an insulator in maintaining the animal's body temperature. The thickness of this blubber layer varies with the seasons and the food supply.

Near Florence, Oregon, is a large rookery of Steller sea lions, which are primarily inhabitants of arctic waters. In an enormous cave carved out by the waves the huge beasts play and slumber, apparently unmindful of the visitors who come to watch. The rookery is a bedlam of sounds: the pounding of the surf, the calls of sea birds, the guttural booming of the bulls, the wails of the cows, the whines of the pups. The sea lions are as restless as the waves: they dive off rocks and ledges; they scramble after each other; they leap out of the water like porpoises. More than any other animals, in their total mastery of the breakers they typify the wave-swept Pacific shore.

Monterey also marks approximately the southern limit of the range of the arctic sea otters. Of all the North American mammals and birds that have trod the hairline border between survival and extinction, none has made so dramatic a comeback as the sea otter. This species once ranged from Japan across the north Pacific to the Aleutian Islands and down the west coast of Canada into the United States. But the otters were so prized for their velvety brown fur that they were relentlessly hunted for as long as any could be found. The species was believed extinct, but in 1938 one small band was discovered. Since then it has been conscientiously protected against hunting or disturbance; today four groups, numbering in the thousands, live between Carmel and Point Sur.

The otters live offshore in the great undersea forests of kelp, a ribbon-like seaweed that may grow to a length equal to the height of a large tree. In the haven of the kelp they sleep floating on their backs, with a few fronds twisted about them as anchors. They use the kelp as a break-water against waves, and they flee into it when danger threatens, particularly from the killer whales that prowl the coast. When the newborn otter is two days old, the mother moors it to a frond of kelp while she hunts in the depths. The otter's diet consists of marine invertebrates— sea urchins, mollusks, crabs, and especially the red abalone. No one knows exactly how the otters manage to dislodge this mollusk from the

ARCH on the Oregon coast serves as a basking place for hordes of sea lions.

rocks, but it is believed that they pound its shell with a stone. When an otter emerges from the depths with an abalone or a clam, it also brings up a stone. Rolling over on its back, the otter then rests the stone on its belly as it if were an anvil, and proceeds to smash its prey.

The eternal battle between the forces of sea and land, and their tentative relationship at the water's edge, is best symbolized by certain trees that grow nowhere but along the Pacific coast. The rarest tree in North America, and possibly in the world, is the Torrey pine, which is found growing wild only near La Jolla, California, and on the island of Santa Rosa, off Santa Barbara. No more than about thirty feet tall, these little trees seem to fling themselves against the slopes to escape from the wild ocean winds. The wind has so sculptured their branches that the trees resemble tattered banners flapping in the breeze.

No coastal tree is better known than the Monterey cypress, whose contorted branches are the very emblem of the Pacific shore. Only about 10,000 of these cypresses survive today in the wild state; they are all found at one place in the world, on the rocky headlands around Monterey. Monterey cypress, unlike the mangrove or the swamp cypress, belongs wholly to the land. It possesses no special adaptations for life near the sea, yet it is never found growing more than a mile inland. High winds and salt spray nip at its buds, twist its trunk into writhing shapes, and shear off its leaves. But only while it endures the hardships of the sea cliffs does the Monterey cypress attain its full beauty. Many people who have taken a fancy to this tree at Monterey have planted it on their own property. Seedlings planted far from the moisture-laden winds of a large body of water soon perish; and those that survive develop into prim specimens totally lacking the grotesque beauty of their kin at Monterey. No gardener has yet been able to re-create the combination of salt spray, gusty winds, and rocky soil that nurtures this tree in the wild.

As the cypresses mature at Monterey, they become more and more heavily draped with beards of "moss"—actually a lichen. The growth of the lichen suppresses leaves and weakens the tree; but it is a boon to the birds of the Monterey Peninsula, since it furnishes an excellent nesting material. When the tree dies and stands leafless, the bleached skeleton serves as a platform for the hosts of birds that fly before the sea winds. Eventually, the dead roots relax their grasp on the cliff, and the trunk crashes to the watery rim. It may be claimed by the tide as driftwood or it may lie on the beach where it has fallen. Shorn of bark and whitened by the spray, it becomes yet another symbol of the constant pull and tug between sea and land.

III

THE INLAND
WATERS

6 : Rivers and Waterfalls

O NLY IN THE MOST ARID SECTIONS of the continent is it possible to travel more than a few miles without crossing a bridge or catching sight of a pond or stream. Water is everywhere on the land. It trickles from springs and rushes down mountains; it is captured momentarily in mountain lakes or flows in silt-laden rivers through yawning canyons. All of this water is ceaselessly on the move toward the sea. On its journey across the continent it is the prime agent of erosion, and much of the variety of the landscape owes its origins to the paths taken by water across the land.

Inland waters are the result of a greater amount of water falling upon the land than the soil can absorb or the plants can use immediately. This excess water has the power to carve an uplifted block of the earth's surface into a mountain scene of valleys, foothills, and jagged summits— or to excavate a canyon through rocks more than a mile thick. Even in the arid regions where rainfall is a rare event, it is water that has carved the nightmarish shapes of Bryce and Zion, the mesas, and the natural bridges and arches. It is scarcely believable that mere water can wear down rock, the very epitome of permanence. But water falling on the land creates scenery in two ways: first, it undermines and washes away rocks and soil; then it uses the debris as tools to cut further into the land. Water with a speed of only one foot per second will transport gravel; a current traveling four feet per second will move a rock weighing two pounds. A speed of 25 feet per second will transport huge boulders.

Water is able not only to pit and peel the surface of even the most resistant rock, but also—as it enters cracks and joints and then expands due to freezing—eventually to shatter it as well. It also breaks down rocks by chemical erosion: it reacts with minerals in the rocks to form compounds that lead to their decomposition. Water erosion is the great leveler of the surface of the continent, continually wearing down the high places and depositing the debris in the valleys until a level plain is created. It has been estimated that water erosion lowers the entire surface of the United States by about one foot every 10,000 years.

The rivers and lakes of North America form a blue trelliswork on the pages of an atlas. They seem to be permanent features of the landscape, but their true history is one of appearance and disappearance, increase and decrease in size, and constant alteration of course. Some rivers are ancient by man's reckoning, but they are all youthful by the scale of geologic time. Many of them, indeed, have come into existence within the historic period of man's life on the continent.

Every great river system has been molded by the conditions of the land through which it flows—climate, soil, rock structure, and even vegetation. Rivers constantly make adjustments to these conditions, but eventually they find their way to those parts of the landscape where the rocks are weakest, and as these are gouged out and worn away a channel is formed. The Rio Grande on the Texas-Mexico border, for example, is shallow and sluggish over much of its course, yet at the Great Bend it seems to have parted the cliffs to cut a channel 1500 feet deep. This was not such a mammoth rock-moving job as it might appear; the river has simply located itself along the line of a huge fracture in the rocks.

Few streams flow haphazardly, although many appear to do so. The varied patterns they assume are actually a response to the conditions of the landscape. One of the less usual patterns is that of parallel rivers. Anyone who has driven along the Atlantic coastal plain between Virginia and southern Georgia will probably have noticed that dozens of rivers flow parallel to each other with a monotonous regularity. So rigid is this arrangement that even the tributaries themselves follow parallel routes before swinging in to join the mainstreams. Parallel rivers occur elsewhere on the continent and around the world, but nowhere else on such a scale. This pattern is not due merely to chance. It occurs only on land that is flat with a gentle slope, like a roof with a slight pitch. Rainwater running off such a roof flows in a series of parallel rivulets. The gradual slope of the south Atlantic coastal plain from the Appalachians to the ocean resembles just such a roof. Parallel rivers also exist inland —in Nebraska, for example—and the origin of these is the same. Vast quantities of soil eroded from the Rockies have been carried down to form a sloping plain that extends eastward for more than 500 miles.

There are many other river patterns, such as those of the "lost" rivers that disappear into the earth midway in their courses, and of the radial systems that follow a pattern like the spokes of a wheel down the slopes of a symmetrical mountain. Another pattern, which is most easily seen from the air—especially in flying over the ridges of the Appalachian Mountains—is that of a trellis. This one has a certain resemblance to a climbing rosebush, with smaller branches often developing at right angles to the main branches. A trellis system usually develops in places where the rocks have been twisted and folded into ridges in such a way that wrinkles of resistant rock alternate with weaker ones. Water flowing across such a surface cuts its channels only into the weaker rocks, and a trellis pattern is the result.

River patterns are complicated by what may be called the piracy of one stream upon another. Rivers lengthen their channels by extending into new territory upstream, at their headwaters. In the process the headwaters of one river may cut across the channel of another river and divert the waters of the latter into its own channel. The Shenandoah River of Virginia is an outstanding example of such piracy. At one time a number of rivers—the largest being the Potomac, Rappahannock, Rapidan, and James—all originated on the western side of the Blue Ridge and flowed through gaps in these mountains toward Chesapeake Bay. Also flowing on the western side at that time was an insignificant tributary of the Potomac—what is now the Shenandoah. Gradually, as the headwaters of the Shenandoah began to cut upstream in a southwesterly direction, along a belt of soft rocks, it cut into the headwaters of the other rivers, one by one, and captured them. The Rappahannock and the Rapidan yielded their headwaters to the Shenandoah, and today they both rise on the eastern slope of the Blue Ridge. The Shenandoah has not yet captured all of the James River; but since it is steadily cutting upstream, one may safely predict that it will do so in time.

At first glance the lower Mississippi and its tributaries from Memphis southward appear to form a system of parallel rivers similar to those of the south Atlantic coastal plain. The tributaries of most rivers join the mainstream at the nearest convenient point, but the tributaries of the lower Mississippi flow alongside the big river for great distances; some of them never reach the Mississippi at all, but instead flow directly into the Gulf of Mexico. A number of other midwestern rivers follow a similar pattern.

The parallel flow of the Mississippi tributaries has, however, a different origin from that of the rivers of the south Atlantic. These midwestern rivers carry great amounts of sediment stripped from the easily eroded soils of the plains and prairies. In the spring these rivers usually rise and spread out beyond their normal banks. As a result, the banks of the rivers in time become elevated to form natural levees, effectively isolating the mainstream from its tributaries. A tributary stream thus can only flow alongside the mainstream until it finds a weak place in the natural levee. The Yazoo River, for example, flows about halfway through the state of Mississippi before it joins the main stem at Vicksburg. On the western side of the Mississippi, the White and the Arkansas have managed to remain connected with the main stem, but only by splitting into little channels that meander through a network of narrow openings before finally reaching the Mississippi.

The beginnings of the mighty Mississippi are unimpressive. At Lake Itasca in Minnesota, about 2500 miles north of the Gulf of Mexico, it comes into being as a gurgling little brook that would ordinarily attract little attention. From the time Europeans first sighted its mighty lower reaches, many attempts were made to trace the great river to its source. As expedition after expedition pushed far up the river, many a likely lake or brook was proclaimed to be that source. But a young geologist named Henry Schoolcraft, who had gone on one of these expeditions, remained convinced that the true source had never been discovered. Accompanied only by an Indian guide, he followed the twisting, narrowing channel until he proved in 1832 that it originated in a little lake in Minnesota. Using the middle syllables of the Latin for "true source"—*veritas caput*—he coined the name Itasca.

Between its source and the St. Anthony Falls below Minneapolis–St. Paul, the upper Mississippi is a winding stream that flows through a landscape smoothed out by the glaciers. At the falls the character of the landscape changes, and the river enters a channel between high rocky bluffs. South of Tennessee the bluffs end, and the great river, joined now by the Missouri and the Ohio, wanders toward the Gulf of Mexico through a broad flood plain. From the sparkling little stream that left Lake Itasca's blue waters it has become transformed into a vehicle for carrying countless millions of tons of silt. In fact, the river's whole lower course is through a land that the river itself helped to create by depositing loads of sediment. In a past geologic age, the bluffs marked the southern boundary of the continent.

Throughout most of its lower course the Mississippi is notable for the endless windings and shiftings of its course. It often jumps its channel, swinging to the right or to the left, and cuts new channels into the flood plain. Much of the Mississippi down which La Salle floated 300 years ago is now solid ground, for since then the river has altered its course many times. The neck of any one of the numerous horseshoe bends may grow narrower and narrower, until at some flood season the river takes the shortest course and cuts through it, thus straightening its channel. The bend is now cut off from the river, but it is still filled with water. It has become what is known as an oxbow lake, a temporary feature of the

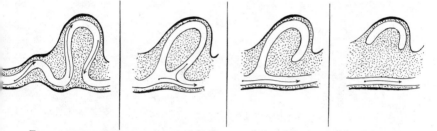

FORMATION OF AN OXBOW LAKE. At left, the meandering river forms a horseshoe bend. Later, it cuts across the neck, taking the most direct route and leaving behind a semicircular lake whose shape suggests an oxbow.

landscape that soon becomes marshy and silt-filled. At some future time, however, the river may change its course again and reclaim the oxbow, making it once more a part of the channel.

Geologists often describe rivers as young, mature, or in their old age, referring not to their actual years of existence but to the stage of development they have reached. The Mississippi has a youthful headwater in Minnesota, a mature middle section between the bluffs, and a lower river that follows the meandering course of old age. A Maine river rushing toward the Atlantic usually lacks the meandering stage; some rivers elsewhere may be in old age throughout much of their course. Not every river possesses all three valley stages at the same time, but most rivers pass through each of them eventually.

The youthful river may begin as a shallow groove in the rocks, as a little outlet from a lake, or as a carrier of spring water. It expends most of its energy in cutting downward into its channel; as it does this, the swiftly flowing water carves steep, sloping banks that meet at the bot-

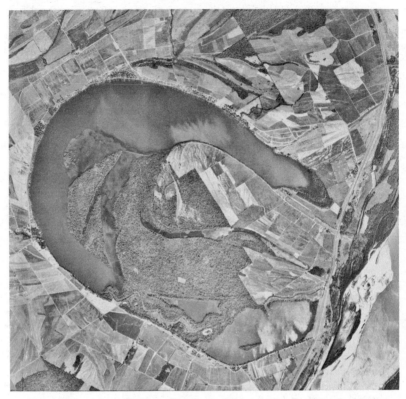

AN OXBOW LAKE near Hughes, Arkansas, was formed when the Mississippi River (lower right) took the shortest route across a horseshoe bend.

tom of the stream like the sides of the letter V. Usually present in youthful valleys are rapids and waterfalls that alternate with pools and marshes; there are few tributaries. A youthful river such as the Mississippi above the St. Anthony Falls is rarely navigable. The Yellowstone River at its falls in Wyoming, the Niagara, the Red River of North Dakota, and the Grand Canyon of the Colorado are all youthful valleys. Although these rivers have already impressively cut through the land, the major part of their work still lies before them.

The youthful river expends its main energies in cutting downward into its bed rather than in widening its banks. But gradually the youthful river begins to grow broader, and along the banks occasional deposits of sand or gravel can be seen. A point is finally reached at which down-cutting is negligible; the velocity of the river decreases, and the sediments form a continuous strip on both sides of the channel. The valley sides become less steep; the lakes and pools of the river's more youthful stage have now merged with the widened stream channel or have been filled with sediment. This is the mature valley, and in cross section it resembles the letter U. In its old age the river meanders lazily across a flood plain, the creation of the silt deposited by its waters in times of flood. The river in old age is characterized by a wide flood plain, natural levees, oxbows, and sandbars.

During a day's hike a small stream can be followed from the upland forest where it is born to a mature stage downstream, and even sometimes into its old age. The birthplace of such a stream might be a damp spot in a forest, shaded by tall trees and surrounded by ferns. The trickle of water is often so inconspicuous that it may be scarcely noticeable. As one walks farther down the slope, it may be seen that the stream has cut a little furrow and is quickly deepening its bed. Along a typical stream this little V-shaped ravine is bordered by trees, which stabilize the banks, furnish shade, and reduce evaporation. The little ravine is a world in itself, with its own climate and a quite different vegetation from that of the surrounding forest. It is damp and cool, much like the climate farther north. Oaks and cedars, which grow in warmth and sunshine, may populate the surrounding forest, but the little ravine harbors a more northerly plant community—hemlock, yellow birch, beech, and witch hazel, for example.

Much about the procession of plant life on the planet can be observed in this little ravine. Growing closest to the water are liverworts, plants lacking true roots and therefore little suited for life on dry land. Ancestors of these humble growths were among the first plants to make the transition from a water to a land existence; one botanist has labeled the liverwort "the Christopher Columbus of the plant kingdom." Slightly higher on the ravine grow the club mosses or ground pines, and these are followed by the lacy ferns. Low-growing plants today, during the Coal Age, roughly 300 million years ago, they towered to the height of trees. At the edges of the little ravine can be seen still another advance in the parade of plant evolution: the conifers, whose ancestors flourished after the decline of the coal swamps. These plants represented a marked improvement, for they were among the first to bear seeds. And everywhere around the ravine, adapting to sunlight as well as to shade, to wetness and to dryness, are the present rulers of the plant kingdom. These

THE LOWER FALLS of the Yellowstone River in Wyoming make a drop of 306 feet and rejuvenate the valley into a youthful V-shape.

are the trees, herbs, and grasses that bear flowers and whose seeds are encased in a protective container. They developed during the time of the dinosaurs, but they did not assume leadership of the plant kingdom until after the extinction of the great reptiles.

As one continues to trace the channel of the little stream, the ravine gradually widens, and the sides become less steep. At first the same kinds of plants inhabit both sides of the ravine; but as the valley increases in width, one side is flooded with sunlight while the other is in shade. Two strikingly different plant communities develop at a distance of only a few feet from each other. The shaded north-facing slope remains moist and cool, and maintains a vegetation much like that of the steep ravine. But the rays of the sun beating on the opposite, south-facing slope produce conditions that are hot and dry. The sun-bathed rocks are pioneered by the crusty growths of lichens. Red cedar and hickory may replace hemlock and beech, and the smaller plants may include grasses, blueberries, wild aster, and goldenrod.

Occasionally the character of the stream at this stage of development is affected by the intervention of the beaver. Other animals of the forest accept the conditions it imposes upon them. A bird may construct a nest in a tree, or a woodchuck may dig a hole in the ground; but these are trifling enterprises compared with the elaborate engineering works of the beaver. In building its home this enterprising animal also markedly alters both the stream and the several acres of land surrounding it. The beaver's way of life calls for an underwater lodge and an underwater food cache where supplies of twigs can be stored against the winter famine. The problem of finding suitably deep water is solved by damming a stream. The beaver selects the site for the dam with what appears to be uncanny engineering skill. It digs to this site a series of canals, which are used as waterways for the transport of the logs it obtains by gnawing down large numbers of trees. The trunks of the largest of these are used as the foundation for the dam; occasionally they are propped in place with stones. Then a maze of thinner trunks and branches is piled on to form the internal supports for the application of the beaver's own concrete: a mixture of mud, leaves, and small stones.

Like a man-made reservoir, the dam impounds a permanent pool of water, which lasts through dry seasons as well as wet, by storing the water from spring rains and melting snow. Soon the little pond becomes a focal point for the varied life of the forest. Water plants find their way there, and so do frogs, snakes, and aquatic insects. Migrating birds often pause near the beaver pond, and the mammals of the forest come there to drink.

The pond alters the face of the land around the stream. Many of the surrounding trees are used by the beaver to construct its lodge and dam; others are quickly killed by the standing water. In no more than a few years an area several acres in extent may be leveled. At the same time, however, the pond collects the silt brought down from the hills by the stream. At first the beavers raise the height of their dam to perhaps five or ten feet in order to maintain deep water; but they cannot combat the inevitable process of filling in. As the water level drops, they depart,

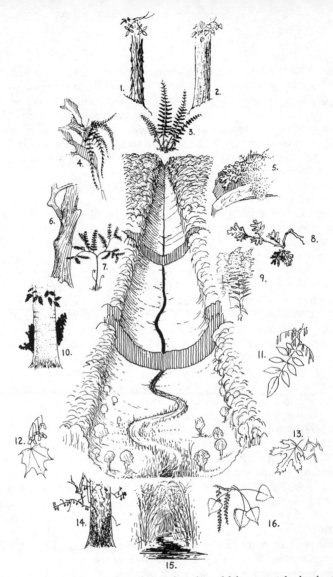

MANY RIVER VALLEYS pass through a V-shaped youthful stage at the headwaters, a U-shape at maturity, and then meander in old age. Among typical plants in the youthful stage are (1) shagbark hickory, (2) basswood, (3) Christmas fern, (4) bladder fern, (5) liverworts and mosses. Typical of the mature stage are (6) hornbeam, (7) maidenhair fern, (8) white oak, and (9) goldenrod. Typical of the meandering stage are (10) beech, (11) white ash, (12) sugar maple, (13) silver maple, (14) sycamore, (15) sandbar willow, and (16) cottonwood.

and the dam falls into disrepair; there remains a flat meadow that much resembles a man-made park in the midst of a forest.

The waterfall created by the beavers' dam may rejuvenate the stream, causing it to dig down into its bed once more. But farther downstream it widens again, and strips of sediment appear along the banks—signs that the stream has entered middle age. The growing flood plain alongside the channel is taken over by a new community of life, developing around those plants that can endure almost constant wetness: nettle, willow, cottonwood, black maple, and others. The stream may remain a mature one, or it may become a fountain of youth once again by plunging over a waterfall, to begin anew the cutting of a youthful valley. In fact, the mature stream may be rejuvenated several times, with alternating rapids, falls, and quiet pools, until finally it settles down into the trough-shaped channel of maturity.

As the river makes its way down the valley, it cuts through rocks of varying resistance. Soft rocks are eroded much more rapidly than resistant ones, and the result is the creation of a waterfall. Waterfalls are only temporary features of the landscape. As a river plunges over a fall, its youthful energy is renewed. The falling water strikes at the base of the resistant rocks, undercutting them until a lip or overhang results. Eventually the lip collapses, and the undercutting of a new lip begins again farther upstream. The lip steadily retreats upstream, until the falls have disappeared and are replaced by a deep gorge.

Almost all waterfalls, including Niagara, have been created in this way. At the time of the melting of the glaciers, water flowed from Lake Erie through the Niagara River until it reached the lower elevation of Lake Ontario, where it formed a waterfall. The Niagara River's course was over a plateau of weak, easily eroded shales, but these shales were protected by a cap of very resistant dolomite rock. As the falling water plunged over this plateau into Lake Ontario, it struck against the easily eroded base of the plateau. The weak shales there were washed away, leaving the dolomite cap as an overhang which eventually collapsed. The cliff of the falls thus became vertical again, but at a place farther upstream. Falling water undercut the dolomite once more, leaving another overhang which likewise eventually collapsed. Constant undercutting has caused Niagara Falls to retreat seven miles upstream since it came into existence, leaving a deep gorge to mark the successive retreats. Today the falls are only about 160 feet high and are retreating upstream at an average rate of some four feet a year. Some day the dolomite cap will be completely undercut; Lake Erie and Lake Ontario will then be connected by a river that flows downhill rapidly, but without any falls. All that will remain of the grandeur of Niagara will be rapids, and they, too, will disappear eventually.

All along the rivers of the Atlantic coastal plain, there are water-falls: the Great Falls of the Potomac, the Schuylkill Falls at Philadel-phia, the falls of the James River at Richmond, and many others. In fact, if the locations of the waterfalls of the Atlantic coastal plain are

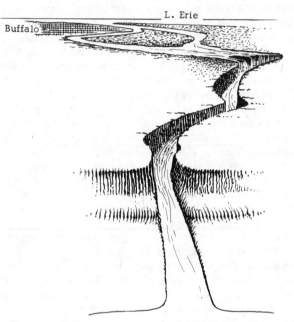

AERIAL VIEW OF NIAGARA FALLS shows the escarpment, the deep gorge produced by the undermining of the falls, and the location of the falls today—seven miles upstream from their former location near Lake Ontario.

plotted on a map—starting at Columbus, Georgia, and continuing north-ward through Macon, Augusta, Raleigh, and so on—it will be seen that they follow a straight course; this is the "fall line." The fall line marks the most easterly boundary of the Appalachians, the place at which the rivers leave the resistant granite of the mountains to flow over the yielding sedimentary rocks of the coastal plain. The reason that so many cities lie astride the fall line is that for the pioneers the falls marked the end of river transportation inland. There, abandoning their boats, they set up trading centers, which eventually grew into some of the major cities of the southern and eastern states.

The greatest waterfalls on the continent are man-made; they are the approximately 3000 large dams that dot the landscape. No natural waterfall on the continent can rival the cascade that pours over the spillway of Grand Coulee Dam on the Columbia River. It is about as long as Niagara, and four times as high. Every second an average of

Fall Line ·······

Piedmont

Coastal Plain

THE FALL LINE is the place where rivers pass from the resistant granitic rocks of the Piedmont to the weak sands and clays of the coastal plain, producing falls.

117,000 cubic feet of water pours over the dam and through its outlet tubes, exerting energy equal to almost three million horsepower. During the spring, when the snowpacks on the flanks of the Rockies melt, the torrent may reach four times that quantity of water. The storing of water prevents floods, permits the irrigation of crops and forms artificial lakes for recreation. As the water flows out of the dam, it drops through long tubes to huge powerhouses nestled at the dam's base, where it spins turbines and thus generates electricity.

The rivers of the northern Pacific are the ancestral homes of the salmon that now surmount the dams by means of fish ladders. The ladders are actually a series of pools of water, each pool a step above the one before, which enables the fish to make successive leaps from the bottom of a dam to the high water in the reservoir above. About a year and a half after it is hatched from the egg in a small tributary stream, the young salmon, then the size of a sardine, begins an extraordinary journey. Suddenly, an impulse overtakes all the salmon in a stream to head in the direction of the sea, which may be a thousand miles distant, twice that in the case of the Yukon River of Canada and Alaska. They swim downstream, reach the mouth, pause momentarily—and then head for the pastures in the ocean whose exact location is unknown. After roaming the Pacific and growing to tremendous size on the abundance of food there, the salmon seek out the very rivers where they were hatched. They gather at the entrances to the rivers for their last meal, then in a churning mass launch themselves upstream against the current. They display an uncanny singleness of purpose as they surmount the obstacles in their path—the ancient hazards of waterfalls, rapids, and predators, the modern hazards of human fishermen and dams.

At first all is confusion. Five species of salmon—chinook, silver, sockeye, chum, and pink—swim up these rivers in a milling mass. As they penetrate the rivers they tend to separate. Each species has its own place for spawning; each species is subdivided into groups that search for a particular tributary; each group is further subdivided into bands that seek a particular stretch of the tributary. The tagging of young salmon has revealed that 90 per cent somehow manage to find the very stream in which they were born. Propelled by an untiring instinct to reach their home waters, they battle currents, and at a single jump leap waterfalls as much as ten feet high. They maintain an unswerving course upstream at a speed of about six miles a day, although sometimes they swim at twice that speed. Many do not survive the long journey. They may perish from sheer exhaustion, or flop onto rocks where they struggle unsuccessfully to get back into the water; many are caught by bears, minks, and otters that come to the banks for an orgy of feeding on the salmon.

No one knows for sure how the salmon manage to recognize the stream where they were hatched. There has been no shortage of theories: the differing velocity of the current in each stream, the characteristics of the stream bed, the chemical "taste" of the water have all been suggested as landmarks. Many experiments have demonstrated that the knowledge of the parent stream is not inherited. The young fish learns to recognize its native stream during the first year of its life, just as a young bird is enabled by learning to return, after a migration of thousands of miles, to the very tree in a forest in which it was fledged.

The final answer to the mystery of the salmon may be in their remarkable ability to detect chemical substances in the water. Salmon are so sensitive to the "taste" of the water that a fish coming up a small stream has been known to halt or even turn around when a man has dipped his hand into the water a considerable distance away. Experiments in which the nostrils of salmon were plugged revealed that these fish did not have the same ability to locate the parent streams as did salmon whose nostrils were left unplugged. This much, at any rate, is certain: once the salmon have reached the spawning places and laid their eggs, their lives are over. Not a single adult ever survives to make the return journey downstream to the Pacific. But in the pebbles of innumerable brooks and streams are the countless billions of eggs that will produce the next generation.

The Pacific salmon is the most dramatic of the living links between the oceans and rivers, but it is not the only one. Atlantic salmon have a similar life history, although the adults return to the sea instead of dying on the spawning grounds. The Atlantic eels reverse the procedure by living most of their lives in lakes and rivers and then returning to the ocean to spawn. And each spring when the sun's path crosses the equator and the lengths of night and day are equal, the alewives (members of the herring family) enter the innumerable inlets and tidal estuaries from Newfoundland to North Carolina to spawn.

7 : Lakes and Bogs

ENRY DAVID THOREAU once wrote: "A lake is the landscape's most beautiful and expressive feature." Just what a lake expresses may be different for each beholder; but for the geologist it expresses the impermanence of all landscapes. Every lake is destined to grow shallower and smaller, and eventually to become dry land. In all the world only ten lakes, five of which are in North America, have surface areas greater than 10,000 square miles. Most lakes are very small, and even the deepest are relatively shallow. As soon as a lake appears on the landscape, whether it is a crater on a mountain top or an oxbow along a meandering river, natural forces set about filling it up and decreasing its area. The streams flowing into a lake deposit sediments that form a gradually tightening noose. And as the stream that carries water out of the lake continually deepens its channel, the level of the lake is lowered. Throughout the White and Green Mountains of New England, for example, one often comes across former lake basins, now filled in and drained of water, which are almost the only patches of level land amidst the rocky terrain.

A look at a detailed map of the continent will show that there are swarms of lakes in Canada, Minnesota, Wisconsin, and New England. In some mountains, for example the Adirondacks of New York, lakes are common; in others farther south, such as the Great Smokies, they are rare. One is not surprised that flat and dry Texas should have few lakes;

but North Dakota, although equally level and arid, is covered by swarms of them. Much of this distribution pattern is due to the glaciers, which created lakes in many ways. Sometimes the glaciers simply dammed the rivers. Occasionally a glacier traveling down a mountain valley dug out long hollows, thus producing "finger lakes," as at Glacier Park on the Montana-Canada border, in western New York, and at many places in the Rockies and southern Alaska.

Other lakes were formed near the moraines. They are unusual in being kettle-shaped, and in having no inlet or outlet streams. The formation of kettles, as these lakes are called, began when large blocks of ice were buried in the debris of the moraines. As the blocks melted, the moraines collapsed at those points, producing depressions that soon filled with water. Many of these lakes still hold water thousands of years after the retreat of the ice. The reason is that watertight bottoms were created for them by the glaciers; masses of clay particles collected by the moving glaciers were deposited in these hollows, and then compacted by the immense weight.

A large swath of the Canadian landscape, to the northwest of the Ottawa River, as well as an adjoining section of northern Minnesota and Wisconsin, is covered by almost innumerable lakes. In fact, in many parts of this region as much as a third of the land is covered by water—speckled with the blue dots of lakes and meshed with twisting rivers. A few of the lakes, like Great Bear and Great Slave, are huge, but most of them are hardly more than ponds. Typical of this whole area is Minnesota, whose slogan, "Land of 10,000 Lakes," is no exaggeration. A map of Minnesota reveals that the lakes, ponds, and swamps do not lie haphazardly on the landscape, but rather seem to be arranged in a series of sweeping arcs.

Each of these arcs marks the location of a glacial moraine. The last glacier did not melt back at a uniform rate, but alternately retreated and advanced. Each time its front halted or changed direction, it dropped a load of debris that formed a belt of low hills with hollows between them, and the hollows filled with water from the melting ice. The shallowest of those depressions have long since dried out or been filled with sediment; some are well along the route to extinction and hold water only during the wet season; others remain as lakes the year round.

One of the most magnificent lake regions of the continent lies in western Minnesota and eastern North Dakota, extending northward into Manitoba and Saskatchewan; here Lake of the Woods and Lake Winnipeg are the largest bodies of water, but there are swarms of others. This is a land of spruce, pine, and aspen, and of waterways so complex that the land seems to be a series of islets floating in one immense lake. And in fact this whole area was at one time covered by the waters of a single immense lake, larger than all the present Great Lakes combined, to which geologists have given the name of Lake Agassiz.

Lake Agassiz came into existence when the Red River, which forms the boundary between North Dakota and Minnesota and flows northward to the Arctic Ocean, was blocked by the ice sheet. The ice functioned as a dam, impounding the waters of the Red River and backing them up into what is now South Dakota. At its maximum, Lake Agassiz was about 700 miles long and 250 miles wide. After the ice retreated northward to Hudson Bay, most of the water drained northward again, and Lake Agassiz disappeared except for a remnant of scattered smaller lakes and ponds. But while the land was covered by the lake, silt filtering to the bottom filled in many of the depressions in the landscape, bequeathing to present-day agriculture an extraordinarily level plain with fertile soil. Today that plain—the floor of the ancient lake—is the bountiful wheat-growing land of the Dakotas, Minnesota, Manitoba, and Saskatchewan.

Northeastern Minnesota and the Canadian lands that border upon it form another lake-laced wilderness, much of which is preserved in an unspoiled state as part of the international Quetico-Superior Wilderness Area. Nearly half of the 16,000 square miles of the area is covered by lakes and connecting streams. This labyrinth of water forms a large jigsaw puzzle that has bewildered many geologists, for the drainage system left by the glaciers is enormously complicated. Many streams flow not in channels they have cut, but rather along the beds of old lake basins. There is little pattern to the direction of stream flow; many of the lakes have no visible outlet; rapids and waterfalls are abundant.

All lakes are being filled in, inevitably turning into bogs as the vegetation creeps in from shore. Any lake that is surrounded by a ring of vegetation will not long endure. At first the lake shows little apparent change; nevertheless, submerged plants are taking root unseen, and as generations of these plants gradually raise the level of the bottom, they create a seedbed for the next stage, that of the pondweeds. These are plants adapted to a life in perpetual moisture; as their roots ramify along the shore, straining out the debris of the lake, they are imperceptibly creating land, tightening the noose of the shoreline upon the water.

There comes a time when the pondweeds can no longer survive on the dry land they have created, and they are followed by a succession of other plants. Each of these stages is made up of plants increasingly better adapted to a life on dry land, until finally the mud along the former shore has become dry enough to support the growth of trees and shrubs. While this has been happening, other pondweeds have been building new land closer to the center of the lake. Finally, all that remains of the lake is a small circle of clear water. This clear patch is soon bridged by the sedges, which form a floating mat of plants. In time the water under the mat is filled in by dead plants and sediments, and the lake disappears utterly. So recent is the retreat of the last glacier that the complete

THE MAZE of waterways in Quetico-Superior is a legacy of the last glacier.

succession of steps from lake to dry land can be seen in only a few places in Minnesota. But the final steps in the obliteration of a lake can be witnessed in lands farther south from which the glaciers departed earlier; nearly all of the glacial lakes in Indiana, for example, were filled in before the first settlers arrived.

When one comes from dry land to a bog, one pays a visit to an alien world. The underpinnings of much of the bog are pure peat, formed by the partial decay of plants under the cold waters. The soil of the bog is

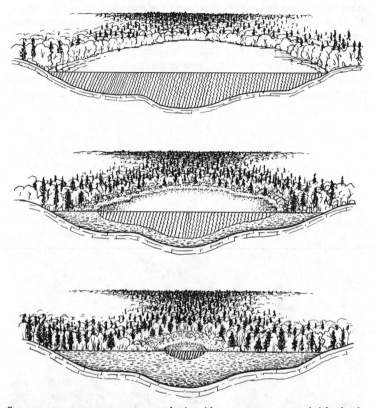

STEPS IN THE FILLING IN OF A LAKE begin with open water surrounded by hard-woods (such as in a beech-maple forest) and a few conifers (such as tamarack) farther back from the water. The accumulation of humus from water plants makes the lake shallower and forms soil around the shoreline in which shrubs can grow, followed by willows and poplars, then by the surrounding forest trees. Eventually, as the forest pushes toward the center, the former lake is represented only by a small marsh of sphagnum moss and sedges; this, too, is finally filled in and the forest stretches unbroken.

usually depleted of many such essential nutrients as nitrogen, phosphorus, and lime, for these are absorbed by the peat. Those plants that possess modifications to survive where there is a scarcity of such nutrients—such as on the arctic barrens—can live in the peat bogs. In addition to starvation, the plants suffer another hardship in the extreme cold of the waters, which is due not only to the severity of the winters but also to the insulating effect of the peat and sphagnum moss. Only plants inured to these conditions can endure—such hardy species as Labrador tea and other heaths, black spruces, and tamaracks, which are all natives of the northern part of the continent. It is not only their presence that makes the bog look different from the surrounding countryside, but also the absence of many familiar weeds and flowers of the uplands. Those intruders upon landscapes everywhere, the cosmopolitan weeds, can endure many hardships, but not the combination of undernourishment, icy water, oxygen shortage, and sun scald that are the lot of plants growing in a northern bog.

Typical of these northern plants is sphagnum moss, which forms floating gardens on the waters. This northern moss, the main constituent of peat, is practically unassailable by decay. It is responsible for much of the acidity of the bog soil and for the clear amber color of the waters. Although it is the very emblem of the bog, forming quaking mats on the surface, it cannot float alone, but requires the partial support of other plants in the bog community, particularly the little sedges. Sphagnum is equipped with casklike cells that permit it to absorb water as few other plants can, up to as much as a hundred times its own weight.

The bog represents an ancient association of plants and animals which has changed little since it was established in the wake of the glaciers. Because of the persistence of bog conditions, the plants and animals from the far north have had no reason to alter the association even though the glacier has long since disappeared and the climate is now much warmer. Strangely enough, growing among these inhabitants of the north are other plants representing the southern flora, such as the insectivorous sundew and pitcher plant. They are at home here for the reason that certain conditions in the southern swamps—continual moisture and a deficiency of nitrogen in the soil—approximate those of the northern bogs.

Although the pitcher plant had been known as a botanical curiosity since its discovery in the sixteenth century, it was not until about 150 years ago that the reason for its strange shape was understood. As its name suggests, it has pitcher-shaped leaves, which are attractively marked with red veins; inside each pitcher is a pool of water, in which dead insects may often be seen floating. Close study of this plant has revealed that it is an ingenious trapline for capturing insect prey. The lip of the pitcher is colored red, just as are many flowers that attract insects upon which they depend for cross-pollination. Red veins act as trail markers that lead the insect from the lip into the pitcher. The trail ends abruptly at the neck of the pitcher, which is steep and glassy smooth.

Here, unable to gain a foothold, the incautious insect hurtles down a toboggan slide of downward-pointing hairs and into the pool of water. If the insect attempts to climb out, the hairs, which now point directly toward it, form an impassable tangle; the victim soon becomes exhausted by its struggles to escape. The water in the pitcher contains enzymes that break down the tissues of the insect; then the plant absorbs minerals and nitrogen directly from the water.

The little sundew, a plant that is usually less than an inch high, adorns the ground of the bog like a cluster of jewels. The innocent-looking hairs that rise from the leaf are actually tentacles, each holding a droplet of sticky fluid, in which an unwary insect is quickly entangled; the tentacles bend inward, surrounding the prey, which is then digested by the plant. In addition to the flypaper technique of the sundew and the pool of the pitcher plant, there is also the method of snaring prey used by the insectivorous plant known as the Venus's flytrap. This plant does not inhabit the northern bogs, and in fact is found in only one region in the world, the coastal bogs of North Carolina. An unwary insect alighting on the shiny leaf of a Venus's flytrap brushes against one of the leaf's six short trigger hairs. The leaf snaps shut, imprisoning the insect, which is then digested by enzymes. Later the leaf opens again and the indigestible parts of the insect are blown away, leaving the trap prepared for the next victim.

To the east of the bogs and lakes of Minnesota lies a chain of gigantic basins, arranged in a series of descending levels like a vast watery staircase. These are the Great Lakes: Superior, Michigan, Huron, Erie, and Ontario. Superior, the most western of the lakes, forms the top step, 602 feet above sea level. Thence the water drops by stages from lake to lake, passing through rapids at Sault Ste. Marie and making a deep plunge over Niagara, until finally it reaches the St. Lawrence River. Superior is the largest body of fresh water in the world; so great is the total volume of the water in the Great Lakes that it has been estimated to equal nearly the flow of the major rivers of the world in a year.

Before the time of the glaciers, an ancient river system probably flowed through the land now covered by the lakes. The ice sheets rearranged the drainage pattern of this river system and scooped out five great

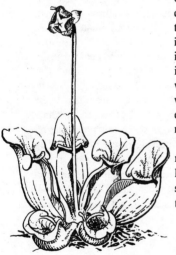

PITCHER PLANT

basins along its valleys. At times, as the glaciers advanced, withdrew, and finally melted, the lakes were considerably larger than they are to-day; the cities of Chicago and Detroit, for example, are built on what were once lake bottoms. The waters accumulating in these basins sought outlets to the sea. At one time the Grand River flowed across the lower peninsula of Michigan, carrying water from Lake Huron into Lake Michigan, and then down the Mississippi River. At other times the Great Lakes found an outlet through the Finger Lakes of New York and thence into the Susquehanna River. The broad valley lying across New York State, in which the Erie Canal is located, was cut by churning waters from the Great Lakes seeking to reach the Hudson River.

About 10,000 years ago the ice cleared sufficiently for the St. Lawrence River to become established as the outlet for the Great Lakes. Released from the crushing pressure of the ice sheet, the land around the Great Lakes has tilted upward. The uplifting of the area to the northeast of the lakes resulted in the dumping of the waters toward the southwest, just as happens when a basin filled with water is raised at one side. The shorelines to the north and northeast, on the raised side of the basin, have emerged above the water to distances of several hundred feet. The tilting of the water to the south and west has caused the land on those sides of the basin to be submerged. The uplift is still taking place at the rate of a few inches a year. Small as this figure seems, it has been estimated that in hardly more than 1500 years water from the Great Lakes will no longer be able to reach the elevated St. Lawrence River. It will then seek an outlet to the west, probably through the Chicago River and thence into the Mississippi.

The lowering of the water after the retreat of the ice, and the steady tilting of the land, have exposed great cliffs to the winds and waves. Conditions on the Great Lakes are favorable for the building up of waves: there is a high wind velocity, the winds can sweep long distances across the lakes, and the water is very deep. Waves have been produced here that rival those pounding the seacoasts; heights of more than twenty feet have been reported by ships plying these inland seas. When waves such as these break against the cliffs, they explode up the rock faces for distances of nearly a hundred feet. The sculpturing caused by the waves can be easily seen almost anywhere along the eastern margins, but an especially vivid example is the Picture Rocks near Munising in the upper peninsula of Michigan. There waves have carved the sandstone cliffs into shapes reminiscent of those in highly eroded desert areas: steeples, pulpits, arches, ship prows, and so forth. So great is the reverberation of the waves smashing into the caverns at Picture Rocks

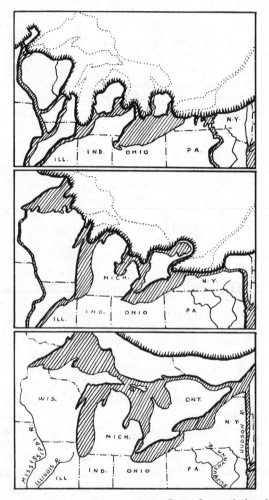

THREE STAGES IN THE DEVELOPMENT OF THE GREAT LAKES during the retreat of the last ice sheet are shown here. Water from the melting ice finds successive outlets through (top) the Mississippi, Illinois, and Susquehanna rivers; (center) the Erie valley to the Hudson River, and the Mississippi and Illinois; and (bottom) the Champlain valley, the Hudson, and the present outlet, the St. Lawrence River.

that the Indians used to regard these caves as the home of the gods of thunder.

Although most of North America's lakes are clustered in the glaciated areas, they are not entirely absent from the south. One of the largest lakes on the continent is Okeechobee in southern Florida. (Any place name in Florida and southern Georgia that ends with a double *e* is likely to pertain to water. Okeechobee means "Big Water" in the Seminole language; Kissimmee means "Winding Water"; any place ending in *hatchee* is a river.) In its primeval state, Okeechobee was shaped like a shallow saucer, with several chips along its edge into which streams flowed. Maurice Thompson, writing in the last century, described Okeechobee as "a large spider from whose elliptical body radiate short, crooked legs." Much of the former eeriness has now departed from the lake, for a levee has been built around its shores to prevent damage by its escaping waters following a hurricane; a navigable waterway has been dredged from the lake to the Gulf of Mexico, and drainage canals have been dug to reclaim the rich soils lying along its borders.

Okeechobee is the liquid heart of Florida, and its main vein is the muddy water that drains from the Kissimmee Prairie, an area of about 4500 square miles lying immediately to the north. Since similar habitats attract similar kinds of animals, these Florida prairies are suprisingly like those of the western states, and unlike the rest of Florida, in their animal population, which includes burrowing owls, sandhill cranes, Audubon's caracaras, and mountain lions.

No river serves as an outlet for the waters of Okeechobee; instead, the surplus water simply drains down into southern Florida, creating the soggy region known as the Everglades, the "river of grass." The sawgrass that distinguishes the Everglades from other southern swamps and marshes is not a grass but a sedge related to those of the northern bogs; growing nearly ten feet high, it has edges set with teeth. Sawgrass is present everywhere throughout the 5000 square miles of the Everglades, and its level stretches are broken only by clumps of trees that rise out of it like islands from the sea. Along the coast, where the river of grass meets the salt tides from the sea, it gives way to mangroves and buttonwoods.

Underneath the sawgrass, the mud-stained waters of Okeechobee that have created the Everglades move almost imperceptibly toward the coast, cutting a curving swath, about 60 miles wide and some hundred miles long, through southern Florida. This sawgrass river actually has banks and a bed, although they are scarcely distinguishable to the casual eye. The Everglades is underlain and surrounded by limestone rock, whose encircling rim is the only solid thing that stands between the sawgrass and the sea. Along the eastern and southern rims the projecting limestone provides the foundation for a number of cities which ring the Everglades: Palm Beach, Fort Lauderdale, Miami, and Homestead, among others. The Tamiami Trail and all the other roads that cut across the Everglades were built by digging up this rock from under the muck.

The limestone also protrudes from the surface of the muck at many places in the river of grass. Each outcropping of the rock is a potential site for the formation of an island of trees, a "hammock," as it is called in Florida and Georgia. These outcroppings provide platforms above the muddy water and the competition of sawgrass. At first, only humble plants are able to grow in the sparse soil caught among the ridges of the porous limestone. Their decaying leaves, stems, and roots are all added to the mineral particles, and the amount of soil is gradually increased. As more and more soil accumulates from the decay of generations of plants, trees take hold. Gumbo limbo, blolly, cabbage palm, saw palmetto, and other species grow close together, sharing the pedestal that raises them above the limitless horizon of wind-rippled grass.

The Everglades have now been stripped to a mere shadow of their primeval magnificence. They have been crisscrossed by man-made canals, designed to carry off their water to the sea and thereby to claim the land for agriculture. But instead of the outflow of fresh water, in many places the result has been the inflow of salt water up the canals. The salt has killed plants, poisoned the soil, and driven many Everglades animals deeper into the interior. In other places the lowering of the water by drainage has left the sawgrass high and dry, an inflammable mass of dead vegetation; sawgrass fires are so numerous during the dry season of late winter that a pall of smoke often lies over the Everglades.

Many people, visiting the Everglades for the first time, expect it to be a jungle. But only in the disturbed portions, on the hammocks, and along the fringes do the Everglades ever resemble the tangled tropical growth of the storybooks. Most of it is an open solitude, a study in varying tones of green and brown. Nevertheless, it contains several distinct habitats; representatives of each have been included in Everglades National Park, a preserve about the size of the state of Delaware. Trails have been laid out, enabling the visitor to leave his automobile and penetrate with ease into the strange life of the Everglades.

Perhaps the most fascinating of these is the Anhinga Trail, a boardwalk that penetrates into a typical Everglades slough. In an exploration of only a few hundred yards along this boardwalk, it is possible to observe closely an amazing concentration of wildlife, all going about their business unmindful of the intrusion. The anhingas, or water turkeys, which have given the trail its name, swim rapidly through the water, spearing fish with their needlelike bills. Stalking the lily pads are the spectacularly-colored purple gallinules, which seem to have no fear of visitors and are possibly the most photographed birds in the park. And soaring overhead are the glamor birds: wood storks, egrets, bitterns,

HAMMOCK of trees in the Everglades seems to float on a sea of sawgrass.

herons. Almost everywhere in the slough, what one takes for a dark log suddenly quivers or sinks under the surface, and turns out to be an alligator. These reptiles are found only in fresh water; inhabiting salt water on the edge of the Everglades is the much rarer crocodile, recognizable by its sharp snout and lighter color.

A southern coastal swamp of a much different sort is Okefenokee, in southern Georgia and western Florida. It was formed when a low barrier of land emerging from the gulf isolated a portion of the broad, level coastal plain. Today a large part of that depression is choked with plants which act like a sponge, soaking up water. When the sponge is filled to capacity, the excess water overflows into the two outlets from Okefenokee, the St. Marys and Suwannee rivers. The St. Marys forms the southern boundary of Georgia for about a hundred miles, and finally empties into the Atlantic Ocean; the Suwannee winds through the cypress forests of Florida, eventually emptying into the Gulf of Mexico.

Okefenokee possesses a remarkable diversity of habitats, which accounts for the richness of its fauna: bears, bobcats, alligators, and many kinds of unusual birds. In the eastern part of the area, the visitor sees open marshlands, called "prairies" by the natives, on which innumerable islands of pines and cypresses appear to float. To the west the water becomes shallower, and trees dominate the scene: magnolias, cypresses, and red bays. At the western margins appear wide stretches of open water, which are part of the looping and almost indefinable course of the Suwannee.

The overwhelming impression of Okefenokee is much the same as that made on a visitor by the salt marshes and lagoons fringing the Atlantic —one of land winning out over water. Toward the center of any of the area's innumerable lakes the surface of the water is largely concealed by gardens of lovely aquatic plants rooted in the deep muck. Forming a ring around these water gardens, in shallower places where the muck lies closer to the surface, are other plants adapted more nearly to a terrestrial existence. The actual shorelines of these lakes are not easy to determine, but where there are extensive beds of ferns, the water's margin coincides with the line beyond which these land plants do not venture.

Another way of locating the shoreline is to trace the dying forms of the bald cypresses. These trees are adapted for a water existence. Their trunks are vase-shaped, sometimes with a diameter of ten or more feet at the base and only a fifth that wide a dozen feet above it. Projecting from their bases are a tangle of arching roots and the curious structures called "knees," actually extensions of the underwater roots that reach above the surface for air. Soil particles collect between the roots and gradually build dry land around them, thus paving the way for the creation of a habitat for other trees, better adapted to life on dry land, but also for the destruction of the water-demanding cypresses themselves.

Many of the cypresses are shrouded with Spanish moss, the emblem of the southern swamps. It is actually not a moss at all, but a member of the pineapple family. Nor is it a parasite, for the only thing it takes from the tree is the elevation that allows its fragile strands to grow closer to the sun. The roots of Spanish moss never connect with the ground; rather, they consist of a series of grapples that spread into crevices in the bark and provide firm anchorage for the plant. It takes the moisture it needs directly from the atmosphere, and thus it can grow only in humid areas.

At first glance, Spanish moss has little apparent structure. It seems merely to drape itself over the boughs of oaks, water elms and cypresses, even over telephone poles; at a distance its soft, furry growth looks like hoarfrost on the trees. But if the grayish outer cover of the plant is

CYPRESSES, festooned with hanging curtains of Spanish moss, mark the shoreline at Okefenokee. Their roots trap soil that enables other trees to grow later.

parted, green chlorophyll cells can be seen—evidence that this plant labors in the sun and manufactures its own food by the process of photosynthesis. If one continues to search among the strands, one will also find little yellow flowers and seed pods. Spanish moss proliferates in another way, also. Whenever a part of a plant breaks off, the loose strands are easily carried by the wind to other locations, where they develop into new hanging gardens.

In the dim, brooding world of Okefenokee, the visitor's worst imaginings about the world of reptiles are no more dreadful than the reality. The cypress knees are favored haunts of cottonmouth moccasins; these venomous snakes are occasionally also seen twined in great numbers around the lower limbs of trees. Plowing through the tangled plants of the watery prairies are alligators. The trails blazed through the nearly impenetrable growth by the powerful reptiles are later used as waterways by the swamp people in their pole-boats. Alligators at Okefenokee grow to a length of nearly fifteen feet, reaching a greater size there than anywhere else on the continent—and also a greater degree of aggressiveness. When the pioneer naturalist William Bartram traveled through this area he labeled it "the most blissful spot of the earth." But he qualified his enthusiasm by adding that his boat had been attacked by huge alligators; many other reliable reports since then have confirmed his experiences.

Okefenokee is derived from a Seminole Indian word that means "trembling water." All bogs and swamps, since they have their underpinnings in yielding plant matter, seem to shudder and quake, but nowhere else in so pronounced a fashion as at Okefenokee. There are actually places where a visitor who stamps hard on the ground can set a large tree quivering. At Okefenokee it is also possible to see whole portions of the swamp come apart and turn into floating islands. Sometimes this happens because of a rise or fall in the water level, which detaches a spongy mass of plants and sets it adrift; but there is another force at work in the creation of the floating islands. Microscopic bacteria in the soil produce methane or "swamp gas," which expands with heat and contracts with cold. As the weather warms in the spring, the gases trapped in the tangle of vegetation expand. In so doing they may break off a mass of plants and create a floating island, which usually disappears with the onset of cold weather later in the year. The floating islands are reminders that although the lakes and swamps are destined eventually to become dry land, the advance of the land is not one continuous victory.

8 : Springs, Geysers, and Caves

T HE VISIBLE WATER SUPPLY in lakes and rivers represents but a small portion of the water on the continent; the rest of it lies hidden in natural reservoirs underground. Most lakes and rivers would dry up if they depended solely upon precipitation for their store of water. It is the continuing supply from the underground sources that keeps lakes high and rivers running even during periods of drought. Water is stored underground by the percolation of rain and snow water into porous soils and rock crevices. In addition to moving downward through the layers of rock, it may also move sidewise when it encounters non-porous rock, through which it cannot filter. It may flow for long distances underground, or it may emerge promptly as a spring which flows into a lake or river. Like the water in lakes and rivers, the final destination of underground water is the sea.

The only contact most people ordinarily have with underground water occurs when they drill a well. But the effects of underground water are plainly visible. Geysers, a phenomenon consisting of tons of hot water gushing out of the earth, are the most arresting of these effects. The three outstanding geyser regions in the world are in Iceland, New Zealand, and Yellowstone National Park in Wyoming; two lesser geyser areas in North America are at Beowawe and Steamboat Springs, both in Nevada. However, neither Iceland nor New Zealand can boast such a concentration of geyser phenomena as is found at Yellowstone, where there are at least 10,000 geysers, hot pools, pots of boiling mud, and fumaroles (vents of steam).

Several special conditions are necessary for the formation of a geyser. There must be seething liquid rock (volcanic magma) deep under the surface of the ground. Lying between the magma and the surface there must be hollow tubes of rock sufficiently strong to endure the explosive force of the geyser. Finally, there must be an underground source of water that will strike the magma in such a way that it is heated and forced upward. The primary difference between a hot spring and a geyser is in the degree to which the water has been heated by the liquid rock; geysers occur only when the heat and pressure are sufficient to produce steam.

While geysers and hot springs appear to be spread at random throughout Yellowstone's 3472 square miles, they are actually arranged in definite belts. These belts occur along faults or fractures that have caused one section of rock to move up, down, or sidewise in relation to the section alongside it. These faults provide passageways for the escape of steam and hot water. Geysers bring tremendous amounts of heat to the surface; the combined heat from the geysers and hot springs at Yellowstone would be sufficient to melt three tons of ice in a second. The geysers have created favorable living conditions for animals, which cluster around them. Many bears have sensibly located their dens near geysers, thus obtaining steam heat during the winter. Numerous birds have been observed to nest in the same warm areas; while all around is frozen, ducks are often seen in the pools of water kept free of ice by the warm water issuing from the geysers. The temperature of the Yellowstone River rises by an average of six degrees as it flows through the geyser area; this increase in temperature ensures a food supply for the trout, and in that stretch of the river they remain active all winter long.

Old Faithful is not the most powerful geyser at Yellowstone; others have produced greater eruptions, and Steady Geyser almost never ceases to play. Nor is it the most beautiful. But no other geyser combines reliability of eruption with great height and beauty to the same degree as Old Faithful. This geyser has rarely missed an eruption in the hundred years it has been under observation, nor has the height to which its waters are cast diminished during that time. It is a youthful and vigorous geyser, whose age is estimated to be less than 300 years.

Old Faithful is located in the center of a mound which it has created, measuring about twelve feet in height and as much as 55 feet across. The source of the moɪ ɪd is the underground water itself. Geyser waters are extremely rich in dissolved minerals. They are what is commonly

BISON at Yellowstone find forage in the warmth created by a steaming geyser.

called "hard water," and anyone who lives in a hard-water area knows that a coating of minerals soon forms inside kettles; the minerals are the residue left by the water when it evaporated by being heated. Precisely the same sort of thing occurs around the jet of a geyser. The rocks formed by Old Faithful are not so striking as those around numerous other geysers at Yellowstone. Formations of rocks have been created in the shapes of cauliflowers, sponges, chairs, flowers, and necklaces; sometimes graceful terraces are created, as at Yellowstone's Mammoth Hot Springs, where they rise to astonishing heights. The brilliant streaks of color in these deposits are due to the great variety of minerals carried to the surface by the geysers, and sometimes as well to certain algae that are able to survive in the boiling temperatures.

Old Faithful's eruptions do not occur like clockwork, as many people believe. They take place, on the average, every 64½ minutes; but although the geyser is rarely very much off schedule, the interval may be anywhere between 30 and 90 minutes. The waters almost always give advance warning of an eruption. There is a short spurt, then a graceful column begins to rise. At first it seems to grow with great effort, but soon a jet shoots upward to a height varying between 115 and 150 feet. At its crest the jet is broken by the breeze, and the water unfurls into a shower of droplets that capture the light and transform it into a rainbow. The entire display lasts between two and five minutes, and about 12,000 gallons of water may be expelled during a single eruption.

This is only the visible spectacle of Old Faithful. Underground is an intricate plumbing system which connects the liquid rocks with the surface. As water seeps into this system, it is heated first at the bottom, just as water is in a teakettle. But whereas in a teakettle the heated water can rise and change places with the cold water above it, the narrow tubes of the underground geyser system do not allow the free circulation of water to take place.

GIANT TERRACES have been created around the jet of a hot spring. Minerals dissolved in the steaming water were left as a residue after the water evaporated.

Instead, the water at the bottom of the tube grows hotter and hotter, eventually rising much above the boiling point, because the vapors are prevented from escaping by the overlying weight of cold water. Finally the heated water produces such tremendous pressure that a spurt of the overlying water shoots above ground—the signal of a coming eruption. The escape of this water decreases the pressure from above upon the heated water, and it can now blow out of the tube. It is remarkable that Old Faithful is so regular in its eruptions, for only a slight variation in the amount of water seeping down, or in the temperature of the liquid rock, could alter its schedule. Most other geysers are irregular by comparison, with intervals varying in some instances from minutes to years.

Yellowstone also has thousands of springs that do not erupt as geysers; they range from quietly steaming pools where there is only the slightest turbulence to hot springs that bubble like caldrons. They are all potential geysers which lacked one or another of the conditions producing an eruption. Often the reason they do not erupt is that the shape of their underground passageways does not permit the heated water to build up the tremendous pressure necessary. Some of the most attractive of the non-eruptive pools are the sulphur springs; many of them discharge only a comparatively small amount of water, but large amounts of sulphur have rimmed the pool with brilliant yellow.

Hot springs and geysers are characteristic of areas in which volcanic action was recently present but is now on the wane. A cold spring, on the other hand, depends on the presence underground of an aquifer, or water-bearing rock. A drilled artesian well is nothing more than a man-made spring that penetrates downward to water-bearing rock. In some areas, wells must be drilled very deeply before water is reached—to about 4000 feet near St. Louis and Pittsburgh, for example. Along the Atlantic coastal plain, aquifers are usually reached before depths of 200 feet, but the well that supplies St. Augustine, Florida descends to 1400 feet.

The greatest aquifer on the continent underlies the Dakotas and large portions of Kansas, Nebraska, Wyoming, Montana, and Saskatchewan. Here a vast layer of porous rock absorbs water from the flanks of the Rockies, the Big Horn Mountains, and the Black Hills, building up tremendous pressure against an overlying layer of impervious rock; when that layer is penetrated, a flowing well results. Throughout this vast stretch of the northern plains the traveler is likely to see a landscape studded with windmills pumping water out of this underground source. It is tapped by tens of thousands of wells, with the result that the pressure of the water has been drastically reduced in recent years.

Aquifers that reach the surface are known as artesian springs, and they are more abundant than most people realize. The vast majority of them flow unseen, reaching the surface either in remote places or under the surfaces of lakes and rivers. Some rivers owe their origin completely to artesian springs and most of their flow consists of spring water. One such river is the Current, born at Montauk Springs, high in the Missouri Ozarks. Nearly a dozen springs rise here in a level, parklike area only a few acres in extent; they are joined by others flowing from the rocks on the surrounding hillsides. Altogether these springs, which form the head-waters of the Current, produce some 45 million gallons of water a day. All along its valley, the Current is replenished by other springs; in fact, about 60 per cent of its total volume is made up of spring water. Only the Snake River of Idaho rivals the Current in the number and volume of springs that feed it.

In areas where the rocks are predominantly limestone, underground water has many effects on the landscape. Limestone is a highly soluble rock compared to granite or shale, and water running over it seeps downward through multitudes of tiny openings. Streams with the name "Lost River" can be found almost any place where limestone lies close to the surface; these are the rivers that suddenly disappear in mid-course, filtering into the limestone rocks only to reappear some distance downstream. (There are also rivers that disappear into desert sands and lava rocks.) Surface streams are usually few in number in limestone areas, even though the rainfall is abundant; most of the water flows underground, appearing occasionally, then disappearing again.

When viewed from a low-flying airplane, limestone areas often appear to be riddled with funnel-shaped holes, some of them containing ponds. The northern half of Florida, for example, swarms with little lakes, for here a belt of very soluble limestone rocks is combined with high rainfall. The rain seeps into the limestone and gradually dissolves the rocks, forming underground channels and caverns. As the caverns increase in size, the land above them may collapse, forming funnel-shaped "sink holes." In the Florida lake belt, many of these sinks have fused, with the result that the whole landscape is a series of lakes, large and small, that often nearly touch. Sinks are extraordinarily abundant in the lost-river areas of southern Indiana and Kentucky, which may have as many as a thousand to the square mile.

The best-known effect of underground water on limestone rock is the formation of caves. Limestone caves are exceedingly abundant, although most of them are inaccessible. The vast majority are also extremely small, but one chamber at Carlsbad Caverns, New Mexico, is nearly a mile long and 350 feet high. The chambers are usually linked by intricate shafts and passageways; Mammoth Cave in Kentucky has at least 150 miles of explored passages, and many times that number that are as yet unexplored.

Before there can be a cave, a series of events must have taken place. The first of these is the formation of limestone, by the accumulation and compaction under the sea of the skeletons of small marine animals. Second, movements in the crust of the earth must have raised this limestone out of the sea so as to convert it into dry land. Third, some of the limestone must have been dissolved by the action of water. As rain descends through the air, it combines with carbon dioxide to form a weak carbonic acid solution which seeps through cracks and dissolves the limestone. In addition, the underground waters carry sediments that enlarge passageways and scour out chambers. Finally, the level of the underground water must drop, leaving dry shafts and chambers in the limestone.

A great number of caves are concentrated in a curving arc from Pennsylvania to Virginia, almost all of them near a single highway, Route 11. Here are some of the most-visited caves on the continent: Crystal and Indian Echo in Pennsylvania, and such well-known Virginia caves as Luray, Virginia Caverns, Shenandoah, and Weyers. In addition, there are dozens of smaller caves, visited only by spelunkers (amateur cave explorers), which are not shown on tourist maps. Obviously it is no accident that all these caves lie precisely in a single valley, with the Blue Ridge to the east and the Appalachians to the west. The rocks from the Blue Ridge eastward to the Atlantic coastal plain are composed of resistant granite and quartzite; the Appalachian ridges were formed from similarly resistant rocks. Between these two mountain ranges lies the cave country of the Great Appalachian Valley, where the rocks are composed primarily of limestone.

Because the limestone layers have been warped and folded by massive movements of the earth's crust, these Appalachian Valley caves are particularly beautiful. The passageways, as they twist and turn and wind up and down, following the folded limestone layers, are quite unlike those of Mammoth Cave, which was hollowed out of horizontal beds of limestone. A visit to a new cave is never disappointing, for caves have an almost infinite variety as a result of the varying solubility of the limestone. Caves intrigue visitors not only because of the mystery that surrounds a descent into the earth, but also because the winding passageways open suddenly into chambers of awesome beauty. Most limestone caves are elaborately decorated: their walls appear to be hung with draperies and festooned with garlands of colorful flowers; ornate pedestals and columns rise from the floor, and huge stone icicles hang from the ceiling. All of the numerous cave formations, whether they be massive thrones or airy sheets that seem to flutter down from the ceiling, are composed of solid rock.

Although it is water that creates caves, water is also at work to fill up every cave with rock once again. Rainwater seeps through the soil and rocks overlying the cave until it penetrates the ceiling. In its slow passage downward it dissolves infinitesimal amounts of calcium carbonate. Each droplet of water, carrying its load of dissolved minerals, hangs from the ceiling before it drops to the floor. Even in that brief time some of the water in the droplet evaporates, leaving behind on the ceiling a ring of calcium carbonate. Later, another droplet hangs from this spot, and in the same way it adds a layer of mineral to the ring.

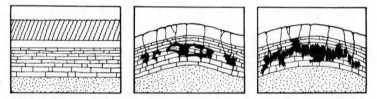

THREE STEPS IN THE FORMATION OF A CAVE. Left: limestone is laid down in a layer under the sea. Center: the limestone is uplifted by shifts in the earth's crust, and water seeping through cracks begins to dissolve the limestone. Right: the hollows have merged into large caverns containing stalagmites and stalactites.

After countless years of slow drip after drip, these rings form a hollow, strawlike cylinder. As the cylinder develops, droplets run down the inside as well as the outside and merge at the tip in a formation with the shape of an icicle, known as a stalactite. A similar process occurs on the floor of the cave. When the water droplet falls to the floor, some of the water evaporates there also, leaving behind another ring of calcium carbonate. Ring is added to ring, building totem poles, domes, beehives, thrones; these formations that rise from the floor of the cave are known as stalagmites. The stalagmites and the overhanging stalactites may eventually merge in a formation resembling an hour glass; a number of stalactites growing across a crack in the ceiling may become fused in a graceful, swirling pattern across the cavern; columns of combined stalactites and stalagmites may grow alongside and resemble the pipes of an organ. The building up of dripstone rocks is exceedingly slow. According to estimates obtained by measuring amounts of dripstone that had collected on tools left in caves by explorers, the time required to build a single inch is upwards of 750 years.

FANTASTIC FORMATIONS at Carlsbad Caverns, New Mexico, resulted from the trickle, during thousands of years, of water carrying dissolved minerals.

The visitor to a cave rarely fails to observe that it is either warmer, if the season is winter, or cooler, if it is summer, than the temperature outside; this is due to the insulating effect of the surrounding rocks and soil. Regardless of the season, a thermometer placed in a cavern shows only slight changes during the year. Mammoth Cave in Kentucky is an almost constant 54 degrees, Carlsbad in New Mexico a constant 56 degrees. As an environment for life, a cavern has many advantages: no extremes of hot or cold, no storms, and a constant high humidity. The only thing it lacks is sunlight. However, while green plants require sunlight for photosynthesis, other plants, such as the molds and bacteria, are able to live in darkness by feeding on the debris of plant and animal matter. This once-living matter may have been carried into a cave by underground rivers, or it may consist of the droppings of animals that spend part of their lives there. Bats, for example, spend the daylight hours in caves and thereby become foundation for a community of living things: flesh-eating beetles that subsist on the dead bats, insects that eat the bats' fur, spiders that snare the insects. Feeding on the detritus of this community are still other permanent inhabitants, such as millipedes and crickets.

Many of the underground dwellers are blind and lack pigments; the blindfish of Mammoth Cave, two inches long and nearly transparent, are an example. Sightless, their heads are equipped with sensitive nerves that allow them to detect slight stirrings in the water. According to an early theory, these fishes became blind through lack of use of their eyes in the caves; but this theory is probably incorrect. It is now supposed that the ancestors of these fishes were already blind while they were living in the world above ground, where they must have been at a disadvantage in competition with fishes with sight. When some of them were carried into cave streams, presumably by floods, they found an environment free from competition by other fishes and predators, and they flourished.

Of all cave inhabitants, the bats of Carlsbad Caverns have attracted the most attention. Incredible numbers of them, estimated at upward of three million, pour out through a cave opening at the rate of some 300 a second. It may require nearly three hours for all the adult bats to leave the cave, spiraling upward, always in a counterclockwise direction, and streaming off in great flocks to forage for insect prey. The return flight occurs just before dawn. The bats dive into their entrance hole, find their places, and spend the daylight hours asleep, hanging head down from the ceiling and walls.

Bats are among the most maligned of all the animals with which we share the continent. The eleven species that live at Carlsbad are all immensely beneficial. In a single night's foraging they consume an estimated 25 tons of insect prey. The bats' unique sonar allows them to locate their prey in complete darkness: they emit high-pitched sounds, most of them inaudible to human beings, which bounce off the smallest surfaces and send back an echo into their keen ears.

Over the centuries, bats have built up thick deposits of guano at Carlsbad and in other caves. After many thousands of years, the guano would markedly decrease the size of the cave. At the same time, dripstone is also filling in the opening. Eventually the cycle of the constant battle between water and land runs its full course, and the cave has disappeared.

IV

THE MOUNTAINS

9 : Appalachian Backbone

MOUNTAINS ARE THE MOST IMPOSING ELEMENTS of the landscape, yet even these mightiest of earth forms are anything but permanent. They rise in their youth, are sculptured in their maturity, and are leveled in their old age. The maturing of a mountain leaves much evidence of its disintegration: rocky streams, landslides, jumbles of boulders. At every stage of their development, mountains have a beauty and majesty that are uniquely their own. There is beauty of a different sort in the youthful Sierra Nevada, in the mature southern Appalachians, and in the aged Laurentians of eastern Canada, which are now worn down to gently rolling hills.

Mountains come into existence in many ways. Some have originated as volcanoes, by the building up of successive layers of lava and ash. Others, for example the White Mountains of New Hampshire, came into being as a result of underground volcanic action. The White Mountains are the product of molten rock which rose from a crack deep in the earth but which, instead of reaching the surface, formed a blister just under the overlying layer of rocks. This outer dome of softer rocks was in turn eroded away by the action of wind and water, to reveal the once molten material, which meanwhile solidified into resistant granite. The White Mountains are so named because they consist almost entirely of light-colored granite rock.

A third mountain-building process is the crinkling of the crust of the earth. Just as the surface of a carpet wrinkles when it is pushed together, rocks pushed by earth movements into a smaller area may accommodate themselves by buckling and wrinkling. The result is a series of parallel ridges or "folded mountains" such as the western Appalachians. Or, instead of wrinkling, the rocks may be split in the process; as a result, one block will rise and be thrust over the neighboring block. The splitting usually occurs along a line of weakness known as a fault. The uplifted block now forms a mountain range characterized by a steep wall, the escarpment, alongside the uplifted block. The imposing east face of the Sierra Nevada, rising abruptly out of the desert, is a spectacular example of "fault block" mountain building.

Most mountain ranges are complex, the result of more than one mountain-building process. The North American continent is endowed with mountains displaying all of these methods in any number of variations. Although isolated patches of mountains occur in various parts of the continent, most of its mountains belong to three great chains: the youthful Pacific coast ranges and Sierras, the Rockies, and the older and more subdued Appalachian chain in the east.

The Appalachians of today are part of an ancient chain that once extended unbroken from Newfoundland to Alabama, and possibly included the mountains of Missouri, Arkansas, and Oklahoma; the chain

FOUR TYPES of mountain building are illustrated here. Faults (left), caused by clean breaks in neighboring blocks of rock, produce mountains such as the Sierra Nevada and the Grand Tetons. Folded mountains (second from the left) are the result when the edges of the crust are pushed together and wrinkled. Domes (second from right), as seen in the Rockies, are formed from blisters of molten granite. At right is the cone of a volcano, built of layers of cinders and lava.

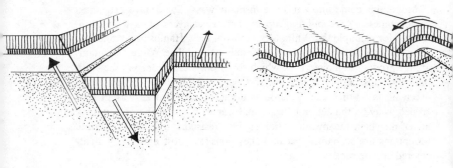

must have been three or four hundred miles wide. This part of North America was raised from the sea, after repeated floodings and upliftings, some 200 million years ago; but never since, despite the numerous earth movements on the continent, has the sea reclaimed these mountains. They were planed down and then uplifted again, and are now deeply sculptured. The deceptively tame and subdued appearance of these eastern mountains is due to the green, velvety mantle of their luxuriant vegetation; anyone who hikes among these ridges receives a very different picture of precipices, deep valleys, and rugged terrain.

To the west of these older Appalachians there was once a shallow sea into which rock particles washed down from the mountains. Over millions of years deep layers of rock accumulated and then were uplifted. As the waters of the interior sea retreated, the rocks were deformed and folded to form parallel ridges. These are the newer Appalachians, which extend from southern New York to Alabama, paralleling the older Appalachians, from which they are separated by the Great Valley.

The Appalachians of the present day have their northern anchor in Newfoundland; they cover parts of New Brunswick, Nova Scotia, and Prince Edward Island in Canada, and extend southwestward like a backbone through the eastern United States. The portion between Mount Katahdin, Maine, and Mount Oglethorpe, Georgia, is traversed by the Appalachian foot trail, which winds for some 2000 miles through the valleys and up the summits. In the Canadian portion of the Appalachians, the mountains appear only as scattered hills 1500 to 2000 feet above sea level, although on the Gaspé Peninsula some mountains rise to heights of more than 4000 feet. Many of the Canadian Appalachian peaks are washed directly by the sea, which has entered the valleys and laps against their flanks. Only farther south, in Maine, does a coastal plain intervene between the mountains and the sea; south of New England the coastal plain becomes increasingly broad.

The New England Appalachians are but the stumps of mountains that have been greatly worn down. It has been estimated that if all the rocks eroded from the New England highlands could somehow be replaced, New England would rear as a mountain block more than 25,000 feet high. The mountains of course never actually reached that height, for as they rose they were attacked by the forces of erosion.

The summit of Mount Monadnock in southern New Hampshire is 3165 feet above sea level, and it towers some 2000 feet above its immediate surroundings. This mountain is a classic example of its kind: a peak of resistant rock that stands above the general level of the land, like an island overlooking the sea. For this reason any mountain of the same kind is called a monadnock. Anyone who climbs to the summit of Mount Monadnock on a clear day is greeted with a spectacular view, and a clear picture of the geological structure of New England. As one looks to the south, the landscape of Massachusetts appears level, except for a number of monadnocks that rise imposingly above the plain: Mount Wachusett near Worcester and Mount Watatic near Fitchburg, among others. To the southwest the summits of the Berkshire Mountains appear remarkably level, with Mount Greylock, another monadnock, rising above them. Similarly, the summits of the Green Mountains of Vermont form an even skyline.

The explanation of the level New England skyline is in the fact that at one time this land was a vast, gently rolling plain. Rising above it were several conspicuous mountains of very resistant rock, including the higher peaks of the White and Green mountains, Mount Katahdin, Mount Greylock, and Mount Monadnock. This plain was tilted slightly to the south, buckled by earth movements, dissected into valleys by erosion, and gouged by the ice sheets; yet in the level skyline the remnants of the original plain are still visible.

The highest mountains in New England are the White Mountains of New Hampshire. Several of the peaks in its Presidential Range—Jefferson, Madison, Adams, Monroe, and Washington—rise above 5000 feet. Mount Washington looms 6290 feet above sea level—only a hill when compared with the western mountains, but the highest point east of the Black Hills of South Dakota and north of the Smokies. What makes it particularly imposing is that it rises about 4500 feet above the surrounding plain; it is so lofty that explorers cruising the Atlantic coast 400 years ago were astonished to see its summit projecting above the horizon. So exposed is the summit that winds strike it with terrifying

CRAGGY FEATURES of New Hampshire's Old Man of the Mountain are due to the plucking of rocks from five separate ledges by the last glacier.

force; the highest wind velocity on the planet, 231 miles per hour, was recorded there.

The White Mountains are actually a string of peaks that extend westward from Mount Katahdin in northern Maine for some 150 miles. Everywhere the land shows the former presence of the ice sheet. The

Old Man of the Mountain is, geologically speaking, a Young Man of the Mountain. His visage on a cliff at Franconia was sculptured by the most recent of the glaciers, probably between ten and twenty thousand years ago. In the White Mountains are numerous notches—Franconia, Pinkham, and Crawford, among others—that cut dramatically through the range. They do not twist and turn as do many of the valleys cut by streams, but are surprisingly straight. Moreover, in cross section they are shaped like the letter U, rather than the V of many stream valleys. The straightness and the rounded sides of the notches are proofs that they are legacies of the glaciers, gouged out by prongs of the ice sheet armed with the cutting tools of boulders plucked from the mountains.

One cannot fail to notice the arena-like basins on the sides of many of the mountains; these amphitheaters, known as cirques, are earmarks of glaciers in mountainous areas. The best-known cirque in the White Mountains is Tuckerman's Ravine on Mount Washington. It was formed by a snowbank that accumulated at the headwaters of what was once a stream valley. In the warmth of the sun the snowbank melted somewhat, and the water seeped into the rocks; during the cold nights the water froze, thus expanding and producing more cracks in the rocks. Year by year, small chunks of rock were dislodged and washed away, leaving a depression beneath the snowbank. As the snowbank grew into a valley glacier that began to ooze down the mountain, the depression was further enlarged by the plucking out of fragments of rock. In some cirques, a small lake or tarn may remain in the basin after the glacier has melted.

These little valley glaciers were everywhere in the mountains before the main ice sheet arrived and incorporated them into itself. It is now clear, although for decades there was doubt about this, that the ice sheet covered every mountain peak in New England. The reason for believing that the height of the ice sheet was not more than 5700 feet was that the scratches and grooves usually cut into rocks by glaciers were not to be seen above that altitude. It has now been established that frost action at these high elevations had obliterated the signs. Nevertheless, until recently some geologists continued to maintain that the upper few hundred feet of Mount Washington were an exception, and remained free from the ice. The final proof to the contrary came when a broadcasting tower was constructed on the summit of Mount Washington; during the excavation, rocks were discovered that were not native to Mount Washington and could have been transported there only by the ice sheet.

Anyone who has climbed a mountain, even a peak of modest size, has probably noticed that it becomes colder as he ascends. One might rather expect it to get warmer, since the summit of a mountain is closer to the sun. However, at high altitudes the air is thinner and absorbs less radiation from the sun, with the result that the thermometer drops about three degrees for every thousand feet of ascent. Not only the climate but the plant and animal life changes also. The changes in plants are so marked that a mountain-wise naturalist can usually calculate his altitude merely by noting the plants around him. The reason is that an ascent of a thousand feet up a mountain is roughly equivalent to driving due north at sea level for a distance of 300 miles. An ascent to the treeless summit of Mount Washington is the same as a 2000-mile trip to the barren lands

U-SHAPED TROUGH at Crawford Notch, New Hampshire, resulted from the passing of a glacier through a former river valley.

GLACIERS SCULPTURE mountains by gouging out rocks. At left is an unglaciated mountain, with rounded peaks and V-shaped river valleys. Glaciers move down the valleys, etching the peaks into a sawtooth profile and making the valleys U-shaped (center diagram). The melt of the glaciers leaves behind cuplike cirques (right), which have been hollowed out at the heads of streams. Often the cirques contain small lakes.

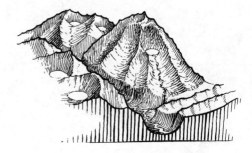

inside the Arctic Circle. Many species of birds also are largely restricted to specific zones. At the foot of Mount Washington redstarts may be seen; as one ascends, these disappear and are replaced first by wrens and white-throated sparrows, then by hermit and Swainson's thrushes. After further climbing, these also are left behind, and near timberline one sees Bicknell's thrushes and slate-colored juncos.

At the foot of the trail leading to the summit of Mount Washington the forest is a luxuriant collection of maples, beeches, birches, and some conifers. But as one climbs even a short distance, the heavy, dank smell of the deciduous forest is replaced by the sweet odor of balsams. A little farther on, the deciduous species almost completely disappear, except for a few birches and mountain ash; they are replaced by a dense forest of red spruce and balsam fir in whose dark shadows little else can grow. The air begins to grow detectably colder and the wind—almost unnoticed at the beginning of the ascent—to increase. Soon the forests of spruce and fir are interrupted by patches of black spruce, magnificent trees when they grow under hospitable conditions, but as seen high on the slopes of Mount Washington, twisted and stunted from their battle with the wind and their attempt to find sustenance in the thin, rocky soil.

It is easy to detect the direction of the prevailing winds: for a few hardy spruces have poked their tops above the general level, and their growth is all on one side, the leeward, so that they look like banners unfurled in the wind. They are pioneers; if the winds should remain at a generally low velocity for several years, the protection these taller trees afford may allow other spruces to lift their tops also, and thus the whole forest may increase several feet in height. But it is more likely that the tops of the taller trees will be mowed back to the general level; possibly they may be killed by the scythe of the wind, leaving a bleached skeleton polished as smooth as ivory, the only reminder of their adventure above the collective security of the forest.

As the hiker continues up the mountain and nears the summit, the height of the spruces steadily decreases, until they grow almost horizontally, crouching on the ground and forming a tangle close above the stony soil. They are joined by little oaks, birches, pines, and other trees that have abandoned their spreading shape and instead grow dense and squatty. Finally, as one reaches timberline, even these dwarf thickets disappear, and the landscape resembles the frozen tundra of the Arctic. No trees can survive on the windy summit of Mount Washington, where snow falls during every month of the year. The maximum temperature on the summit is 70 degrees, the same as might be expected on a hot summer day in the arctic barrens.

During the struggle at timberline, the tenacious trees are made to yield to the wind, first appearing like supplicants on their knees, then crawling ignobly, and finally lying spreadeagled, hugging the rocks for protection. They are whipped by wind and slashed by ice, yet they endure. These stunted timberline forests are known as *Krummholz*—a German word meaning "crooked wood." The elfin forests are produced in much the same way as a dwarf Japanese bonsai tree: by starvation and pruning. At first the little trees of the timberline grow like those in more hospitable locations, sheltered behind a rock or other low-growing trees. During its first few winters, the tree is mulched by snowdrifts, which provide a protective blanket. But in subsequent years, as it grows, the mulch no longer covers all the shoots; the highest ones are exposed to the drying effect of sun and wind, and are killed. During the following summer, other shoots grow to the same height as those that have been killed, and they in turn are nipped back.

But while the top growth is being suppressed, the side shoots, mulched by snow and sheltered by a rock, continue to grow. They have their difficulties also. On the windward side their bark is torn off and branches are stripped away. But summer after summer, the branches on the protected leeward side continue to put out side shoots. These shoots grow so long that they cannot hold themselves upright, and the weight of the winter snow presses them tightly against the rocks. After several decades, the tree may be only a few inches high, but the branches may have grown many feet in length.

The flowering plants above timberline have similarly adjusted to the harsh conditions there. Nearly all mountaintop plants are perennials, for there simply is not enough time for an annual plant to sprout, grow, flower, and produce seeds for the following year. Many of the plants of timberline take the form of a cushion only a few inches in height, from which their roots often spread out between the rock crevices for distances of several feet. Each little cushion is a tangle of present and past growth. The current year's growth surrounds the decaying structures of the plants of previous years, which provide humus that soaks up water like a sponge. The little cushion so completely fills the cranny that there is very little evaporation of water from the soil. The tangle retains heat remarkably well, and thus furnishes a refuge for mountaintop insects, which repay by performing the service of cross-pollinating the flowers. Timberline herbs possess other adaptations that protect them against the loss of water in the cold dry air. Some are covered with a fuzzy down that acts like an insulator by trapping air; others have hard outer coats, or fleshy parts which store up liquids.

A number of plants found atop Mount Washington also grow on summits of the Rockies, and in Greenland and Alaska, but are found nowhere else. One wonders how these isolated patches came into existence, separated by thousands of miles of deserts or plains. They surely could not have been blown such immense distances by the wind, nor carried in the digestive system of birds. The explanation is to be found, as are so many of the other phenomena of these mountains, in the cold brought by the glaciers. During the periods of glacial advance, northern plants were pushed steadily southward. The land immediately south of the glaciers, although not covered by ice, must have had a climate re-

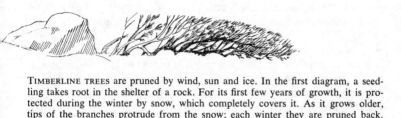

TIMBERLINE TREES are pruned by wind, sun and ice. In the first diagram, a seedling takes root in the shelter of a rock. For its first few years of growth, it is protected during the winter by snow, which completely covers it. As it grows older, tips of the branches protrude from the snow; each winter they are pruned back. But the tips of branches growing outward, not upward, survive under the snow mulch. Year after year, the upward growth is killed, while the outward growth survives. The tree may live for hundreds of years, but it will never grow taller.

sembling that of the arctic tundra. Thus, these plants were able to find a sanctuary in the deep valleys between the southern mountains as well as on the summits. As the ice retreated northward, however, the valleys warmed first and conifers were able to take hold. They filled the valleys, isolating the patches of tundra vegetation on the hillsides from each other. As the climate continued to grow milder the trees marched up the hillsides, pushing the tundra plants ever higher toward timberline. The little plants disappeared completely on the summits of the low mountains, but they continue to endure above timberline where few other living things can survive.

Mount Washington is the only New England peak that clearly displays a timberline, and under different conditions even it would be too low. In the western mountains timberline does not occur below an altitude about twice that of Mount Washington; but Mount Washington is an unprotected peak, with no barrier to break the winds that whip its summit, carrying with them frigid temperatures and snow, drying out the scant pockets of soil and the leaves of plants as well.

West of the White Mountains is a north-south chain of worn-down mountains which in Vermont are known as the Green Mountains, in Massachusetts as the Berkshire Hills, and in Connecticut as the Litchfield Hills. If the valleys between their summits were filled in, there would be revealed a sloping plain with an elevation of about 3500 feet in Vermont, tilting down gradually to about 2300 feet in the Berkshires. Rising above the general level of this sloping plain are a number of prominent monadnocks, notably Mount Mansfield (4365 feet) in Vermont and Mount Greylock (3505 feet) in the Berkshires.

The Green Mountains form practically the whole surface of Vermont. In some places their beauty is due to the green that mantles their slopes, in others to their aged and wrinkled faces of exposed rock. Much of the exposed rock of the Green Mountains is known as gneiss, which is similar to granite but often can be distinguished by the bands of color that run through it. At one time these bands were horizontal layers of various minerals; now their contorted folds are evidence of the changes they have undergone. These are among the oldest rocks on the continent, and they almost always attract attention. There are numerous outcroppings of gneiss in the southern Green Mountains and in Massachusetts; one of the most impressive occurs at the gorge of the Housatonic River, near Cornwall Bridge in western Connecticut.

The Green Mountains are a land of ferns, and it is only the most hurried traveler through the state who fails to notice them creeping down to the roads, waving their fronds from the edges of fallen rocks, and bordering the streams. Upwards of 80 different kinds are native to Vermont; in the multitude of environments offered by mountains, each of these species has been able to find conditions in which it thrives. Plant life is likewise an attraction of the southern extension of the Green Mountains, the Berkshire Hills, a crossroads for plants growing at the extremes of their ranges. They are the eastern limit of growth for a number of plants; they are the southern terminus for trees more familiar in northern New England, such as balsam fir, black spruce, and red spruce; they are approximately the northern limit for flowering dogwood and other southern species.

As mountains go, the Berkshires are not arresting. They have no backbone of high peaks, as do the White Mountains with their Presidential Range. The Berkshires are only about twenty miles wide, and they extend only about 50 miles down western Massachusetts before they dwindle off into the Litchfield Hills of Connecticut. The appeal of the region is in its concentrated beauty. It is so irregular that there are scarcely any extensive plateaus.

The Adirondacks of northern New York have many features in common with the New England mountains: slopes strewn with boulders, lakes, and many streams that pour out of the mountains. The traveler who approaches these mountains from the west or the north scarcely notices that the land is rising. But at the eastern border, along Lake Champlain, a steep slope rises as much as 3000 feet from the lake to the summits. The heart of the Adirondacks is a circle with a diameter of about 120 miles, which touches Alexandria Bay on the St. Lawrence River and the western shore of Lake Champlain. Within this circle lie the most enchanting of the Adirondack lakes and the highest peaks: Marcy (5344 feet), McIntyre (5112 feet), Whiteface (4872), and forty others with elevations above 4000 feet. Outward from this ancient core the rocks are younger. The explanation is that these mountains were formed by an internal pressure that thrust upward to the surface the older, underlying rocks, thus surrounding them with layers of younger rocks.

Although they are in many ways similar in appearance to the New England mountains, the Adirondacks have a different history. The rocks of which their core is composed are among the most ancient exposed rocks on the planet. They form an extension into the United States of the remarkable rocks that mantle the whole Labrador Peninsula, much of Quebec and Ontario, northeastern Manitoba, Saskatchewan, and parts of the Northwest Territories. Prongs of this great formation extend into the United States in the vicinity of the Adirondacks and Lake Superior. The island of Greenland also appears to be a part of it, but one now separated by water and largely covered by an ice cap.

One does not have to be a geologist to see that these rocks are unlike most others; they are hard and crystalline, often with twisting streaks and bands of colored minerals. These rocks cover two million square miles in Canada and the United States, and if their limits were traced on a map, they would present a shape somewhat like a shield. For that reason, this tremendous area is known as the Canadian Shield. Except in the eastern Adirondacks and a few other places, the landscape throughout the Canadian Shield is a distinctive one made up of low rolling hills and thousands of lakes and swamps.

The Canadian Shield is part of the great system of rocks that make up the basement for the overlying rocks of the continent. Though they are well over a billion years old, they have not been covered by the sea and overlaid with sediments, as have the basement rocks elsewhere in North America. During all this vast stretch of time, these rocks have endured the inundations of repeated lava flows and have kept themselves above the sediments that have buried similar rocks in other places. These rocks have yielded precious ores—iron, copper, nickel, silver, and gold in enormous quantities. The Mesabi Range in Minnesota has been a primary source of iron for decades; more recently the Labrador iron deposits have been developed. The Sudbury region north of Lake Huron is the source of much of the world's nickel supply. Farther north, in the Cobalt region, silver has been mined; between Cobalt and James Bay are huge deposits of copper, zinc, and gold.

The skyline of the shield is monotonously even. Its shape is somewhat concave, with Hudson Bay forming a central depression, and with the highest land along the margins. There are a number of monadnocks that give variety to the landscape. The Laurentian Mountains rise abruptly to a height of about 2000 feet above the St. Lawrence River; the Torngat Mountains of Labrador, soaring to nearly 5000 feet, are the highest in eastern Canada. The high peaks of the Adirondacks are all monadnocks. All these are but the stumps of mountains that once must have rivaled the Rockies.

The Appalachians to the south of New England stand in sharp contrast to the rugged northern mountains. Instead of presenting faces of bald rock, they are mantled by deep soil, an indication that they were never scraped bare by the ice sheet. Nor were the rivers of the Appalachians south of Pennsylvania dammed by glacial deposits and scooped out to form lake basins; while the northern mountains teem with lakes, south of Pennsylvania the lakes are few. Lack of glaciation also explains the contrast between the sawtooth profile and rugged peaks of the north and the gently rounded slopes to the south.

Much of the central Appalachians consists of long parallel ridges with deep valleys between them. The Pennsylvania Turnpike, running east and west, penetrates these ridges through long tunnels; the older roads follow a northeast-southwest route through the valleys, probing for low places in the ridges where they can cross. At one time the layers of rock that compose these ridges were horizontal, and had a width of some 80 miles. Earth movements have compressed them to a width of only 65 miles. The rocks responded by forming eleven parallel ridges or "hogbacks," in much the same way that a rug would wrinkle if the two ends were pushed toward the center.

In Pennsylvania the easternmost of these ridges, which borders the

Great Appalachian Valley, is the Kittatinny—an Indian word meaning the "Endless Mountain." It extends from the Shawangunk Mountains, northwest of New York City, into Georgia, and is the ancestral highway for the migration of numerous kinds of hawks and eagles. As the wind strikes the flanks of this ridge, powerful updrafts of air are set in motion. On nearly motionless wings, the hawks and eagles ride the invisible air currents. These birds are among the most accomplished fliers on the continent, but they save energy by making part of their migration flight as gliders on the air currents.

Hawk Mountain, near Drehersville, Pennsylvania, is a promontory overlooking a narrow portion of this ridge. Hawks and eagles funneling down from Canada and New England become concentrated in great numbers at this narrow place in their highway; as a result, the ledge on Hawk Mountain each fall affords the most spectacular view of hawks to be had anywhere on the continent as thousands glide by, almost within touching distance. Late August brings the vanguard, bald eagles and ospreys on their way to Florida and the Gulf Coast. Then come the hordes of little broad-winged hawks that fly to Central and South America. Starting in mid-October, the flights include large numbers of red-tailed hawks and a number of golden eagles. The spring migration northward is not so spectacular, for the birds return in small groups and usually take a different route through the ridges.

Anyone who climbs to the top of one of these ridges will find spread before him a vista of hogbacks, all of approximately the same height. They are interrupted only by water gaps, sudden openings through which a river flows. The Susquehanna, for example, cuts through no less than six deep, narrow ridges in 40 miles, although by swinging only a few miles out of its way it could have avoided two of these. The Potomac River forms a picturesque gap at Harper's Ferry, West Virginia, and the Delaware River cuts a spectacular gorge along the New Jersey–Pennsylvania border. One Pennsylvania river actually appears to have gone out of its way to cut a water gap through a ridge. Many people who visit these water gaps are convinced that the rivers were once so powerful that they were able to bore their way through the ridges. That is quite untrue, for rivers always take the route of least resistance. How, then, is one to account for the behavior of these rivers, which seem to have gone out of their way to blaze trails through the rocks?

The explanation goes back to the formation of the ridges themselves. When the rocks were compressed and as a result the hogbacks came into existence, the formation took on a pattern resembling a series of waves. The high points of the waves were worn down by wind and water, and

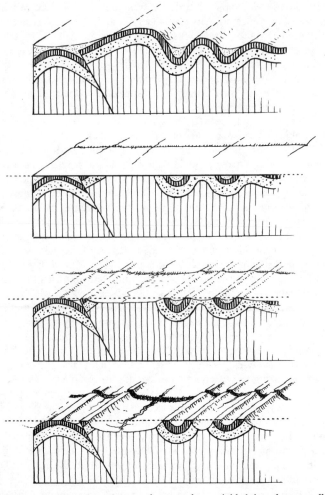

FORMATION OF WATER GAPS. At top, the crust has wrinkled into long parallel ridges of resistant rock. In the second diagram, ages later, the region has been worn down to a level plain, across which a river flows, cutting down into its bed. Then erosion wears away the weaker rocks, allowing the resistant ridges between them to emerge once again. Finally, the tributary streams form broad valleys in the weaker rocks. Gaps through the ridges were formed as the river cut downwards, not, as is commonly supposed, by pushing through the ridges.

the debris gradually filled in the troughs, until a level plain had been formed. Rivers flowing through this plain cut in exactly the same way across the stumps of the ridges and the filled-in troughs. It was at this time that they formed their channels. However, since the debris collected in the troughs was easily eroded, tributary streams gradually carried it away, with the result that eventually the resistant ridges had once again emerged; but now the rivers had found routes through them.

Two of the most attractive mountain chains in the east, the Blue Ridge and the Great Smokies, form the southern anchor of the Appalachians. The construction of the Skyline Drive and the Blue Ridge Parkway allows the traveler to follow the crest of the Blue Ridge for 105 miles, and then to travel for another 335 miles through some of the most magnificent parts of the Smokies. The Great Smokies are the jewel on the entire Appalachian chain. This lofty range, with a score of peaks higher than Mount Washington, includes the highest mountains east of the Mississippi River and forms a mighty barrier between North Carolina and Tennessee.

Untouched by the ice sheet, the rounded contours of the Great Smokies are a sharp contrast to the craggy features of the New England mountains. Very little of the underlying rock is exposed to view; almost everywhere it is covered by plants that clothe these hills from base to summit. In this land of deep soil and plentiful moisture, trees grow vigorously. The antiquity of these eastern mountains is shown by their rounded contours and low elevation as compared to the youthful mountains of the west. Here, all the lines are gentle curves; in the west, everything is angular. In the Smokies, immense stretches of time and heavy precipitation have rounded off the sharp peaks, washing down rock from the high elevations and filling in the slopes with a gentle profile. In the arid Rockies the process is much less advanced, for in that youthful land, as yet untamed by erosion, there has been comparatively little time for the leveling and smoothing down of the peaks.

10 : The Great Divide

ONE MUST SEE the Rocky Mountains from the air to realize fully what an agonizingly contorted mass of rock they form. Peak after peak rises nearly 8000 feet above the level of the plains, and many are more than 14,000 feet above sea level. Their summits project through dense clouds into a sunny atmosphere, like volcanic islands from a billowing sea. Many of the peaks carry immense snowbanks near their summits that remain through the year. Unlike the mountains of the east, the Rockies have thousands of feet of barren rock lying fractured and crumpled above timberline. The only tame portions are the areas known as "parks"—natural basins between ranges where the topography somewhat resembles a rolling New England countryside.

Of all the Rockies' many spectacular views, few are more impressive than the view from Estes Park, 65 miles northwest of Denver in the Rocky Mountain National Park. It is a summation of the Rockies—their raw, exposed summits, placid lakes, dark green forests, and oceans of wildflowers. Standing in the village of Estes Park, one is at the bottom of a deep basin. To the west is a semicircle of some of the most jagged spires of the Rockies, some with patches of lingering ice, others with bald tops. Within the 400 square miles of the Rocky Mountain National Park are fifteen peaks more than 13,000 feet in elevation. Everywhere on these peaks the handicraft of the valley glaciers can be seen. To the east, the view is a sharp contrast. Here are the foothills: lower, rounded, covered by trees to the summits, never touched by the glaciers.

The Rocky Mountain system is the longest mountain chain on the planet; in North America it includes the Brooks Range of Alaska, the Rockies of Canada and the United States, and the Sierra Madre Oriental of eastern Mexico. The growth of this present system began about 60 million years ago, in a period of upheaval that witnessed the cooling of the climate, the extinction of the dinosaurs, and the rise of the mammals to eminence. The uplift of the Rockies took place so gradually that it would have passed unnoticed had any human beings then been alive to observe it. The uplift raised towering domes made up of granite and schist. In some places the rising dome of rock was fractured, and one block slipped over the other. These fractures formed outlets permitting magma to pour forth from the earth's interior. As the central core rose, it caused the buckling of the sedimentary beds, thousands of feet thick, which had been deposited by the inland seas that periodically en-

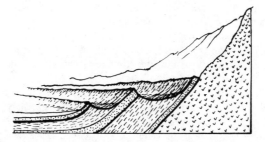

HOGBACKS of the Rockies were formed by the edges of resistant layers of rock.

croached on this area. Folded together, these sedimentary rocks fringing the central core buckled and formed the hogbacks of the Front Range that rise dramatically out of the Great Plains. Another period of uplift began some ten million years ago, and may still be in progress. This comparatively recent uplift has tilted the mountain streams, thereby rejuvenating them, deepening the mountain canyons, and hastening erosion.

Such was the shape of the Rockies before they underwent the sculpturing of the ice age, at about the same time that the ice sheets covered the New England mountains. The glaciers of the west, however, were not a part of the continental ice sheet; rather, they were local valley glaciers, which originated near the heads of mountain valleys but never reached the lowlands. Valley glaciers are much like slow-moving rivers. They originate in cirques, as some rivers originate in mountain lakes. Like rivers, they move down valleys; indeed, these valleys were originally cut by rivers, and the glaciers merely took advantage of existing routes. The valley glaciers poured like waterfalls over precipices, and were sometimes broken up into deltas. They ground and polished the bedrock as they flowed over it. Boulders captured under the moving ice were ground to a smooth, flat finish; every time the ice encountered an obstruction, these rocks would be turned over and polished from another angle. As a result, numerous huge boulders of the Rockies resemble the many-faceted shape of a cut diamond.

As the ice continued down the valleys, a number of glaciers merged to form larger ice masses. Eventually they reached the warmer low altitudes, where they stopped advancing and began to melt; that is why the low hogbacks of the Rockies show no signs of glaciation. Each time any of the valley glaciers paused during its retreat, it dropped some of its load of debris, forming a moraine and damming the valley. Behind many moraines a little, deep-blue lake was formed; the pools are often strung so closely together as to resemble the beads on a rosary, and thus geologists have named them "paternoster lakes."

Running from north to south through the Rockies are a series of peaks and ridges that form the Continental Divide. A drop of water falling to the east of the divide flows into the Atlantic Ocean or the Gulf of Mexico; another drop falling only slightly to the west flows toward the Pacific Ocean. In the Tetons of Wyoming is a small lake, called Two Ocean Lake, that has two outlets: one, Atlantic Creek, flows into the Yellowstone, and thus eventually by way of the Missouri and Mississippi into the Gulf of Mexico; the other, Pacific Creek, flows into the Columbia River and thence into the Pacific Ocean. From the snowdrifts and the glaciers of the Colorado Rockies rise six of the great river systems of the United States: the Missouri, which flows into the Mississippi; the Columbia and its main tributary, the Snake; the Colorado and its tributary, the Green River; the Arkansas and the Platte, both of which flow eastward across the Great Plains; and the Rio Grande, which empties into the Gulf of Mexico.

The variety of altitudes and climates of the Rockies have made possible numerous communities of plants and animals. Entirely different life zones exist on a north slope and a south slope, near a stream and on an exposed ledge, or near a stream at a low altitude and near a stream at a high altitude. At the Rocky Mountain Park and elsewhere in Colorado, the lowest of these life zones occurs at elevations between 4000 and 6000 feet. The Plains Zone is at the foot of the mountains; it is the land of short grass, and is nearly treeless except for stunted pines, willows, and cottonwoods along the streams.

Between 6000 and 9000 feet is the Montane Zone. In it ponderosa pines, the botanical indicators of this zone, grow in open stands of equal-age trees, their long boughs not quite touching, almost as though they had been set out by a gardener. But no gardener planted these trees. Their arrangement is the result of frequent small fires caused by lightning. Each even-age grove springs up in the space left by the death of its elders. The first fire consumes the dead trees and the litter of the forest floor, leaving a seedbed of ash for the growth of young trees. Seeds from neighboring pines drift in and germinate; the young pines provide no fuel of needles for another fire for a number of years, and so they become established. After a few years the soil is again littered, and sooner or later there is a small fire that kills the smaller seedlings but leaves the larger ones. The roots of the survivors appropriate the soil once held by the burned seedlings, and the result is an even-aged stand, with wide spaces between the larger trees. As the stand matures, pine needles accumulate, and a heavy fire results that begins the process anew.

Trees requiring greater moisture than the ponderosa pine grow along the streams of the Montane Zone: alders, willows, birches, and the Colorado blue spruce, which has been widely planted elsewhere on the continent as an ornamental tree. Its distinctive bluish color comes from a powdery substance which covers the needles, and which is particularly noticeable in midsummer. On dry, exposed sites in the Montane Zone grow little pinyon pines and junipers (commonly miscalled "cedars").

Beginning at 9000 feet and ranging up to timberline, at about 11,500 feet, is the Subalpine Zone. The slopes at this elevation are clothed with a completely different kind of forest, typified by the tall, steeple-shaped Engelmann spruce. Spruces can grow where pines cannot because their shallow roots permit them to survive in the thin soil of high altitudes. Wildflowers of rare beauty grow in almost every open space in this zone: Colorado blue columbines, globeflowers, monkshoods, marsh marigolds, and primroses.

The Alpine Zone begins at approximately 11,500 feet, the altitude above which trees cannot survive. However, timber does not meet bare rock in an even line around the mountains. Trees grow higher than 11,500 feet where there is a sheltered ravine on a southern slope; they do not grow even at that altitude on an exposed northern ridge. Timberline thus undulates around the mountain, sometimes sending long prongs up the slopes. The trees relinquish their hold with reluctance, but they eventually give way to the meadows where carpets of alpine flowers bloom. Growing in the Alpine Zone of the Rockies are some 250 kinds of flowering herbs that are found nowhere else. In the Rocky Mountain

PONDEROSA PINE FORESTS of the southwest achieved their parklike, even-aged appearance due to fire. At the left is a mature stand; the debris littering the floor provides fuel for a lightning-ignited blaze, which creates openings in the forest where seedlings can take hold. As the seedlings mature (second from right) they drop needles, providing fuel for a small fire, which in turn eliminates new seedlings and keeps the stand open.

National Park these alpine meadows can be visited with ease by taking the Trail Ridge Road, which ascends to an altitude of more than 12,000 feet and is the highest through road on the continent.

Animals also are stratified into zones, although less rigidly than plants since they are mobile. The Alpine Zone, for example, has a year-round population of birds and mammals—rosy finches, ptarmigan, and pikas—which is very nearly exclusive to it, and which is augmented in summer by horned larks, pipits, elk, mule deer, and bighorn sheep from lower altitudes. Similarly, the Subalpine Zone has its own community, including the pine grosbeak, olive-sided flycatcher, Clark's nutcracker, hermit thrush, Rocky Mountain jay, pine marten, and bobcat. The Plains Zone is the habitat of numerous kinds of animals that rarely extend their range into the mountains, such as pronghorn antelopes, prairie dogs, and rattlesnakes. In addition, there are other species that range all the way from the foothills to the alpine meadows: mule deer, marmots, coyotes, and chipmunks.

The structure of the Colorado Rockies is similar to that of many other parts of this chain, including the outlying Black Hills of southwestern

South Dakota. This range, a hundred miles long and 50 miles wide, rises not quite 4000 feet above the plains. The most picturesque feature of the central dome is Harney Peak, an immense mass of pink granite that is one of the most beautiful rock faces on the continent. Rain falls in greater amounts on the Black Hills than on the seared plains below them. As a result, pine and spruce have taken hold on their slopes and in their rugged, rocky canyons; from a distance the trees appear so dark by contrast to the arid landscape that the pioneers called these mountains the Black Hills. They form a crossroads for trees from the north, east, and west. From Canada have come the paper birch and the white spruce, which grow on the high slopes. Ponderosa and lodgepole pine, which dominate the lower flanks, are from the Rockies. Species from the eastern forests include ash, elm, and, most notably, bur oak—all of them distributed as a scrubby growth below the evergreen forest.

Just as the Black Hills are its eastern outpost, the northernmost extension of the Rockies is the Brooks Range of Alaska, whose summits rise to heights of about 5000 feet above sea level. The area has been little explored on foot, and it is mostly covered with perennial snowfields. This land, still in the grasp of the ice age, is a picture of what the Rockies might have looked like 10,000 years ago. Between the Brooks Range and the United States border, the Canadian Rockies swerve westward until they all but press against the Pacific coast ranges. The Canadian Rockies display a sawtooth profile, with sharp spires and castlelike summits. A vast segment of this majestic region has been set

YOUNG ENGELMANN spruce overtop aspen in the high Rockies.

aside in four Canadian national parks: Banff and Jasper on the east slope, Kootenay and Yoho on the west. Their boundaries meet along a string of icefields that follow the crest of the Continental Divide and form a white spine for the Canadian Rockies.

Banff is almost a textbook lesson in the formation of mountains. The Cascade and Sulphur ranges have been carved out of a large fault block that was uplifted and tilted toward the west. Their eastern face is thus much higher than the western; the traveler approaching from the east sees it looming out of the plains as an abrupt escarpment. In the Sawback Range are mountains that were formed by being uplifted into an arch; and some of the peaks to the west are of limestone rather than granite.

The glaciers in the Canadian Rockies are much more extensive than the small white patches to be seen farther south in the mountains of the United States. A number of icefields within Jasper National Park can be visited without difficulty; but the most impressive sight is the lower end of Athabaska Glacier, which originates in one of these icefields and follows a mountain canyon for at least ten miles. This glacier has come to a virtual standstill, for its advance is balanced by its melt. The uneven rate of melting has formed huge caves; water trickling into them freezes, creating a fairyland of icy stalactites whose ever-changing colors are due to the refraction of the light.

WINDSWEPT Engelmann spruce grows prostrate at timberline in the Rockies.

No one who has visited the lakes fed by this and other glaciers can have failed to notice the varying colors of the lakes and streams. The ice as it moves is continually grinding rock fragments into powder. When they have been ground sufficiently fine most types of rock, particularly limestones and shales, yield a whitish powder. Water flowing from the melting glaciers becomes clouded from its load of this rock flour, which similarly whitens the lakes closest to the glaciers. Although most of the rock flour is deposited in the higher lakes, some is occasionally carried downstream, thus giving the lakes below a light gray tint. Only the lower lakes remain a clear blue. Occasionally, when the glaciers have ridden over red shale rocks, the lakes they feed acquire a pinkish tint.

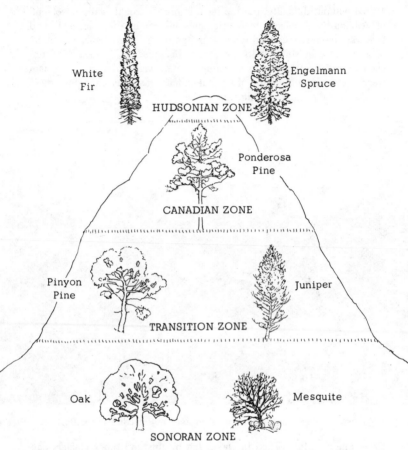

White
Fir

Engelmann
Spruce

HUDSONIAN ZONE

Ponderosa
Pine

CANADIAN ZONE

Pinyon
Pine

Juniper

TRANSITION ZONE

Oak

Mesquite

SONORAN ZONE

LIFE ZONES on a typical mountain in the southern Rockies of New Mexico, and the species of trees primarily found in each zone.

Athabaska is a glacier still in action; on the other hand, there is no better place to witness the past effects of glaciers than at the Waterton-Glacier International Peace Park, which straddles the border between Montana and Alberta. Here the glaciers have been at work so recently that some of the valleys are still bare of soil. Cirques gouged out of the heads of valleys hold quiet lakes that flawlessly mirror the peaks. Here are precipices thousands of feet high, deep canyons, turbulent streams, and waterfalls. Since much of the park is above timberline, the earth forms are in full view, not clothed by vegetation. At present there are less than 50 small glaciers in the park; they have fluctuated greatly in size, probably reaching their maximum about a hundred years ago. Since then the climate has warmed, and they have shrunk steadily. The retreat of the ice fronts is very noticeable: Sperry Glacier, for example, retreated an average of 62 feet annually during a recent eight-year period. Anyone who visited Glacier National Park several decades ago and carried away with him a recollection of vast white expanses would be disappointed if he were to return today.

Many questions occur to visitors at Glacier and Waterton parks. What is the origin of the bright bands of rock? What has caused these mountains to rise so precipitously above the plains? A visitor as he first enters the park might regard the white, red, and purple bands across the mountains as an optical illusion. But he soon realizes that wherever he looks, the mountains are composed of layers of variously colored rocks. These are sedimentary layers, formed by the accumulation under the sea of the skeletons of sea animals and of mud and sand, which were later compressed into limestones, shales, and sandstones. Similar banded rocks can be seen in the mountains of western Montana, northern Idaho, and southern British Columbia. The visitor who has traveled widely in the southwest will also recognize their similarity to those occurring at Grand Canyon and in the Uinta Range of Utah.

All of these widely distributed sedimentary rocks were formed under a long, narrow sea that extended from the Arctic Ocean to California. About 60 million years ago a series of movements of the earth's crust, most of them pushing from the west, compressed and uplifted the sediments, converting what had been the bottom of the sea into mountains. Increased pressure caused the rocks to break along a fault line into two huge blocks. The block to the west of the fault was pushed upward and then eastward for twenty miles, so that it lay on top of the rocks to the east of the break, tilted like one half of a raised drawbridge. This placed the layer of oldest rocks to the west of the fault directly on top of the youngest rocks to the east, in much the same way that the bottom card in a deck ends up directly above the top card when the deck is cut. The bands of rock seen by the visitor to the park are almost completely the rocks of the overthrust, which have buried those to the east. Because of the overthrust, the mountains appear to rise straight out of the plains, without any intervening foothills.

These sedimentary layers did not all accumulate quietly under the sea. Periodically, while the sediments were still under water, molten rock was squeezed up from the interior of the earth and spread out over the layers of sediments. The product of one such lava flow can be seen clearly as a thin black layer at Granite Pass. The lava flow was fed from underground by a vertical passageway that cut through the sedimentary formations. Some of these dikes, as they are called, remain as vertical chimneys or chutes on the mountainside. One dike, about 1500 feet high and 30 feet wide, transects the Pinnacle Wall at the outlet of Iceberg Lake.

A number of other well-known mountain ranges originated as fault blocks, just as did the mountains of Glacier Park. The Grand Tetons of Wyoming are a classic example. The level plain approaches to the foot of these mountains with scarcely a ripple; then, abruptly, the peaks rise from the plains to the height of a mile; from the east, except at Teton Pass, the range presents an insuperable barrier. But because this overthrust block has been tilted to the west, a traveler arriving from that direction climbs gradually, passing through a series of foothills that slowly increase in elevation. Before the assault upon the Tetons by the glaciers, the contrast between the gentle western approach and the remarkably steep eastern face must have been even more striking than it is today.

As the Teton block was uplifted, air currents from the west were forced to rise so high that their moisture condensed, thus greatly increasing the precipitation on that side. The streams, already rejuvenated by the uplift, now had to carry an increased amount of water. Compared with those of the gentle western slope, the streams flowing to the east had far shorter, steeper courses. Thus the eastward-flowing streams not only cut deeper canyons, but also extended their headwaters farther to the west, encroaching upon the western streams and often capturing them. As a result, the eastern slope has been widened at the expense of the one to the west

The streams of the eastern slope, as they flowed out onto the plains, carried loads of sand and boulders that spread widely as an outwash plain. In a number of places the outwash plains are alongside the glacial moraines left by the retreating ice. The moraines are composed of a mixture of rock particles that are compact and retain moisture, but the cobbles spread by the streams do not hold moisture. Thus, while forests of lodgepole pine grow on the moraines, only the hardy sagebrush has been able to take root on the outwash plains alongside them.

The western mountains built by faulting are but one demonstration of the constant unrest of the earth. Around the world, more than a million earthquakes are recorded every year. The continual changes in the earth's face—the retreat or advance of ice caps, the accumulation of sediments, the uplift of mountains—set up stresses that distort rocks be-

THE EASTERN FACE of the Grand Tetons, a sheer wall rising out of the plains, is typical of a fault-block mountain.

yond their limits of resiliency. When that happens, they yield along the line of a fracture or fault and an earthquake is the result.

The regions of North America where earthquakes occur have been compared to a poorly laid cement pavement. As such a pavement settles, cracks develop, breaking it up into many individual blocks. Some of the blocks sink, others rise, and still others tilt in various directions. Many of the mountains of the western states can be visualized as parts of such an uneven pavement on a continental scale. The Sierras, the Tetons, and many of the plateaus of Nevada and Utah are blocks resulting from the settling of this pavement; the boundary of each of these is a crack or fault. Sometimes there are numerous faults, as at the eastern edge of the Sierra Nevada, where faults descend for 5000 feet into the Owens Valley of Nevada like a flight of stairs.

Earthquakes occur when new faults are created or old faults are abruptly displaced. Often the ground breaks along faults, and the actual displacement of the earth can be seen in the warping of highways and fences. The San Andreas fault is easily observable from the air along much of its 600 miles between San Francisco and southern California. It was this fault that caused the disastrous San Francisco earthquake in 1906, when the land to the west of the fault moved northward as much as twenty-one feet. The slow movement of the blocks on both sides of the San Andreas fracture had already been under way for years before the earthquake. The rocks had been slowly deformed and bent until the strain could be borne no longer; then they straightened with the speed and abruptness of a spring. The earth trembled as energy that had accumulated for decades was instantaneously released by the rebound. Studies indicate that the block to the east of the San Andreas fault is today steadily inching southward, building up stresses that can be relieved only by a future earthquake.

In 1959 an area of some 550,000 square miles around Yellowstone National Park suffered a severe earthquake, one of the strongest tremors ever recorded in the United States. The energy released was equal to that of 200 Hiroshima bombs. Great changes took place as a result of the quake. Mountains sent awesome rock slides tumbling into the valleys; boulders the size of automobiles bounced down the slopes like marbles. The underground plumbing system of some 300 geysers was altered; some were plugged up, new ones spouted. At this writing, Grand Geyser, previously one of the most active, has almost ceased to play. Some thermal springs that had been inactive for years began to bubble again. Within minutes, more changes occurred than would normally take place in thousands of years.

Volcanoes are another sign of unrest, and in this respect Yellowstone has had a violent and fiery past. Everywhere the visitor is greeted by the sights of vulcanism. Much of the rock at Yellowstone is either a light-colored lava rock known as rhyolite, or a dark basalt. Mount Washburn, 10,317 feet high, is a volcanic mountain. Obsidian Cliff, one of the most striking features of the park—a shining wall of glass, flawlessly black and so hard that the Indians used chips of it to make arrowheads—was formed from a lava flow that cooled exceptionally fast.

At times the volcanic fires at Yellowstone subsided, and forests took root. But when the showers of ash and lava commenced again, these forests were buried. On Specimen Ridge the petrified remains of 27 forests, each growing atop a smothered previous one, have been counted —proof of the periodic violence of the volcanic caldrons. The forests must have flourished for long periods, for some of the trunks are very large. Some of these petrified forests are nearly perfect reproductions that preserve roots, bark, annual rings, and even insect holes.

Even the mightiest of recent volcanic outpourings have been puny affairs compared to the eruptions of previous ages. The most dramatic of ancient volcanoes are those that have built layer upon layer to form a single towering cone. An example is Capulin Mountain in New Mexico, extinct for some 7,000 years. Like a giant anthill it rises nearly a thousand feet above a level plain; its rim is a mile in circumference and contains a cup-shaped crater about 415 feet deep. Similarly Sunset Crater, near Flagstaff, Arizona, has built an almost perfectly symmetrical cone a thousand feet high. It is the youngest volcano in a field which spreads over two million acres, and which produced the nearby San Francisco Peaks.

Sunset Crater erupted for the last time about 900 years ago. Earthquakes must have warned Indians living in the vicinity of the imminent disaster, for they appear to have fled, leaving their huts and fields to be buried under the fall of cinders and ash. When the Indians returned they found that the cinders had improved their fields by acting as a mulch that lessened the evaporation of water from the soil. Land previously untillable because it was parched now produced good crops of corn and beans. Word spread, and an Indian land rush began. Within a few years the Indian population on the cinder blanket is estimated to have numbered about 4000. But the same desert winds that had evenly distributed the cinder mulch began to sweep it up; the cinder carpet soon grew threadbare, and crop failures followed. Within 40 years after the eruption the area was deserted, except for a few families who were able to eke out a crop in the moister areas. The ghost towns left by the Indians can be seen in nearby Walnut Canyon and the Wupatki National Monuments in Arizona.

Most volcanoes are fed from individual underground reservoirs probably not more than twenty miles deep. The deeper down into the earth one penetrates, the higher the temperature becomes. The temperature at a depth of twenty miles is high enough to produce liquid rock or magma, were it not for the fact that the pressure exerted by the overlying rock raises the melting point above what it would normally be at the surface. For example, rock that would melt at 2300 degrees Fahrenheit on the surface would not melt twenty miles below the surface until its temperature reached 2600 degrees. Most rock at this depth is solid, but a small additional amount of heat will turn it into magma. Friction caused by earthquakes might be all that is needed to raise its temperature to the melting point. This might explain why all volcanoes occur in fault zones, although there are many fault zones that lack active volcanoes.

When magma appears at the surface of the earth, it is known as lava. The kind of rock it becomes when it solidifies is governed by two things: how fast it cools, and the amount of gas it contains. Immediate cooling produces a glassy texture. Where there is no gas content, immediate cooling produces obsidian; where the gas content is very high, the result is pumice, which is so light in weight that it floats. Basalt and the lighter-colored rhyolite are produced by flows that do not solidify immediately, but instead crystallize later into fine-grained rock.

The greatest of all flows reach the surface not through volcanoes but along fissures in the earth's crust. In this way vast molasses-like outpourings formed the Columbia Plateau, an area of more than 200,000 square miles that stretches from the Grand Tetons of Wyoming westward to the Cascade Mountains of Oregon and Washington. Flood after flood of lava has poured out of cracks in the surface, as recently as a few hundred years ago; it can be assumed that the present lull in this activity is merely temporary. The flows built up a level surface which in places is thousands of feet deep; the lower hills were inundated as by a flood, leaving only the higher peaks jutting out of a sea of lava.

The steep vertical walls of the canyons cut by the Snake and Columbia rivers, which are comparable in depth and magnificence to Grand Canyon, reveal the structure of the Columbia Plateau. The flows varied individually from ten to 200 feet in thickness; in some places as many as twenty layers have been exposed by the down-cutting rivers. It has been estimated that in the process about 100,000 cubic miles of volcanic material was transferred to the surface.

An impressive blanket of volcanic material covers much of southern Colorado and northern New Mexico between Gunnison and Sante Fe. In places the blanket is a mile and a quarter thick at present, but before erosion stripped off the upper layers its depth must have been closer to two miles, making it one of the major accumulations of ash and lava in the world. At the eastern border of this San Juan country rise those great monuments to volcanic action, the Spanish Peaks of Colorado. West Spanish Peak soars to an altitude of 13,623 feet, and nearby East Peak is only a thousand feet lower.

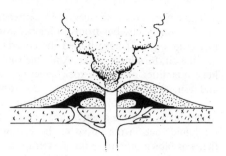

SYMMETRICAL VOLCANOES are built up by alternating layers of lava and cinders that rain down on the volcano's flanks. The building of the cone may be followed by a violent eruption that blows off the top and forms a gaping crater.

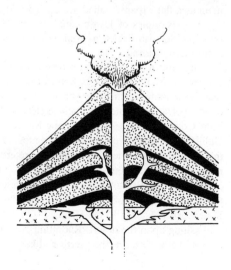

There were no human beings in existence to watch the formation of the Spanish Peaks, but from geological evidence it is inferred that the first eruption must have hurled the covering layer of sedimentary rock into the air, forming a crater. Amid the rumbling of violent earthquakes, huge quantities of molten rock, emerging as globules of lava, cinders, and ash, must have burst repeatedly from this crater. The heavier materials fell back around the vent, increasing its height, while the lighter materials were evenly spread out by the wind. From time to time the liquid rock in the throat of the volcano solidified, forming a crest that was blown off during the next eruption, thus hurling fragments into the air. The light gray or reddish volcanic rocks known as "tuff" or "breccia" are composed of such fragments, which have become welded together. The dark bands seen in the rocks are the result of outpourings of lava. Thousands of such explosions and flows went into the building of the Spanish Peaks.

Not all flows of molten rock lie at the surface or produce volcanoes. Instead, the flow may remain as a sheet between layers of rock; or it may reach the surface and then be covered by sediments. When erosion occurs, sedimentary rocks tend to weather quickly; but the volcanic rocks remain as ledges that project out of the mountain slopes or as the towering vertical monuments called dikes. When the lava flows out in a sheet, it forms a cap of resistant rock that protects the weaker underlying rocks from erosion. Thus, while the surrounding country becomes lowered by weathering, the rocks protected under the volcanic cap remain as a flat expanse called a mesa (the Spanish word for table). Outstanding examples of lava-created mesas are Raton Mesa, a few miles from the Spanish Peaks, as well as Grand Mesa and Flattop Mountain in northern Colorado.

Long after a volcano has become extinct, and the weaker rocks have washed away, its skeleton remains: the routes of the solidified magma that never quite reached the surface, including the thick neck, the core of the volcano. Numerous such skeletons exist in the vicinity of the Four Corners, where Arizona, New Mexico, Utah, and Colorado meet. Unlike the youthful volcanic fields in most of Arizona and New Mexico, this is an area of ancient volcanoes where erosion has almost completely removed the outer cones, leaving only the internal plumbing systems as chimneys or castles towering above the desert. Outstanding among approximately three dozen excellent examples of volcanic necks around Four Corners is Ship Rock. Rising 1400 feet, it looks like a giant black ship sailing upon the desert. Radiating out from Ship Rock and forming a wavelike pattern are thin vertical dikes.

SHIP ROCK is the skeleton of an ancient volcano, the rest of the cone having eroded away. Visible in the foreground is a smaller and more recent cone.

Another pillar of lava is Devil's Tower in the northeastern corner of Wyoming. Nearly 1300 feet high, it looks much like the gigantic stump of some petrified tree. What makes this stump so spectacular is that it is composed of vertical columns with anywhere from three to eight sides, although the number is usually six. At the top of the tower, the ends of the columns form a pattern that looks like the cracks that form in mud as it dries. Such cracks are the result of shrinking caused by the loss of water; when lava cools under certain conditions, it shrinks and cracks in the same way. Columnar jointing, as this sort of vertical fluting is called, may be seen elsewhere, notably at the Devil's Postpile in California and in Yellowstone Park.

The flat top of Devil's Tower covers about an acre and a half, and upon this pedestal there is a bountiful community of life. Grass and shrubs grow on the summit, fed upon by an abundance of rodents such as mice, pack rats, and chipmunks. Prairie falcons have their eyries at the tops of the columns and a constant food supply in the little rodents. The falcons never take so much prey as to exterminate their food source —a striking lesson in what wildlife experts call population balance.

The Craters of the Moon in southern Idaho indeed resembles a moonscape. It is a dark, lifeless world, produced by volcanic activity that appears to have taken place only recently, although the last eruption was at least 500 years ago. Here are cones composed of cinders thrown out by volcanoes; the largest, Big Cinder Butte, rises about 800 feet. There are places where the lava has flowed gently out of fissures to produce low, rounded domes. There are flows that have oozed onto the surface and frozen into the shape of long rolling waves, with billows and cavernous troughs. There are also long hollow tubes, formed when the molten stream hardened on the outside, allowing the liquid interior to drain away. Some of these lava tubes are 30 feet high. Here and there the roof of a tube has collapsed, forming a cave that may retain winter snows until late in the summer.

At first glance the Craters of the Moon appear to be a scene of utter desolation and barrenness, as though the lava had stopped flowing so recently that there has been no time as yet for life to develop. But although it seems impossible that life could exist at all in this scorched land, it has in fact taken hold everywhere. Little heaps of dust and organic matter have accumulated in the lava cracks; windborne seeds have taken root and begun the long process of building soil, adding their dead leaves and roots to the dust and thus making it hospitable for larger and more demanding plants. In some places the invasion by plants is well under way, and such shrubs as rabbitbrush, sage, and bearmat have taken hold; even an occasional limber pine or chokecherry lifts its head above the shrubs. The cinder fields during certain seasons are speckled with little flowers, as for example in late spring, when the red monkey flower grows out of the black cinders in a way that seems miraculous. The plants have attracted butterflies and other insects; even deer now come into the area to browse.

Currently the most extensive area of volcanic activity on the continent is the Valley of Ten Thousand Smokes, at the base of the Aleutian Island chain. In June 1912, it was rent by a series of violent earthquakes, which were followed by one of the greatest eruptions in history. A thunderous blast spewed forth rock fragments; white-hot ash poured from the main vent and from numerous nearby fissures. Within minutes, enough ash had been expelled to form a cube two and a half miles long on each side. This ash swept down the Katmai Valley like a tidal wave, burying more than 40 square miles of the valley floor beneath as much as 700 feet of ash; more than a foot of it fell on the town of Kodiak, about a hundred miles away. Subsequently, steam from buried streams and springs began to rise to the surface through countless small holes and cracks. It was estimated at the time that some 10,000 fissures were giving off plumes of hot gases, but the correct number may have been closer to a million.

Today, volcanic activity in the area has greatly lessened. Mount Trident produced some lava flows in 1953 and 1957; the Valley of Ten Thousand Smokes has dwindled into a valley of less than a hundred smokes, although some of these plumes are still more than 500 feet high. The Ukak River and its tributaries have flowed swiftly across the ash, cutting canyons as much as 200 feet deep. The cliffs are being eroded by wind, and have already begun to resemble the fantastic spires of Bryce Canyon in Utah. Vegetation, which has been unable to develop on the

STEAM still issues from one of the active volcanoes in Alaska's Valley of Ten Thousand Smokes.

deep blanket of ash, has taken hold along the streams, and there are now luxuriant thickets of willow and alder. Should no further eruptions occur, the area will gradually come to resemble other, older volcanic landscapes; but, although the valley is quiescent now, there are omens of possible future activity.

Recent volcanic activity has occurred almost entirely in the western part of the continent, but in the distant past the east also had its volcanic eruptions and lava flows. Although many of the remnants of vulcanism have eroded away or been buried under sediments, a striking one can be seen from Manhattan Island in New York City: directly across the Hudson River in New Jersey is an imposing ridge of volcanic rock, the Palisades. Three rocky eminences that loom over New Haven, Connecticut—East Rock, West Rock, and the Sleeping Giant—are basaltic ridges, the protruding edges of tilted lava sheets that still lie buried. The Hanging Hills of Meriden, Connecticut, and the Watchung Mountains of northern New Jersey are also the result of past volcanic activity. Granite, the most abundant rock of the ancient Appalachian backbone, is itself volcanic in origin—an indication that the caldrons of Vulcan have been steaming since the continent was young.

11 :   The Pacific Rim

T HE WESTERN MOUNTAIN RIM of North America begins on the north with the long string of Aleutian volcanoes and continues in an unbroken chain southward through Canada, Washington, and Oregon to southern California. The Aleutian Island chain forms a sweeping arc, 1600 miles long, that points toward Siberia. Although there is now no connection between Siberia and Alaska, at various times in the past these two continents have been joined by a land bridge.

The New World is new not only in the sense of being a recent discovery, but also in that man traveled to it across the Bering Strait land bridge a mere tens of thousands of years ago, and many animals and plants are likewise relatively recent arrivals from Asia. Until recently the Bering land bridge had been visualized as a narrow gateway or isthmus, but the latest evidence seems to indicate that it was at times as much as 1300 miles wide, completely linking Alaska and Siberia. Soundings made from ships crossing the Bering Sea reveal that beneath the water is a level plain covered by less than 200 feet of water. If the sea were lowered by this depth, there would emerge a land connection broader than the entire present length of western Alaska from north to south.

The level of the sea has been lowered repeatedly in the recent history of the continent. Each successive advance of the ice sheet has locked up vast amounts of water that otherwise would have returned to the sea.

It has been estimated that during the height of the last glacial advance the level of the oceans dropped between four and five hundred feet, more than twice as far as would have been necessary for the Bering Strait bridge to emerge. Since this drop occurred when the ice sheets were most extensive, one might suppose that the land bridge, although liberated from the sea, must nevertheless have been blocked by ice. However, that did not happen, for neither western Alaska nor eastern Siberia was glaciated during the last advance.

The first men who crossed from Siberia to Alaska a few tens of thousands of years ago must have followed the paths already taken by the Asiatic animals which they hunted: mammoths and mastodons, mountain sheep and goats, bison, elk, moose, wolves, and bears. In fact, North America's fauna and flora are very much more Asiatic than American, for the reason that North and South America were long separated from each other. During that time, each developed its own highly specialized plants and animals. When the two Americas were joined by the emergence of the Panama land bridge, South American species were able to invade North America; but the southern animals could not compete with the vigorous ones already established in North America, and only a few southern mammals have been successful in the north: the porcupine, armadillo, and opossum are the most familiar of these.

Where the Aleutian Islands meet the Alaskan mainland, the face of the land alters markedly, from a chain of volcanoes to a complex mountain range carved from folded rocks. Typical of the carved mountains is Mount McKinley, the continent's highest peak, 20,320 feet above sea level. The upper half of the peak is clothed in perpetual snow; scores of valley glaciers have their source on its high slopes. Below the cap of the snows is the tundra zone whose brief season of awakening during the summer culminates in a magnificent wildflower display against a backdrop of bare, frost-riven rocks.

Underlying the flowery carpet of the tundra, often a mere few inches beneath the surface, is the permafrost, soil that is perpetually frozen. Only the top layer melts during the brief summer thaw, and it is the only part of the soil that supports life. The tundra in summer appears to be a land of abundant water, but that is an illusion; the melted water merely lies atop the permafrost in which growing conditions are actually drier than in a desert. Few large plants are adapted to this cold environment with its shallow soil, but notable among those few are the willows. More than 30 kinds grow as low shrubs on the open tundra, hiding their prostrate stems underground and thrusting only a catkin and a leaf or two above the surface. Only a little less able to endure the harsh conditions is the white spruce, which ranges across the roof of the continent from Alaska to the Maritime Provinces on the Atlantic coast of Canada. Its range dips down into northern New England and into the bogs around the Great Lakes, but only in the Canadian and Alaskan ranges does this tree achieve its full majesty. There, it shoots up straight as a mast, with great boughs of bluish foliage sweeping out like the tiered roofs of a Chinese pagoda.

These ranges are a land of great herds and extensive migrations. On the lower slopes the white Dall sheep, with their massive, curled horns, give birth to the lambs in sheltered crannies; in June, the herds migrate to the crags of the Alaska Range. No migrating animal is as restless as the caribou, which may, after making the same trek of some 600 miles for several years, suddenly change the pattern of its migrations. The impetus for its nomadism seems to be the search for "reindeer moss"— actually a large lichen. A herd today may include as many as 4500 caribou; but their numbers were much greater in the past, when herds of as many as a million caribou held up paddle-wheel steamers plying the Yukon River for days while the animals crossed.

Many of the living things of the Alaska ranges seem to be perpetually on the move: moose, reindeer, musk ox, elk, bison. The chief predators upon these grazers are the bears and wolves, which keep their populations in check and prevent the herds from stripping the range bare in a single season. The most awesome of these predators is the cream-colored Toklat grizzly, a tremendous beast which may be encountered almost anywhere in Mount McKinley National Park. In its restless search for whatever prey may be available it pursues small squirrels and marmots, stalks Dall sheep and caribou, steals the food caches of wolves, and consumes large amounts of roots and berries.

Wolves prey on all the big game animals except the bears, and are the primary check on the numbers of the caribou. Contrary to common belief, they have rarely molested human travelers. But they were quick to kill unfenced cattle and sheep, and for that reason they have been mercilessly slaughtered. Those who know these animals well report that no other is so admirably endowed with the human traits of courage, loyalty, and affection. Wolves travel in small family groups that consist of a male, a female, the pups, and a few unattached relatives. The adults get along well among themselves, and treat the pups with exceptional kindness. Before setting out on a night hunt, there are various ceremonies of tail wagging and play; and when a mother joins the hunt, one of the unattached females minds the pups.

If one animal were to be selected as the vanishing American, the most fitting choice would be the wolf. It was once widespread throughout the continent; the voices of wolves must, indeed, have been among the first animal sounds heard by the Pilgrims. But wherever the white man penetrated the wilderness, the wolf was an animal to be eradicated by guns, traps, and poison. It retreated reluctantly before the white man's onslaught; the last of its kind disappeared from the eastern United States little more than half a century ago. Today, no more than a few hundred persist, in a scattering of remote places, south of the Canadian border.

The coastal ranges of Alaska sweep southward in a compact arc, joining the mountain ramparts of British Columbia along the Inland Passage. A pair of mountain belts, one forming the islands along the outer margin of the passage—Vancouver, the Queen Charlotte group, the Fairweather Range—and the other the ranges on the mainland, cut down through the United States. As they proceed southward, the distance between them widens. The mainland ranges swing toward the interior, forming the Kamloops of British Columbia, the Cascades of Washington and Oregon, and the Sierra Nevada of eastern California. To the west of these mountains, and paralleling them, is a lowland trough consisting of the Inland Passage, the Willamette Valley–Puget Sound lowland of Washington and Oregon, and the Great Central Valley of California. To the west of the trough the mountains rise again to form the rim of the continent—the Olympic and the Coast ranges of Oregon and California. The same pattern of trough bordered by interior and coast ranges extends from the Aleutians to Mexico, where the trough lies under the water of the Gulf of California.

Few mountain ranges are endowed with so many majestic peaks as the Cascades. Rainier (14,408 feet), Adams (12,307 feet), and Baker (10,778 feet) in Washington; Hood (11,225 feet) and Jefferson (10,-499 feet) in Oregon; Shasta (14,162 feet) and Lassen (10,457 feet) in northern California—all of these impress the beholder with their symmetry of outline. Many of the mountains of the Cascades display, in fact, the classic volcanic shape; for this is a volcanic landscape that has only recently spent its powers. Indeed, Mount Baker, whose last eruption was in 1870, and Mount Lassen, which was active as recently as 1921, are likely to be heard from again. And these are only the most noteworthy of the volcanic peaks; in the southern Cascades alone there are at least 120 others.

One of the most beautiful of all volcanic mountains is Rainier in the northern Cascades of Washington, southeast of Tacoma. What makes Rainier so impressive is that it rises upon its immense base, covering

PERFECT SYMMETRY: Mount Adams, a volcanic peak in the Cascades, soars above a sea of ponderosa pine.

about a hundred square miles, directly out of the tidewater of Puget Sound. On its flanks, like ermine robes on the shoulders of some king of mountains, lie 26 glaciers, a greater expanse of ice than on any other peak in mainland United States. Its majestic bulk, its isolation from the rivalry of other peaks, the fact that nowhere can the summit be seen from the base—these things have made Rainier the most striking of all the mountains in the mainland United States.

Rainier was once also thought to be the country's highest peak. Re-measurement has now given that distinction to Mount Whitney (14,495 feet) in California; but statistics have not diminished Rainier's overwhelming grandeur. It is like the stump of a giant tree, buttressed by huge, gnarled roots, and with a jagged edge showing where it has been decapitated. That is, in fact, exactly what has happened. At one time Rainier was more than 16,000 feet high. Then an explosion, or very probably a series of explosions, blasted 2000 feet of rock from its crest, leaving a deep crater surrounded by a jagged rim. Successive less violent eruptions, the last in 1870, gradually filled the crater and produced a domed summit.

As if all this majestic beauty were not itself enough, Rainier's slopes are girdled with some of the most varied wildflower meadows anywhere on the continent. Few places exceed Rainier in either the sheer number of individual species of flowers—700 of them—or their total abundance. The reason for this wealth lies in the mountain's enormous variety of habitats, which permit nearly every kind of flower to find a place that meets its requirements for growth. A flower that comes into bloom during the spring at a 4000-foot altitude may not bloom until early summer at a higher elevation, and not until late summer at the very limits of the Alpine Zone. Thus the seasons of blossom are like a fireworks display which, just as it seems to have exhausted itself, bursts forth anew at a greater height. Whereas those who live at low altitudes know spring as something that arrives and then goes, in the mountains spring is present nearly all summer long, a little farther up the slope.

The lowland forest encircling Rainier's less elevated slopes is what first attracts the visitor, and many tarry there so long that they are too late for the alpine floral displays. The forest is composed of towering boles of Douglas firs, western hemlocks, and western red cedars, whose tops are invisible from the ground, and which form a canopy so tightly interlaced that scarcely a ray of sunlight penetrates. The ground is soft and yielding from the centuries of accumulated humus; moss seems to festoon everything: the rocks, the fallen branches, and the shade-tolerant plants, such as dogwood, Oregon grape, sword fern, and sorrel. Towering over all else in this green carpet is the Douglas fir; some of its deeply furrowed trunks are ten feet in diameter and soar to heights of more than 200 feet.

Anyone who travels southward among the Cascades must inevitably be drawn to the hidden jewel of these mountains, the deepest and surely one of the loveliest of all the lakes on the continent. The visitor does not see Crater Lake until the last possible moment. Suddenly, after driving uphill for miles, he is on the edge of a volcanic crater, looking across six miles of deep blue water, encircled by a rim a third of a mile high that is splashed with deep browns, yellows, and every conceivable shade of blue. From the middle of the lake projects a miniature volcano, Wizard Island, and at one end another island, called the Phantom Ship, lifts its single mastlike pinnacle.

Crater Lake crowns a volcano that was once considerably higher than it is today. At some time within the past 7000 years that volcano, now referred to as Mount Mazama, erupted with such force that it literally boiled over, spreading out lava to a distance of 35 miles. The volume of lava ejected was at least five cubic miles, in addition to another cubic mile or two of shattered fragments torn from the mountain top itself, and vast quantities of pumice which were blown into the air. In all about ten cubic miles of material were scooped out of this mountain, creating a void that could be filled in only one way—by collapse. Before the eruption Mazama had been about 12,000 feet high and rivaled the other peaks of the Cascades; after the eruption, it had been reduced to a 7000-foot hill.

Even then the volcanic activity did not cease. With its last gasp it produced the perfect volcanic cone of Wizard Island, which rises from the floor of the cavity. Gradually the crater filled with rain and snow, and the lake was created. There is no outlet for the water, yet its depth remains nearly constant, varying only a few feet from year to year. The reason is the lake's almost perfect balance between income from precipitation and outgo from underground seepage and evaporation. The deep blue color of the lake is due to its extreme depth (nearly 2000 feet) and the purity of the water itself. The water acts like a prism, scattering the sunlight that shines upon it, reflecting the blue rays and absorbing the other colors.

The southern terminus of the Cascades is Mount Lassen in northern California, the only volcanic mountain on the mainland United States which has been active in this century. Lassen had been quiet for about two hundred years before 1914, when it broke its slumber and began the first of 212 mild eruptions, which continued sporadically until 1921. Without a rumbling or a twitch by way of warning, the eruption broke from a new crater on the north slope, close to the summit. At first the crater was only 45 feet wide, but within two weeks it had enlarged to a diameter of 1500 feet and was sending ashes and steam to a height of three miles. Then the volcano slumbered again. Almost exactly one year after that first eruption, a tremendous explosion sent lava spilling down the beds of Lost Creek and Hat Creek. The hot blast leveled a forest of virgin timber around Lost Creek, as though the great trees had been nothing more than cornstalks. Farther away, bark was stripped from trees on the sides facing the eruption; stumps of uprooted trees were sandblasted until their polished surfaces shone.

Lassen is an approximate dividing line between the volcanic Cascades to the north and the granite Sierra Nevada of California. (The Spanish word *sierra* means "saw," and is used by the Spaniards to describe ranges that are sawtooth in profile. Sierra Nevada thus means "snowy sawtooth mountains.") The Sierra Nevada is a fault-block range carved out of a massive block which had previously been uplifted and tilted to the west. Its origins are much like those of the Grand Tetons of Wyoming, but on a grander scale. On the west, the Sierra rises gradually through a foothill zone; on the east it looms near the Nevada border as a bold escarpment on the edge of which stands Mount Whitney.

VOLCANIC CONE of Wizard Island rises out of Crater Lake, which itself fills the crater of an extinct volcano.

The Sierra Nevada, constituting a continuous barrier 400 miles long, is America's longest and most impressive single range. The Rockies are in reality a collection of mountain ranges, with many gaps between them; the longest continuous barrier in the Rockies is only about half as long as the Sierra Nevada. The high peaks of the Rockies rise only about 7000 feet above the Great Plains, but the peaks of the Sierra tower nearly 11,000 feet above the Great Central Valley. The Cascade Range is also longer than the Sierra Nevada, but it, too, is broken by numerous gaps. To the pioneers, the Sierra represented an almost insuperable barrier; it was best avoided by going around its southern flank, through the Mohave Desert.

Because of its predominant gray color under the cap of snow, the Sierra resembles an ocean wave rising from the trough of the Central Valley and gradually breaking along the snowy crest of the eastern escarpment. Anyone who has visited the High Sierras must have noticed

ONION WEATHERING is displayed by the layers of granite that compose the dome of Liberty Cap in Yosemite National Park.

that the granite masses are often rounded into huge domes that resemble helmets, a striking contrast to the angular rocks of most mountain peaks. At first glance, it might be supposed that these smooth domes were legacies of the glaciers. But a similar dome at Stone Mountain, near Atlanta, Georgia, is about 350 miles south of the farthest point reached by the glaciers. Thus, a glacial origin for these domes is out of the question.

Instead, these domes are seen to have been built up like an onion, with layer atop layer; the individual layers of rock vary in thickness from a few inches to several feet, although some in the Sierra Nevada are more than a hundred feet in thickness. These shells peel off, one after the other, always leaving another smooth shell underneath. Each time one layer is peeled away by erosion, the removal of the pressure from above permits those underneath to expand, thus loosening the next layer. Exfoliation, as this kind of weathering is called, can be seen also in desert areas where hot days and cold nights alternately cause the rocks to expand and to contract. But nowhere does exfoliation exist on such a scale as in the High Sierras: at Moro Rock, Sunset Rock, and Beetle Rock in Sequoia National Park, and at the magnificent Tehipite Dome in the canyon of the Middle Fork of the Kings River.

If one stands at the crest of the Sierra, one looks down upon two low-land regions—the Great Basin to the east and the Central Valley of California to the west. The actual western limits of the Sierra extend far to the west of the foothills. But these lowest slopes have been buried under the mud and gravel washed down from the higher peaks. Occasional low peaks, which have not yet been completely covered, still rise from the floor of the Central Valley; such are the Twin Buttes north of Visalia. At the time that the Sierra was formed by uplift, the Central Valley came into being by depression. Ever since, it has been receiving immense loads of debris, which now have a depth of at least 2000 feet in some places. Numerous snow-fed streams spill into the Central Valley; many of these have been dammed, and the diversion of their waters into canals has made possible the irrigation projects that checker the Central Valley with orchards, vineyards, and vegetable fields.

Much of the structure of the Sierra is due to faulting, not only along the eastern face where the major fault developed, but also in many places on the uplifted block itself. The canyon of the Kern River, for example, is located in a fault which is nearly parallel to the eastern margin of the range. At the north the Sierra divides into three ranges, each a fault block in itself. Part of the way down the eastern escarpment, another range, the Carson Range of Nevada, has been carved out of a lesser fault block. Lying between the main fault of the Sierra and the Carson Range is Lake Tahoe, 22 miles long, 1600 feet deep, and the largest lake in the Sierra. It had its origin as a depression between the two faults whose outlet was blocked by volcanic action, forming a dam and impounding the water from rain and melting snow. Glaciers added the finishing touches when they built the dam even higher with debris. Tahoe is an exceptional body of water, quite unlike most intermountain lakes produced by the damming of a valley; these are usually shallow, whereas Tahoe impounds even more water than does Lake Mead behind Hoover Dam on the Arizona-Nevada border.

The drainage patterns of the rivers flowing near the eastern fault are extraordinarily confused. The outlet of Tahoe is the Truckee River, which meanders in a northeasterly direction and ends in another lake, Pyramid. Near by, the Humboldt River flows westward, as though aiming for the Truckee; then suddenly it veers and ends in a swamp. In this land of dwindling rivers, the Carson probes among the mountains and shifts its course constantly, eventually finding a grave in a desert sink.

While all is disorder in the faulted eastern section of the Sierra, the rivers of the west slope display a monotonous symmetry. Ten rivers— among them the Merced, Feather, Yuba, American, Bear, and Calaveras —flow down the slope along courses that are almost exactly parallel and equidistant. The same effect can be achieved in miniature by placing ten droplets of water on one edge of a bridge table, then lifting that edge; the droplets will follow parallel routes as they roll toward the lower edge of the table. Before being uplifted the Sierra was somewhat like the flat bridge table; the streams moved sluggishly across the surface. But when the Sierra block was tilted toward the west, the streams gained speed as they rolled down the surface. Because of the increased precipitation after the uplift, they cut deep channels along these routes.

The streams keep a steady course long after they have emerged from the foothills. In fact, they flow nearly three-quarters of the way across the Central Valley before they are gathered into the northward-flowing San Joaquin and the southward-flowing Sacramento rivers. The visitor might well wonder why the San Joaquin and the Sacramento do not capture these mountain streams as soon as they emerge from the Sierra, rather than after they have flowed so far across the valley. The reason is that the mountain streams have actually shoved the San Joaquin and the Sacramento away from the foothills. During the glacial epoch the mountain streams were much larger, and were laden with sand and gravel. This material was unloaded at the base of the Sierra in a series of alluvial fans. Alluvial fans are similar to river deltas, except that they are formed on land: when a river loses speed after emerging from a mountain valley, it drops its cargo of silt in the shape of a fan. As the extent of these fans increased, they spread farther west, pushing the San Joaquin and Sacramento rivers away from the base of the Sierra.

Mile for mile, the Sierra has more basins of water than any other mountain range in the mainland United States. Anyone flying over these mountains will notice thousands of lakes dotting their flanks and crests like blue droplets among the gray rocks. Yosemite National Park numbers within its borders nearly 425 lakes, countless waterfalls, and numerous impressive streams. Many of the Yosemite waterfalls are of the free-leaping type that drop unimpeded by ledges. A leaping fall can occur only where the walls of a canyon are sheer. Those of Yosemite fling themselves over the cliffs and, whipped by the wind, flutter downward to join the river far below. Visitors who come in midsummer often do not see the falls in action, for the snowmelt that feeds them is gone.

Upper Yosemite Falls, which drops in free fall for 1430 feet, hits a ledge, and then tumbles another thousand feet, is the highest waterfall on the continent. Ribbon Falls sends a stream of water plunging down the flanks of the valley for 1612 feet, more than the height of the Empire State Building; among known free-falling torrents, it is second only to Angel Falls in Venezuela. One wonders why these tributary streams hang so high above the mainstem that they must then leap the intervening distance. The explanation is that the glaciers that filled these tributary valleys were not equipped with the cutting power of the main Merced River glacier. When the glaciers melted, the tributary streams were left hanging above the Merced; the only way they could rejoin it was to pour over the cliffs in cascades.

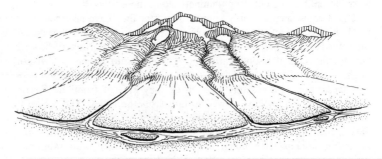

ALLUVIAL FANS, composed of sediments brought down from the mountains, force rivers in the Central Valley of California away from the base of the Sierra.

The broad trough of Yosemite Valley, seven miles long and not quite two miles wide, is a widened portion of the canyon of the Merced River. Twelve miles to the north is the Grand Canyon of the Tuolumne River, a deeper and longer gash. The beauty of the rock sculpture in these two valleys is unsurpassed anywhere in the Sierra. The shapes taken by granite under erosion are determined largely by the pattern of joints in the rocks. Joints are places of potential weakness; they are avenues through which water may enter and pry the rock apart by freezing or by decomposition. Cliffs composed of rocks with numerous joints crumble bit by bit. But the bold face of a cliff unmarred by joints for hundreds or thousands of feet possesses great resistance to erosion and endures as a bold promontory. The walls of Tuolumne Canyon have so few joints that they were able to resist the glaciers; instead of being fractured into a typical U-shaped glacial valley, the canyon retains its V shape. Tuolumne was endowed not only with monolithic walls, nearly a mile high, but with a smoothly sloping floor also, and the ice glided down it as

DEEP TROUGH of Yosemite Valley was cut by the glaciers, which also sculptured El Capitan (left), Half Dome (center, background), and Cathedral Rocks (right).

though along a chute, leaving almost no imprint on this valley.

The variations in the jointed structure of the rocks of Yosemite have made it an ornate, sculptured valley of domes, monoliths, and minarets. Guarding the approaches to the valley are some of the world's greatest monoliths. El Capitan, the boldest of them, sweeps upward for 3600 feet, twice the height of the Rock of Gibraltar. Opposite are the three summits of the Cathedral Rocks, looming one above the other. At the other end of the valley is Half Dome, shaped like an enormous pie cut in half, and rising nearly 4900 feet above the valley. Near Tenaya Lake and Tuolumne Meadows are clusters of domes of a wide variety of sizes and shapes; Sentinel, North Dome, and Basket Dome at Yosemite are among the most perfectly shaped of those in the Sierra.

Typical of this land of rocks and waters is a remarkable bird, the water ouzel or dipper, whose habitat is the waterfalls and swift-flowing streams northward from the Sierra into Alaska, as well as in some places in the Rockies. There is scarcely a waterfall, whether in the foothills or in the High Sierras, that does not have a pair of these little birds flitting about in the spray or plunging headlong into the cascades themselves. The dipper is chunky and short-tailed, blue-gray in color, and about the size of a robin. It is one of the most indefatigable singers of the west, one of the few birds that sing the year round, in a tone as sweet as a flute and as liquid as a stream, with numerous trills and tremolos. The torrents of its song match the yearly flow of the waters; scarcely more than a trickle in the dry fall, it builds up during the winter and unleashes a flood of melody in the spring. Whereas other birds sing in response to the songs of their own kind, the dipper is tuned to the streams that furnish an accompaniment for its solo performances.

The mainstay of the dipper's diet consists of water insects. In search of them it wades upstream, against the current, turning over small stones with its bill. In winter, the dipper dives beneath the semi-frozen surfaces of streams and searches out the unfrozen portions of lakes. It dives under the waters for what seem like minutes at a time, bobbing to the surface like a released cork. The dipper's powerful concave wings enable it to swim under water and to avoid being dashed against rocks; even in a strong current, the underwater wingbeats allow it to hold its course. It can endure an underwater life because of the large size of its oil glands; they envelop the bird in oilskins as efficient as those worn by a New England skipper. Under the skin the bird has a thick layer of fat, insulation against the icy waters.

The dipper is wedded to the waters. It almost never takes the shortest route overland, but instead flies along a winding route that traces the lakes and streams, even following the bends, rather than cutting across the loops. Its nest, a little hut of moss, is usually situated on a ledge alongside a waterfall; but sometimes it is built inside the fall, between the cascade and the cliff, so that to reach it the little bird must fly through the torrent. The nest is always near enough to the water that the droplets of spray keep the moss a glistening green; that serves as camouflage, and the nest is not much different in appearance from any clump of moss growing on a ledge. The young birds remain in their nests for an exceptionally long time, about 25 days. Both adults and juveniles seem as playful as the

WATER OUZEL

dancing waters as they chase each other through the falls and foam, sending out showers of song.

The dipper may be encountered almost anywhere in the Sierra Nevada, the Aleutians, the Black Hills, the Rockies, and even the mountains of Mexico. But nowhere is it more perfectly in harmony with its environment of water and rocks than in the Sierra Nevada.

V

THE FORESTS

12 : Forest Primeval

PLANTS SEEM TO GROW upon the continent more or less at random, but actually each landscape is the result of the complex interaction of many forces. If North America were entirely without oceans or mountains, trees would grow in neat horizontal bands around the continent, since the only influence upon plant life would be solar light and heat. The northernmost band, near the pole, would lack vegetation because it would be too cold, and the growing season too short. South of that would be a band of tundra where only a few dwarfed trees would grow. Farther south would be another belt where the growing season would be longer—the taiga, as it is called, in which flourish the extensive forests of conifers, the pines, spruces, and firs. Below the taiga would be the deciduous forests, composed mostly of broadleafed trees that commonly shed their leaves in winter: oaks, maples, elms, and others.

Now restore to this imaginary picture the oceans and gulfs, but continue to visualize it as a uniformly level land mass. The ocean currents will alter the bands of vegetation. A warm current that sweeps along the coast of Alaska permits the evergreen forests to extend far north of their normal range, into what was formerly the tundra. Similarly, the Gulf Stream warms the southern coast of Florida, the Bahamas, and Bermuda, allowing tropical vegetation to flourish far north of what would otherwise be the limit of its distribution. Finally, restore to the continent its mountains, hills, and valleys. The belts of vegetation are now interrupted by deserts and grasslands in the interior of the continent. As the prevailing winds sweep in from the Pacific Ocean, they are laden with moisture. When they encounter the slopes of the coast ranges, they are forced to rise abruptly and are suddenly cooled; their moisture condenses and falls as rain or snow, more than twelve feet a year in some places on the Pacific coast. This north-south zone of heavy rain and snow has produced the Pacific forests of redwood, Sitka spruce, Douglas fir, and western hemlock.

The winds bring heavy precipitation also to the slopes of the Sierra and the Cascades, giving rise to another north-south forest that includes the giant sequoia. Their moisture now wrung out, the dry winds continue eastward, producing desert conditions in the vast basin between the Sierra and the Rockies. Gradually, the winds accumulate additional moisture, and as they reach the Rockies they once more release their cargo of water, creating a third north-south belt of forests. Dried out once again, the winds pass beyond the Rockies over the arid high plains to the east. The humidifying influences of the Great Lakes, the Gulf of Mexico, and the Atlantic Ocean can be observed in the increasing height of the grasses around the Mississippi River and, finally, in the great forests of the east.

Mountains affect the distribution of plants in yet another way, by creating life zones determined largely by altitude. Thus, by restoring the mountains to this imaginary landscape, tundra plants are able to find hospitable conditions on peaks far south of their usual range. On the other hand, mountains also create sheltered valleys that allow southern plants to endure in regions north of their usual range.

Altitude, climate, temperature, and length of the growing season all help determine where plants will grow. Moreover, there is an interplay between living things and the inert matter of the soil that contributes to the establishment of plant communities. Local soil conditions and the previous plant inhabitants of a particular place also determine to a large extent what will grow there in the future. For example, in a climatic zone where one might expect to find a deciduous forest, a glacial bog may create conditions favorable for conifers and northern plants.

Forests cannot grow everywhere, for they are limited by drought and cold. Forests generally require at least fifteen inches of rainfall a year and a frost-free growing season of at least three months. The survival of forests depends not only on the amount of rainfall, but also on its seasonal distribution. For example, the northern Pacific coastal forests receive immense amounts of rain when the trees need it most, during the growing season, and the result is one of the mightiest forests on the

VEGETATION MAP OF NORTH AMERICA

continent. Farther south, in southern California and northern Mexico, however, the summers are dry and most of the rain falls during the winter, when it is of no use to trees. Although in southern California the annual rainfall, on the average, is sufficient for the growth of forests, conditions during the summer approximate those of a desert; thus, instead of trees, the slopes are covered with a scrubby vegetation known as chaparral.

At first glance, a forest appears to be a haphazard collection of trees, shrubs, vines, and flowers. There may be several dozen species of trees in even a small forest, and they seem to grow at random: the shrubs carelessly scattering themselves over the forest floor and the vines clinging to any convenient tree. To the casual eye, it might seem that other trees than those growing there could be substituted without disrupting the forest. Yet, destroy a forest by fire or ax, and in several centuries it will be replaced by a forest of almost exactly the same kind. The forest may make what appear to be numerous false starts, at first giving rise to trees and associated plants different from those that originally grew in that location. But all of these temporary stages point in one direction, the rebirth of the forest along its original lines; the dominant trees will be almost an exact replica of the old forest, and they will have as companions very much the same plants and animals that are unique to that kind of forest.

One example of the stages through which a reborn forest passes can be seen in Acadia National Park on Mount Desert Island, Maine. In 1947, much of this land was dominated by two kinds of spruce, white and red, together with lesser numbers of balsam fir. Scattered throughout the forest also were a number of different kinds of pine, mostly white and pitch. Such a stable assemblage of trees is known as a "climax" forest. Different kinds of trees have succeeded one another until the forest has reached a stage of relative stability. Barring epidemics of disease, holocausts of fire, or decimation by insect pests, a climax forest duplicates itself from generation to generation, with only minor changes.

But in 1947 a catastrophe did occur. A month-long fire destroyed some 10,000 acres of climax forest. Almost immediately, the rebuilding of a new forest out of the charred remains began. In pockets of soil, a number of species of little plants took hold, among them three-toothed cinquefoil and mountain sandwort. Within only a few years a profusion of blueberries covered the scarred land, crowding out the flowers. The blueberries in their turn were overtopped by a number of kinds of trees, particularly birch, aspen, and staghorn sumac. These trees are pioneering the new forest; for already growing under them are representatives of the original forest, pitch pines and spruce in particular. One can predict with certainty the future of this forest. The conifers will grow above the deciduous trees, and their dense shade will kill the sun-loving birches and aspens; the only seedlings that will be able to take hold will be those of the shade-tolerant spruces and firs. As the older spruces and firs mature and then die, their places will be taken by young spruces and firs. This kind of forest will continue to duplicate itself until another catastrophe strikes.

Every forest passes through a series of stages before it reaches an equilibrium. In southern New England the route to equilibrium is not the same as in northern New England. When a Connecticut farmer abandons a field, numerous kinds of plants attempt to invade it. It is captured, though, by those plants which can germinate most quickly and which can survive the sunlight and drying winds of an open field. These plants provide a nursery for the next stage in the succession, a new forest of white pine and birch. For a while the white pines rule this young forest, but they eventually eliminate themselves: their seedlings cannot survive in the dense shade cast by the older pines. Only trees whose seedlings can endure the lack of sunlight, for example certain oaks and maples, manage to grow suppressed under the white pines.

As the pines fall prey to one or another of the hazards of forest life, they leave openings in the forest which are filled by the oaks and maples. As the forest matures, the oaks and maples, along with the remnant of the white pine pioneers, grow so tall that they shut out even the small amount of sunlight needed for their own seedlings. When that happens, their career as rulers of this forest is at an end. For growing on the dark forest floor are the seedlings of such trees as hemlock and beech. It may be scores of years before the oaks and maples surrender their rule, but eventually the hemlocks and beeches become the dominant species. The forest reaches its climax, for the only seedlings that can survive in the darkness are those of the dominant trees.

Almost all forests in southern New England travel this same path. Some, owing to local conditions, arrive at the climax sooner than others; some are halted along the route by fire or logging; some suffer severe outbreaks of insect pests that put them back a step in the succession. The reason that so much variety exists in the forests of an area is that they are all at different way-stations along the path to the climax. As a general rule, no one can witness all of the stages of succession in a single forest during his own life span. The steps from bare field to climax forest may require hundreds, sometimes thousands, of years. But in one spot the bare-field stage can be seen; in another field near by, the white-pine stage may exist.

North America has a remarkable diversity of forests. The continent spans about seventy-five degrees of latitude, virtually from the North Pole to the Tropic of Cancer. It has mountains, high and low, and soils underlain by a variety of rocks. There are arid regions, and regions where the precipitation is heavy. Part of the continent has been glaciated, part has not. Altitude, latitude, soils, climate, and other factors have conspired to produce numerous distinct kinds of forests.

Clothing almost the whole eastern half of the United States and southeastern Canada are the remnants of a forest that once had few rivals anywhere in the world. Rimming the Atlantic and extending nearly unbroken to the Mississippi River, it then divided into two prongs: one stretching northward to the Dakotas, the other southward nearly to the center of Texas. Between these two prongs, the great eastern forest still sends out exploratory fingers that follow the rivers and streams deep into the prairies.

The forests of this immense area may be divided into three major types. In the northern portion, and on the higher slopes of mountains farther south, the forests are primarily of conifers with a scattering of a few deciduous species. South of this evergreen belt are extensive deciduous forests, in the main of oak mixed with hickory, poplar, beech, maple, hemlock, and white pine. South of the oak forests are the piny woods of the southern states. They begin as a narrow band in New Jersey and follow the broadening coastal plain through the south for more than a hundred miles to the west of the Mississippi Delta. Pure stands of pine are everywhere, their gaunt, desolate silhouettes rising out of the land: shortleaf pine in the northern end of the piny woods, longleaf pine in the southern, loblolly pine toward the interior. In moist locations throughout the piny woods grow the southern hardwoods: sweetgum, tupelo, live oak, magnolia, and cypress.

The eastern forests merge almost imperceptibly into the grasslands, but they do not capitulate easily. Willows and cottonwoods line the stream channels almost to the Rockies themselves. The Rockies are heavily clothed with forests: Englemann spruce and its constant associate, alpine fir, on the high slopes; at lower altitudes, the open parklike stands of ponderosa pine. Between the Rockies and the Sierra-Cascades region is stark desert, but the closer one approaches to the moist air of the Pacific coast, the more luxuriant the forests become. The giant sequoias inhabit the Sierra, but it is along the northern Pacific boundary that the North American forests reach their greatest height and grandeur. Here grow coast redwoods, Sitka spruce, western red cedars, Douglas firs, and western hemlocks, some of them soaring to heights of more than 350 feet.

This is the basic flora of North America, but within each of these sprawling major divisions are much smaller associations. For example, in Ohio, Indiana, and southern Michigan the maple-beech association and the oak-hickory association often grow side by side. They do not merge, but instead propagate duplicates of themselves, forming a crazy-quilt pattern on the land. Although a casual glance usually reveals no great difference in the sites they occupy, closer inspection discloses that the oaks and hickories inhabit the drier soils. The dryness usually is not due to a shortage of rainfall; rather, the oak-hickory association develops on south-facing slopes or on barren sandy soils that do not retain much moisture. Because it is capable of enduring dryness, the oak-hickory forest extends deep into the prairies, following the Missouri basin into North Dakota and the Arkansas River into Oklahoma.

The sites they occupy are not the only differences between these two kinds of forest. Entering a maple-beech forest in summertime is like walking into a cathedral. The heavy columns of the trunks soar upward and are lost in the sunless green vault of the canopy. The sky is very nearly blotted out by the leaves; the sparse undergrowth is limited to species that can live shrouded in darkness, such as dogwood, witch hazel, and serviceberry. Before the canopy closes over in late spring, the forest floor is carpeted with a remarkable abundance of wildflowers; they blossom early, shed their seeds, and then wither. The oak-hickory forest presents a completely different picture. The trees grow widely spaced, the canopy is open, and sunlight dapples the ground everywhere. As a result the undergrowth is dense with shrubs and small trees, such as blackberry, hazelnut, and redbud.

Until recently the role played by fires in altering these forest associations was little understood. When the loggers reached the luxuriant forests of Wisconsin and Minnesota, they found growing there lofty white pines mixed with deciduous species. They logged out the prized white pine and left in their wake holocausts that killed all the standing trees and even their seeds, except for those of the jack pine. This unusual tree does not release its seeds in the autumn, as most pines do. Instead, the cones remain tightly closed for years, opening only when they are heated, as by a forest fire. And then they open so slowly that by the time they release their seeds the fire will have burned out. As a result, jack pine is often the only tree to sprout after a fire. For this reason jack pines cover extensive areas of the lake states today, although they were comparatively rare in the primeval forests. Eventually these forests will probably find their way back onto the path of succession and, if undisturbed, consist once more of climax species.

Many of the forest associations of the east are represented in the Great Smoky Mountains of North Carolina and Tennessee. Although they have a total area of less than a thousand square miles, the Smokies are the home of more than 130 tree species, or about 45 more than are found in all of western Europe. Nearly twenty species of trees reach record proportions in the Great Smoky Mountains National Park. There tulip trees grow nearly 200 feet tall, hemlocks and chestnut oaks reach 100 feet, and buckeyes 125 feet. Among the plants that crowd the Smokies are more than 1400 different kinds of flowering herbs, nearly 350 species of mosses and related plants, and about 2000 species of fungi. The unbroken luxuriance of these forests blanketing the mountains formed as much an obstacle to the pioneers as did the slopes themselves. Even today, when so much of the eastern forests has been logged over many times, the Smokies are relatively unscathed. Their inaccessibility has permitted these forests to remain the last area of extensive virgin timber in the east.

The very name Smokies explains one reason for the richness of these forests. Fog rises from the valleys, and clouds roll through the gaps; there is a haze over everything, as though from continual fires. This is really a water forest. Water squishes from the fallen needles at every step; moss carpets everything; even the petals of the flowers that grow in the open spaces hold droplets of water. The western slope of the Smokies has a higher precipitation than any place in the mainland United States outside of the Pacific northwest; in places, rain and snow average about seven feet a year. There is another reason also. This forest is of great antiquity, with a lineage that stretches back far beyond the ice ages. When the cold and ice pressed down upon Canada and the northern United States, they forced the plants southward. The work of millions of years of building stable forests in the north was erased. But the bulk of the southern Appalachian forests was untouched.

This ancient forest of the Smokies, known as the cove forest, exists in sheltered locations below about 4500 feet. It grew here before many of the mammals had yet evolved and long before the existence of modern man. At one time forests similar to this one spread around the globe, clothing even Greenland and Alaska with many deciduous trees familiar to us today. But then there were movements in the crust of the earth: mountains rose; the climate changed; ice descended from the north. In most places the circumpolar forest was destroyed; that of the southern Appalachians is a small remnant.

The cove forest gives the appearance of being settled, at peace with the land. The great trunks of the trees merge gracefully with the earth, masked at the point of transition by a luxurious growth of ferns and mosses. At first glance, the trunks all seem to have been cut from the same pattern, but when the visitor attempts to identify the species, he becomes aware of their remarkable variety. The cove forests contain some species to remind almost any visitor, whether he be from the gulf states or from Canada, of the woods at home. There are groupings of oaks and hickories reminiscent of the forests of the midwest. Stands of hemlock and sugar maple are typical of New England and Canada; other stands appear to be replicas of the Ozark forests.

Crowded into these coves are some 45 species of trees, about as many as grow native in Great Britain. No one or two trees are consistently so much more common than the others that their names could identify the entire association. A visitor standing in a cove may look in one direction and decide that the basswood is the dominant tree. But a slight shift of his gaze to the right or to the left may reveal towering buckeye, yellow poplar, white ash, hemlock, beech, northern red oak, silverbell, and dozens of others. The sizes of the trees are confusing, too; the silverbell, which grows as a shrub throughout most of its range, here has a circumference of nearly twelve feet.

The flowers of many deciduous trees are inconspicuous; but the char-

WISPS OF FOG and hovering rain clouds produced the luxuriant Smoky forest.

acteristic trees of the cove forests bear large and showy flowers. The tulip tree, as its name implies, is adorned with great-petaled flowers that resemble garden tulips; the magnolia bears blossoms the size of water lilies; the buckeye has large yellow or red flowers; great white clusters of blossoms hang from the black locust. The showy bracts of flowering dogwood and the purple clusters of redbud resemble troops of butterflies flitting through the leaves. Blooms burst from silverbells, laurels, and sourwoods. Nowhere else on the continent can one see the woods lighted up by so many different kinds of flowering trees and shrubs.

In this settled forest, many kinds of trees are botanical antiques. The magnolia, for example, is a primitive species, one of the early attempts by a tree to produce a flower. There are a number of very apparent differences between a magnolia blossom and a modern flower. Each blossom of the magnolia is large and stands aloof from the others; there is no close grouping of many small florets, as is found, for example, in the daisy. Each petal in the broad, cuplike blossom is separate from the rest. Beautiful though the flower is to a human eye, this is a most inefficient way to lead an insect to the interior of the flower to bring about cross-pollination; in less primitive flowers the petals are fused at the base, forming a tube that leads the insect to the reproductive parts of the flower. Even a large proportion of the insects of the cove forests belong to primitive groups; they are descendants of the same insects that the magnolia was originally attempting to attract by this prototype of the modern blossom.

If a traveler were permitted to see only one forest in the eastern United States, that one should be the cove forest. Nevertheless, other forests of the Smokies hold great appeal also. Below the coves, at the base of the mountains and in the foothills, are piedmont forests similar to those of the Carolinas and Georgia. Some of the species are the same as in the cove forests, but they do not grow so tall or so luxuriantly. There are oaks and hickories, but no rhododendrons, hemlocks, or sugar maples. The piedmont forest also includes a number of trees distinctly its own: persimmon, red birch, holly, and sweet gum.

Growing higher than the cove forests, above an altitude of approximately 4500 feet, are the stands of northern hardwoods. Here are sugar maples that rise nearly a hundred feet in height, together with beech, yellow birch, and buckeye. As this forest reaches an altitude of nearly 6000 feet, a transformation takes place. Above that height many of the trees grow squat and spaced far apart. Their gnarled branches, spreading like those of old apple trees, have caused local residents to refer to these highest reaches of the northern hardwoods as "the orchards."

The topmost forest, above an altitude of approximately 6000 feet, is one of spruce and fir—the same sort of forest that grows in northern New England and southern Canada. Only the loftiest peaks in the Smokies are crowned with these noble evergreens. The red spruce and Fraser fir often grow in pure stands, with only occasional intrusions by mountain ash and mountain maple. The trunks stand so close together that their branches interlock. It frequently happens that when one of these trees dies, it does not fall to the ground but remains standing, clasped in the branches of the surrounding trees. It is not only their closeness, but also the thickness of the boughs and the density of the needles that make the summits of the Smokies appear black.

Interestingly enough, this topmost forest shows none of the signs of the dwarfing so noticeable near the summits of Mount Washington and of the western ranges. There is no true timberline in the Smokies. The three highest peaks—Clingmans Dome (6643 feet), Mount Guyot (6621 feet), and Mount Le Conte (6593 feet)—are clothed with forests to their summits. However, there are some treeless lesser peaks—the strange "balds" of the Smokies. Although they lack a forest cover, these mountain tops are not shorn of all vegetation. Some are covered mostly with grasses and sedges; others are mantled with

MAGNOLIA

heaths such as rhododendron, laurel, blueberry, and sand myrtle that provide a spectacular display of flowers in late spring. There is no sure explanation why the heath balds exist in a world dominated by trees, at altitudes where trees ordinarily grow. They were not caused by logging off the hillsides, for the pioneers found them in their present state; they probably were not caused by the work of Indians, either. A number of scientists believe that the heath balds are due primarily to fires started by lightning. Fires would kill the trees, but the rhododendrons and laurels would grow back quickly, suppressing any further tree growth.

This may be the correct explanation for the heath balds, but there are also balds composed of a thick turf of grasses and spring flowers, reminiscent of the western grasslands. It seems impossible that the delicate strands of these plants could hold their own against the encircling spruce and fir, the tangles of rhododendron and laurel. Yet the turf is remarkably thick, testimony to the fact that these are not recent changes in the vegetation of the peaks. Fire damage, ice storms, and local weather conditions have all been offered as explanations for these balds, yet no one answer is entirely satisfactory.

Nearly 250 different kinds of birds have been seen in the Great Smokies, and many of them are residents of particular kinds of forest. More than any other place in the eastern states, the Smokies are the domain of the wood warblers, those jewels among birds, smaller than sparrows and as brightly colored as butterflies. Numerous kinds of warblers either pass through the Smokies on migration or are permanent nesters, returning year after year from their wintering grounds in Central and South America. Waves of them flit through the woods, searching for insects and staking out nesting territories.

All seems chaos in the spring forests of the Smokies. How do the multitudes of birds manage to avoid competition, to find places to nest? To understand the organization of birds in a forest, one must be aware that a forest, like a human city, has many levels. There is the street level, then the level of small homes and shops; above it are the apartment buildings; and towering over everything else are the skyscrapers. A forest displays much the same sort of organization. The forest's skyscrapers are the dominant trees; its apartment buildings are the younger trees and taller shrubs; the low shrubs, ferns, and flowering herbs correspond to the small homes. Some of these Smoky Mountains forests consist of no less than seven layers: soil basement, forest floor, ground-hugging herbs, tall herbs and low shrubs, tall shrubs, low trees, and tall trees.

Each of these levels offers niches for particular species of birds. Blackburnian warblers, for example, inhabit the tops of the conifers. Halfway down these same trees, black-throated green warblers might nest, and magnolia warblers might inhabit the lower levels. The branches of a neighboring deciduous tree might be the home of a redstart. Black-throated blue warblers nest in shaded shrubs; chestnut-sided warblers prefer shrubs growing in the sunlight. The ovenbird nests on dry, shaded forest floors, the Nashville warbler on sunlit ones. Thus, a great many kinds of warblers can live in the same forest, each one inhabiting its own particular niche and scarcely competing with the others. The wood warblers also escape competition by their different methods of feeding. Some pursue insects on the wing, some search in bark crevices, others pick caterpillars off leaves.

Other birds similarly manage to find their own living space in the three-dimensional forest. Four species of woodpeckers might inhabit a forest, but since each hunts for insects in a different part of the trees, there is no conflict. Many birds avoid competition by inhabiting forests at different altitudes. For example, the crow, the wood thrush, and the Carolina chickadee occupy the lower altitudes of the Smokies; at higher altitudes they are replaced, respectively, by the raven, the veery, and the black-capped chickadee. Only in the highest altitudes of the spruce-fir forest are heard the whistle of the solitary vireo and the high-pitched, whispering notes of the golden-crowned kinglet.

During the spring and summer, the most commonly seen bird at the higher altitudes is the Carolina junco; it is dark gray in color and about the size of a sparrow, with a song that suggests a tinkling bell. Many other birds return to the high-altitude forests in the spring after migrations of a thousand miles or more, but not the Carolina junco. Its migration is vertical, from the foothills to the summits—a distance of hardly more than a few miles. Juncos of this species spend the winter in sheltered valleys of the Smokies; by the end of April they have traveled up the mountain, in easy stages, and laid their eggs. The Carolina junco is not the only bird that makes the equivalent of a thousand-mile horizontal migration merely by flying between the base and summit of a mountain. In the Sierra Nevada the Oregon junco, mountain bluebird, fox sparrow, and white-crowned sparrow do the same thing. In the Rockies the pipits, pine grosbeaks, rosy finches, and half a dozen other species move up or down in response to the seasons.

North of the Smokies and the surrounding areas, the forests that had been growing undisturbed for millions of years were erased by the ice sheets. The destruction was complete; not only was vegetation leveled and buried, but the topography itself was altered. All that remained was raw rock, sand, and clay. The forests of the northeastern United States and Canada are relatively new; they began from nothing perhaps 10,000 years ago. Fortunately, a record exists of the forests' northward march after the glaciers. When the ice melted, it left numerous depressions filled with water; ever since then, these ponds have been filling up with leaves and twigs washed in by streams, with pollen grains borne there by winds. All of this debris has settled to the bottom, layer upon layer like the pages of a

CAROLINA JUNCO

book, leaving a record of the kinds of plants that grew around the bogs at different times. By boring deep into these bogs and bringing up samples from all the layers, scientists can reconstruct the sequence of vegetation since the glaciers retreated.

The deepest layers form the earliest chapters of the book; no plant remains are found there, but only the mineral particles that washed into the bogs while the surrounding land was being cleared of ice. Directly above this layer are others containing plant remains; some are so decomposed as to be unrecognizable, but in many cases the pollen grains were able to resist decay because of their protective coats. They tell the story of an inhospitable land being repopulated first of all by plants that are today inhabitants of the far north. These little arctic plants were the only ones that could manage to grow in the wake of the retreating ice; they formed the advance wave of the forests. As the glaciers retreated farther north, the arctic plants continued to follow them, and are still doing so.

The next layer in the bogs discloses the kinds of plants that succeeded the arctic species: birch, willow, alder, and numerous berries. For thousands of years they grew around the bogs, generations of them adding organic matter to the mineral soil, creating conditions in which trees could grow. But as the climate continued to grow warmer, these trees moved northward in the wake of the arctic species. They were followed by the spruces and firs, which had found a refuge in the south.

The spruces and firs eventually moved northward also, and the bogs reveal a rain of pollen from other conifers that live in warmer and drier climates—particularly white pine. At first the spruces and firs lingered, growing alongside the pines, but a subsequent layer of the bog reveals that they have departed completely, leaving the forest to the pines. There is a layer made up almost exclusively of the pollen of white pine; then it in turn dwindles. In its place the pollen of oak, beech, birch, maple, and hemlock become increasingly more abundant. These are the trees that have built the present-day forests of southern New England; but even now the northward march of the forests is not completed. Trees from still farther south are now extending their ranges northward. Southern white cedar, inkberry, holly, and rhododendron have now passed the northern boundaries of New England, in some instances growing as far north as the coastal plain of Newfoundland. In recent years there has been an unexplained dieback of birches and sugar maples in New England; one explanation offered is that the warming trend has made New England inhospitable for these northern trees.

The deciduous forest associations share a common problem. Lying in the temperate zone, they must endure the changes and hazards of the seasons. Even though they grow in the humid eastern part of the continent, during the winter they might as well be growing in a desert; when the soil freezes in winter, water ceases to be available to them. Evergreens are largely inured to drought; their thin needles are covered by a thick waxy coating, and they possess fewer breathing pores than the broadleafed trees. These latter have had to develop a different method of survival. To preserve their moisture, they shut down for the winter and become completely dormant. That is why the trees that have developed this life-saving method of dropping their leaves in the autumn are known as "deciduous," from a Latin word meaning "to fall off."

The process of shutting down the tree's waterworks for the winter is what creates the magnificent colorings of fall foliage. This display is restricted largely to temperate deciduous woods; although the leaves of a few other forests of the world also turn in the fall, they are muted affairs as compared with the North American paint-pot. No other place in the world has such a diversity of tree species combined with climate favorable for bringing out a range of hues. "The whole country goes to glory!" exclaimed Mrs. Trollope, an English visitor of the last century, when she witnessed the spectacle of an American autumn. And so it does, for almost the entire eastern portion of the continent blazes with the fires of autumn. Each forest association has its distinctive hues, and that is why the turning of the leaves in different parts of the continent can be viewed year after year without any sense of repetition. The colors of autumn in the Great Smokies are different from those in the Adirondacks, the Ozarks, or the White Mountains. Even the evergreen forests take part, for against the deep-green backdrop of spruce and fir are clumps of aspen that glisten with the color of old gold.

The turning of the leaves is an event that every year arrives approximately on schedule and in an orderly sequence. First to turn are the berry bushes and the herbs—for the little plants of the forest fly their autumn colors, too. Then come the red maples, living pyres of autumn whose glow is visible for miles. Still later, ash trees and sugar maples burst into purple and gold. Then, just as the whole gaudy display seems about to end, scarlet oaks light up the countryside.

Contrary to the popular belief, frost does not color the leaves. Rather, they turn as a result of changes in the life of the tree. All summer long, the trees manufacture food; their leaves are green with the abundant chlorophyll that enables them to carry on photosynthesis. The shortening days of autumn are a signal to the tree that its laboratory must be shut down. Those immense waterworks, the tree's sap system, must be dismantled to preserve the life of the tree; the leaves that are prodigally evaporating water must be shorn off.

Preparation for the leaf fall is made during the summer. When a leaf first sprouts, a zone of weakness, where the leaf is attached to its twig, determines exactly the point at which the autumn amputation will take place. Just below this layer of cells is another that will eventually toughen and become corky, sealing up the wound on the twig. During the spring and summer, certain inhibiting hormones keep these layers from developing. But the increasing length of the nights of autumn serves as a signal to the tree; the production of the hormones tapers off, and the two layers begin to separate.

While this is going on, the tree is slowing down its production of chlorophyll, until finally no more replenishes what is already in the leaf's cells. It wastes away, revealing the yellow and orange pigments that had been in the leaf all summer long, masked by the greenery. Other pigments—the scarlets, lavenders, and vermilions—are not as a rule produced during the summer, but are added as autumn progresses. No one is certain exactly what function the red pigments serve for the tree, although it is believed that they may be a by-product of the breakup of sugar in the leaves. The red pigments give autumn its true magnificence, and account for the fact that the foliage displays are more brilliant in some years than in others. The yellow pigments are little influenced by the vagaries of weather, but the red pigments are subject to soil conditions, sunlight, temperature, and other factors. Generally, the brighter the sunlight in autumn, the brighter the reds in the leaves. That is why the leaves on the inside of a tree, where the sunlight is less abundant, are usually paler than those on the outside which drink in the full light. An overcast autumn will usually be a yellow one, with little production of red pigments.

A third group of pigments in the leaves is the product of the brown substance tannin. Tannin is abundant in the leaves of a number of tree species, particularly oaks. The browns are the most enduring of the autumn colors, and oak leaves, which persist after other trees have dropped their faded banners, remain a rich brown for months. Various combinations of these three pigments result in an endless variety of tints. The autumn purple of the ash is due to a combination of red pigments with the green of chlorophyll. The bronze of the beeches and of some oaks is due to the overlapping of yellows and browns. By the season's end, the separation layers at the bases of the leaves are fully formed; a breeze or a raindrop is enough to sever their last connection with the twigs. As many as ten million leaves may flutter to the floor of an acre of woodland as the forest shuts down for the winter. But each twig bears a promise of the perpetuation of the forest: the winter buds which will unfurl in the spring, several million to a single large tree.

Preparations by the forest's animal population for the harshness of winter are no less remarkable. The shortening days and lengthening nights of autumn are a signal to many birds to flee the forest by migrating to a warmer climate, where food supply is not a problem. For many other inhabitants the solution is the sleep of winter. The woodchuck enters the sleep of hibernation, during which its body temperature drops nearly to the freezing point and its heart beats only a few times a minute. The sleep of other animals is not so profound. The chipmunk awakens during the winter and feeds on its store of nuts and seeds. The bear is only in a state of torpor, and its young are born during the winter.

The wonders of migration and hibernation are matched by the accomplishments of those animals that remain active in the winter woods. Deer, foxes, rabbits, weasels, and bobcats store no food, yet they manage to stay active and to survive the winter. Deer are protected against the cold by the special coat they grow in autumn. Each hair is hollow and filled with air; the deer thus walks through the cold enwrapped in an overcoat of warm air. The squirrel builds in a tree a nest consisting of a large ball of leaves; the air trapped inside the ball is warmed by the squirrel's own body heat. The rabbit survives the cold by digging an igloo in a snowbank, where it is likewise warmed by its own heat. The porcupine climbs into the crotch of a tree and may spend several days there, lazily stripping the bark from the branches; protected by its tough hide and thick coat, it barely suffers from the frigid weather.

In the spring the forests are replenished: by the birth of young animals, by the return of the migrant birds, by the awakening of the winter sleepers. Throughout the forest, seeds that have lain dormant put out little blanched roots and stems; the sap rises in the trees; the early flowers blossom before the canopy closes over. By the time spring has climbed to the treetops, the buds have unfurled; and thus the forest begins another year.

13 : Western Giants

T HE LOFTIEST, the most valuable, and one of the most extensive forests on the continent lines the Pacific coast from western Alaska to central California. More than 2000 miles long, it consists almost exclusively of conifers. Like the forests of the Great Smokies, this one was little disturbed by the ice age. The glaciers that reached the Pacific coast were valley glaciers, and between those tongues of ice lay many sanctuaries where the original forests were able to survive. Climatic conditions on the west coast are ideal for the growth of trees. Tempered by the Pacific Ocean, the coastal regions rarely suffer subzero temperatures, even in Alaska; in Oregon and California frosts are rare. There is ample moisture brought in by the ocean winds, as much as twelve feet annually in some places. Even in those places that receive the bulk of the precipitation during the winter, summer fogs maintain a high humidity and compensate for the drought.

The coastal forest of the Pacific is divided into a number of sections, each with its own dominant species. In Alaska it is ruled over by the hemlocks and spruces; between British Columbia and Oregon it is the domain of the Douglas fir, which gives way in turn to the coast redwoods in southern Oregon and northern California. In southern California, as the climate grows drier the forest dwindles into chaparral.

Alaska is the land of western hemlock and its constant associates, Sitka spruce and western red cedar. This forest rarely penetrates more than five or six miles inland; the ice-bound mountains entirely isolate it from the forests of the interior, which contain many Atlantic tree species, such as birch, poplar, and aspen. The arrangement of these forests is uncomplicated. Western hemlock and occasional red cedars form the primary forest cover; rising above them like jagged spires are the light-demanding spruces. There is an understory of young hemlocks and cedars, both of which are resistant to shade. The ground cover is composed of great clumps of blueberry, false azalea, and other shrubs.

Sitka spruce is one of the stateliest trees of North America. Its base is swollen and buttressed; the bole that shoots up from it is true as a mast; the branches have a noble sweep. It is an indicator tree of the coastal forests, rarely growing more than 50 miles inland from the moist air of the shore. It reaches its greatest height in Washington, where some specimens grow to nearly 300 feet. Western hemlock does not achieve the great height of the Sitka spruce, but it is the most abundant tree of the northern Pacific coast; in fact, there are few places in the Pacific forest where this tree does not grow. Along the Inland Passage of British Columbia it descends almost to the water's edge; on Mount Rainier it ascends to an altitude of 5000 feet.

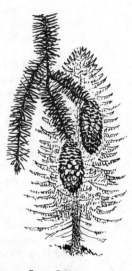

SITKA SPRUCE

The height of the western hemlock is humble by the standards of this lofty coniferous forest; even a very large specimen seldom grows taller than 150 feet. The profile of a hemlock forest on the horizon is one of spires, packed together almost like the bristles of a brush. Because their needles are set so close together on a multitude of branches and branchlets, these trees cast possibly a denser shade than any other. The floor under a mature hemlock forest is not just shaded or dark; it is black. No trees can possibly grow under the canopy except shade-tolerant young hemlocks and cedars. Although Sitka spruce soars above the hemlocks and seems to dominate them, it is but the figurehead of this forest. For the Sitka spruce cannot reproduce its own kind in the shade cast by the hemlocks. When an old spruce dies or falls before one of the hazards of forest life, it is replaced by a smaller hemlock.

Farther south, the western hemlock itself appears to be giving place to another forest giant, the Douglas fir. Indeed, this tree so seems to dominate the forests of the Pacific northwest that in many areas of the Cascades it frequently appears that no other tree is present. Soaring more than 200 feet into the air, the Douglas fir's deeply furrowed bole may be as much as 53 feet in circumference and may grow for more than 100 feet before it erupts in a spray of branches. But like the Sitka spruce, Douglas fir is not the climax species of these forests. When the firs die, the hemlocks and cedars grasp the sunshine and become dominant.

Yet the question arises: why are the virgin Douglas fir forests so extensive if they are not the natural climax? Why do whole forests of them appear to be about the same size, almost like the level pile on a rug? The reason is fire, which molded the forests long before European settlers arrived on the continent. Many fires were caused by lightning; others were due to Indians, who used fire to flush game, and who took no more care to extinguish their campfires than the white man does. Fires retard the natural steps of succession by creating open areas in the forest. Into these the light, winged seeds of Douglas firs are blown from adjacent stands; unlike the hemlocks and cedars, they grow in full sunshine and thus have no competition for possession of the burned area. Since all the seedlings take hold within the few years following a fire, they grow into pure stands of even-aged trees.

At one time the whole Pacific northwest was covered by unbroken forests of Douglas fir. Now, as one drives outside of the national parks where these trees have found sanctuary, one sees huge areas on the hillsides, some as much as a hundred acres in extent, which have been cleared of all trees. To the New Englander familiar with the selective cutting method which harvests one tree here, another there, this looks like despoliation, and he is likely to be indignant. But if the continent is to be supplied with Douglas fir—and it makes up roughly a fourth of the sawtimber in the United States—such "clear cutting" is a necessity. When a stand of these trees matures, after five hundred or a thousand years of growth, the forest floor is totally bare of seedlings; they cannot grow in the dense shade cast by their elders. So the foresters cut out a block, completely leveling it and letting the sun stream in. In a few dozen years the wound is healed, and a new, young forest is in the making.

Although Douglas fir grows throughout the Sierra and the Rockies, it reaches its fullest splendor in the coast ranges of Washington and Oregon. In the southwestern corner of Oregon it dwindles, and is replaced by the tree that for more than 400 miles to the south constitutes the southern anchor of the Pacific coniferous forest: *Sequoia sempervirens,* the "ever-living sequoia," commonly called the coast redwood. The giant sequoia belongs to the Sierra, but its relative the redwood is wholly of the coast, where it is the most distinctive botanical feature.

Redwoods usually grow within twenty miles of the ocean, rarely as far as 50 miles inland. They are never far from the belt of summer fogs that saturate the air in the dry season and become a substitute for rainfall; inland there are groves of redwood wherever there are fog pockets. The fog belt, which consequently becomes the redwood belt, is unbroken from the Oregon border to San Francisco; south of San Francisco, the belt divides into a number of scattered islands. There are some groves near Santa Cruz and in the Santa Lucia Mountains, but south of Monterey County, redwoods grow only under cultivation.

In gardens, their pattern of growth is altered; they become flat-topped and spreading. But in their natural environment, they are the tallest living things on the continent. The Founders Tree in Humboldt Redwoods State Park near Eureka was 364 feet high when last measured, and has probably grown since then. It is not just the occasional specimen that reaches great size; the whole species, on the average, tops the record height of all other contenders. Many grow taller than the Statue of Liberty and weigh at least a thousand tons. The tallest giant sequoia, by comparison, is the McKinley Tree, which measures not quite 300 feet. The giant sequoia lives longer—some known specimens are more than 3500 years old—but even it is not the oldest living thing on earth; bristlecone pines that appear to be more than 4000 years old have been found growing in the White Mountains of eastern California. Nevertheless, the redwood's life span of more than 2000 years still makes it a patriarch among trees. The oldest redwood whose annual rings have been counted was about 2200 years old; a section of the log of this tree is on view at the Richardson Grove near Benbow. So great is the volume of timber in a redwood that whole churches have been built out of a single tree.

The heart of the redwood country lies along a road extending south of Eureka, California, for nearly a hundred miles—the "Avenue of the Giants," as it is called. The traveler approaching from the south, from San Francisco, or from the Oregon border, will have seen other redwood groves, patches of forest broken, however, by open stretches. The Avenue of the Giants, on the other hand, is the single shaft of light that cuts through the impenetrable shade of these groves. Entering the forests is like walking into a cloister; the trunks form the pillars and the spray of branches high overhead the vaults. As in a cathedral, the visitor experiences a sensation of disembodiment. Human steps make no sound on the thick carpet of needles and moss. The human figure casts no shadows in the thick, saturated air.

Even one unacquainted with the slow growth of trees could see that these are aged beyond everyday comprehension. They already formed a thriving forest when Rome was sacked by barbarians; they towered by the time of the Crusades. Many enormous trunks rise out of what appears to be a jumble of boulders. These swellings are burls, lumpy root growths that are sometimes six feet in diameter; smaller burls, a few inches across, rise from the lower part of the trunk and top the jumble like pebbles. No one is quite certain of the cause of the burls, but each contains buds and will sprout into a miniature tree when kept in water. Not only the burls, but also the stumps have the power of regeneration; when a redwood is cut down, a circle of new trees sprouts from the base of the stump.

The group of trees known as the sequoias have an ancient lineage; perhaps 60 million years ago they were widespread trees. They grew around the northern hemisphere, in Siberia and China, Alaska, Labrador, and western Europe. But none grew in California, which at that time was the home of forests much like those growing in the tropics today. But the ice age pushed this California forest to the south; it destroyed all the species of sequoias except the coast redwood and giant sequoia, which found sanctuary in the coast ranges and in the Sierra. One other species, the *Metasequoia* or dawn redwood, previously known only in fossil beds, was discovered growing in central China in 1947.

The redwoods and giant sequoias are irreplaceable. The giant sequoia has been saved from lumbering only by the fact that it grows in inaccessible places and that its wood shatters when a trunk falls to the ground. Redwoods owe their preservation to many organizations and individuals, starting with John Muir, the young Scot who explored the western wilderness and foresaw the threat to the redwoods. "No doubt these trees would make good lumber after passing through a sawmill," he wrote, "just as George Washington after passing through the hands of a French cook would have made good food." The Muir Woods, a quiet grove of redwoods north of San Francisco, are named in his honor. His explorations in the Sierra are commemorated in the John Muir Trail. He was the first to explore Glacier Bay in Alaska; its largest glacier is likewise appropriately named after him.

Except for the heavy boles of the redwoods, everything else in the groves is in miniature. One might expect such giant trees to bear foliage that matched their titanic proportions, but in fact the leaves are delicate, each scarcely a quarter of an inch long. The redwood's cones, smaller than those of any other western conifer, are usually less than an inch long. The companion plants of these trees are mostly the delicate ferns— swordfern, ladyfern, and woodwardia, among others—and the lowly mosses. The wildflowers that manage to grow in the shade are exceptionally fragile: trillium, clintonia, oxalis.

The coast redwoods are rarely found above an altitude of 3000 feet. The Big Trees or giant sequoias that inhabit the western slopes of the Sierra, on the other hand, rarely grow below 5000 feet. The coast redwoods live in an air-conditioned belt under the influence of the Pacific, where there are only two major seasons, wet and dry; the sequoias are exposed to the full hazards of snowstorms and strong winds. At first glance, redwoods and sequoias appear very much alike, but there are numerous differences. Redwoods sprout from stumps and burls; giant sequoias do not. The foliage of the giant sequoia is scalelike, somewhat resembling that of the juniper, while the redwood has flattened needles like those of the hemlock. The shapes of the trunks are different: the sequoia's is like a club and may reach a diameter of 30 feet; the redwood's is like a tapered walking stick, with a maximum diameter of sixteen feet. Redwoods grow in unbroken forests; sequoias are found in isolated groves, of which only some 70 survive. Sequoias almost always grow in the company of other trees, such as white fir, sugar pine, Douglas fir, incense cedar, and black oak. They do not shut out the light as the redwoods do, nor do they produce a silent forest. There is the constant drumming and chatter of woodpeckers excavating holes in the bark—which can be as much as two feet thick—and the scolding of squirrels.

South of the redwood belt, the Pacific coast forest dwindles in stature. Summer sea fogs, on which the security of the redwoods depends, are largely absent; the annual rainfall may be between ten and thirty inches, but only a few inches of that fall during the summer. The result is a desertlike vegetation of evergreen shrubs, the chaparral—a catchall word to describe this scrubby growth. Throughout the chaparral zone, there are patches where the precipitation is heavier, and where small forests grow. A coniferous forest and a chaparral forest may grow almost side by side, but isolated from each other by the difference in rainfall; that invisible barrier prevents any interchange of species between the two communities.

The chaparral community is exceptionally diverse. At least 40 species of shrubs occur in many combinations. Most characteristic is the manzanita, a tough shrub with extremely crooked limbs. Shrubs of this species grow so close together that their branches interlock, forming an almost impenetrable thicket. The chaparral is extraordinarily inflammable; studies have revealed that few chaparral stems are more than 25 years old, owing to the perpetual harvesting by fire. But the fire only temporarily clears the dense vegetation; for chaparral sprouts profusely,

REDWOODS rise out of a green carpet of ferns and evergreen huckleberries, which are among the few plants that can survive in the shade cast by these towering trees.

and in no more than ten years after a fire it is a full-grown shrub forest once again.

The fullest development of the coastal forest is reached on the Olympic Peninsula in Washington, where the ranges of the coastal species, and of many others typical of the interior forest, overlap. It is here that trees often attain their greatest size: the largest known Douglas fir (nearly 18 feet in diameter at breast height), the largest red cedar (more than 21 feet), the largest western hemlock (9 feet). No Sitka spruce has been found that rivals those growing at Olympia to heights of 300 feet.

The Olympic forest is nurtured by the ocean. It forms, as it were, the prow of the continent, against which the Pacific westerlies break, releasing their moisture upon the western slopes. An average of twelve feet of precipitation falls each year on the Olympic Mountains; in some years it may reach eighteen feet, or three billion gallons of water for each square mile. The results are a rain forest in the temperate zone, and numerous low-altitude snowfields and glaciers that provide moisture during the summer months. This forest is dominated by water: it squishes underfoot and drips from the leaves; it is soaked up like a sponge by the mosses—more than 70 species of them—that carpet everything in the forest. Moss lies inches thick upon the ground; it hangs beardlike from the shrubs and trees; it climbs the tree trunks. The forest is filled with an eerie greenish light, the reflection from myriads of water particles in the air. The occasional shafts of sunlight slanting through the forest shine on the moss, heating it and sending up little wisps of fog.

The Olympic rain forest is as dense as any storybook jungle. Shrubs grow so close together that in places they form impenetrable barriers. The weak limbs of vine maple, falling back to earth, take root again and create a maze of branches. Fallen trunks and branches of the giant trees are quickly enveloped by the luxuriant growth of ferns and mosses. The aerial plants of southern swamps have their counterparts here in the hanging gardens of club mosses. They grow like draperies that screen off one forest chamber from the next.

In all forests, dead wood and fallen leaves are broken down by insects and microbes, which release the store of nutrients to feed the living trees. In the Olympic forests, the fallen trees perform another important function. Uprooting of trees in the rain forest is fairly common, since the root pedestals of the giant trees tend to be very shallow because of the abundance of water near the surface. These uprooted trees and fallen branches serve as platforms on top of which seedling trees can take hold, thus acquiring a competitive advantage over the surrounding plants. The seedlings grow in the rotted wood of these nurseries and send their roots

STRAIGHT ROW of trees at Olympia National Park has grown out of the fallen trunk of a "nurse" tree, which has almost completely decayed.

creeping around the flanks of a log until they reach the ground, which may be a distance of more than ten feet below. When the old log finally decays, there remains a straight line of young trees, looking almost as though they had been planted by hand; they stand on stilts, reminders of their youthful years spent atop the nurseries. The nurse trees of the Olympics are but variations upon the endless theme of all forests, that of the old forest nurturing the new.

ONDEROUS SEQUOIA boles grow close together in a grove at Sequoia National ark. The bark of these aged trees is often several feet thick.

VI

THE DRYLANDS

14 : Sea of Grass

As one approaches the western limit of the eastern forests, the dense green blanket becomes increasingly threadbare. For this is a disputed borderland, in which the trees are victorious over the grasses only in sheltered low places and along streams. These woods are sparse by eastern standards; from an airplane, even in midsummer, it is possible to see down through the canopy of leaves to the forest floor. Elsewhere the grasses are the conquerors; rippled by the wind, their long blades appear to be waves that engulf the lingering forests.

The grasses that have wrenched the land from the forests do not possess the bulk, strength, or longevity of trees. But they are the meek that inherit the soil. No other family of higher plants lives under such a wide range of conditions as the grasses; the number of individual grass plants on the continent is probably much greater than that of any other group of higher plants. These humble growths live in the polar regions and on mountain tops; they endure the dry conditions of deserts, and the constant immersion of marshes and tidal flats. They are efficient and uncomplicated mechanisms for survival and dispersal. A grass stem is constructed of solid joints, from each of which arises a single leaf consisting of a sheath that fits around the stem like a split tube. The flowers are minute, attracting little attention either from human beings or from insects. Since they are wind-pollinated, they need neither fragrance nor inviting colors. Their seeds, too, are minute specks that are carried far by the wind.

Between the Mackenzie River of Canada and the highlands of northern Mexico, there is a vast inland sea of grasses, more than 3000 miles long, bordered on the east and the west by forests. As one travels westward from the Mississippi River, the elevation of the land gradually but persistently rises. So gradual is the upward tilt that in western Kansas one seems to be standing on level land, but this is an illusion; actually it is an upward slope that will gain another 1500 feet before it meets the Rockies. And just as steadily as the land rises toward the west, the rainfall decreases. This is not so obvious in Iowa nor in eastern Kansas, but even here, by degrees, the green of the plants takes on a lighter cast, and more bare soil becomes visible between the growths. Then, between the 98th and 100th meridians, there is an abrupt change. This is the boundary between an agriculture where a farmer can depend on the weather and one where he must keep an anxious eye peeled toward the clouds; for here the winds coming over the Rockies have had nearly all the moisture squeezed out of them, and have not yet accumulated a new supply from the Great Lakes and the Gulf of Mexico.

As a result of this decrease in humidity, the grassland falls into two main subdivisions, with a transition zone between. From Ohio to eastern Oklahoma is the tall-grass prairie, where the native grasses once grew higher than the height of a tall man. Such tall grasses once mantled the whole central heartland of the continent, regardless of differences in soil and topography. These diverse lands had in common a flora of waving grasses dotted with colorful flowers. In this sea of grass during the millennia, deep roots had built a sod so dense that in turning it the homesteaders broke their plows. The characteristic native grasses of the prairie are big and little bluestem and Indian grass; nowadays most of the land they covered makes up the corn belt. To the west of the prairie is a transition zone where grasses do not grow so high, nor as a continuous carpet. June grass, wheat grass, and little bluestem grow in clumps, the spaces between the clumps being filled with an abundance of wildflowers; this is the great winter wheat region. Farther still to the west, in the rain shadow of the Rockies, grow the short grasses of the high plains: gramma, needle grass, buffalo grass; today this is an extensive grazing area.

The contrast between the grassland zones is best seen in a drive from east to west across Kansas. At the Missouri border, on the east, the elevation is about 3000 feet below that of the Colorado border on the west; Kansas, in other words, is like a vast tabletop raised toward the west. The eastern portion of the state is rolling and well covered with trees; west of Wichita, around the Great Bend of the Arkansas River, the trees thin out. The westernmost part of Kansas, which is wholly within the short-grass zone, is level and practically treeless. The decrease in the size of plants, owing to the lessened rainfall, is best illustrated as one moves westward by the sunflower, the state flower of Kansas. In the eastern part of the state, sunflowers light up the roadsides from stalks eight feet high. Westward they shrink, not just in the height of their stems, but also in the diameter of their yellow-bordered disks. Finally, at the parched Colorado border, they grow as little wildflowers that one has to stoop down to examine.

Kansas is wheat country, and wheat is a grass—like corn, rye, barley, and oats. From Kansas southward, winter wheat is grown. The seed is sown in the fall and germinates before frost; thus it has a head start and ripens several months ahead of the wheat planted in the spring. Spring wheat is grown north of Kansas, where the climate is too severe for the young plants to survive the winter. Wheat was one of the first plants cultivated by man; ancient kernels discovered in Iraq reveal that there has been little appreciable change in this crop for the last 7000 years. Wheat and the other grains, owing to their remarkable nutritional qualities, have been the cornerstone of many civilizations around the globe. The grain of a cereal is composed of a thin shell that covers the embryo and a food supply for the nourishment of the young plant. This food supply contains carbohydrates, proteins, fats, minerals, and vitamins; that is why a cereal grain comes closer than any other plant to providing an adequate diet.

A corner of northern Kansas was covered by the glaciers; so was almost all of the rich farmland of Iowa. Yet here none of the earmarks of glaciation familiar in the northeastern states are to be seen. There are no boulders that require being piled endlessly into stone fences; there are few glacier-cut valleys. Although moraines are abundant throughout Iowa, Illinois, and Indiana, they are quite unlike those of New England. Whereas the New England glaciers were able to carry huge boulders southward, the rock material carried by the glaciers that descended upon the prairies was made up of fine particles that spread out as a veneer.

Although corn is grown in every mainland state, the tall-grass prairie is the true corn belt; in Iowa one passes for mile after mile through fields of towering deep-green stalks. No other plant, even among the grasses, has a seed-bearing organ quite like the ear of corn. It consists of a specialized flower cluster, enclosed in a husk, which when mature bears several hundred naked seeds. The threads known as cornsilks, which extend beyond the tip of the husk, catch the fine grains of pollen. Each pollen grain develops into a tube that sometimes travels more than ten inches down the silk thread before it reaches the ovary; each ovary in an ear has its own thread and must be fertilized individually in order to produce a kernel. With the aid of man, corn is a most efficient mechanism for producing food; but it would die out if left on its own, because it has no method of seed dispersal. The ear of corn drops to the ground and a hundred seedlings may emerge, growing so closely together that in the competition for water and soil space, all of them die.

Corn originated in the New World and was unknown in Europe until Columbus found it growing in Cuba. The Mound Builders of the Mississippi Valley, the Cliff Dwellers of the Southwest, the Aztecs of Mexico, and the Mayas of Central America all relied almost exclusively on corn. No longer having to hunt and fish for their food, they were given ample time by the abundance of corn to build extremely advanced civilizations, which excelled in mathematics, astronomy, engineering, and art. The oldest fossil remains of corn in North America, which were found in Mexico, date back less than about 8000 years. Much of the development of corn has come within the past three decades, with the widespread use of hybrid corn; today, more than 95 per cent of the corn grown in North America is hybrid. Nevertheless, the idea of crossing varieties to obtain a superior hybrid one was known to the American Indians, who planted rows of different kinds of corn close together, thus effecting cross-pollination. When pollen from different varieties fertilizes an ear, the result is often a varicolored ear, as may be seen in the Indian corn often sold for Halloween and Thanksgiving decorations.

In numerous places throughout the eastern grasslands, trees grow perfectly well when planted by man, even though few trees were found growing naturally by the pioneers. Many theories have been offered to explain why certain places become prairie while others support trees. One of these is that the sod formed by the tall grasses is almost impenetrable to invading plants. A dense network of roots extends many feet down, completely occupying the upper layers of the soil. Many of the grasses may live twenty years or more, and even when they die the soil occupied by their roots is quickly taken over by neighboring grasses. It is nearly impossible for a seedling tree to invade such a soil.

Another theory is that the prevalence of prairie fires in the past favored the growth of grasses over that of trees. A grass fire removes only one year's growth, leaving the roots relatively undisturbed; but when a tree is burned, the growth of decades is destroyed. Within a year or two after a fire, the perennial grasses are flooding the burned area with an abundance of seeds; trees and shrubs, on the other hand, require many years before they reach seed-bearing age. The sharp decrease in fires since this land was settled seems to be tipping the balance in favor of trees and shrubs. The grasslands are at present undergoing an invasion by mesquite and other shrubs, which have spread from their former locations along stream channels into the grassland.

There are still remnants of native prairie that were overlooked by the plow, and that manage to endure as scattered islands surrounded by a growth of alien crops. Only three cultivated plants have been able to gain access to the virgin prairie: asparagus, timothy, and bluegrass. But none of these invaders makes much headway, and they would be promptly eliminated were there not a yearly renewal of their seeds from neighboring cultivated fields. A striking illustration of the endurance of the prairie is seen in railroad and highway rights of way, and along fencerows. These little strips of unbroken prairie have survived as closed communities, although they are bombarded year after year by the seeds of numerous weeds.

The grassland appears almost as monotonous as a placid sea. But its apparent calm is an illusion, for these lands are the scene of a battle each year in which no species is completely victorious, none wholly vanquished. Because the grasses are long-lived, because they reproduce by seeds as well as vegetative growth, and because they all find a hospitable environment in the prairies, there is a continual struggle for light, water, and nutrients. The plant is crowded not only by its neighboring competitors but by its offspring as well.

The result of this competition through the ages has been the development of many compromises among the plants. The root systems of various species grow at different levels in the soil. Each species, as it attempts to enlarge its holdings, meets the opposition of other entrenched species. The struggle for dominance is demonstrated by two major plants of the tall-grass prairie. Big bluestem is able to occupy the good soils and the moist lower slopes, and to exclude its smaller rival, the little bluestem. The little bluestem is only about half the height of its larger relative; but its root system is more efficient for gathering water, and its smaller leaf surface further reduces the total amount of water it needs in order to grow. As a result, little bluestem is dominant on the drier uplands. The ranges of the two grasses overlap on the middle slopes, where there is much jockeying for position. It is only there that they come into conflict; otherwise each fits a niche the other grass is unable to occupy.

Despite the renewal of warfare underground each spring, an undisturbed grassland is a stabilized community. Not by design, but through compromise, each species aids its competitors, and receives benefits in return. The taller plants protect the lower ones from the heat of the sun; the little grasses, in turn, reduce the loss of water from the soil by mulching it with their own prostrate forms. The wildflowers of the prairies are in direct competition with the perennial grasses, but they have made numerous adjustments to ensure their places in the sun. Violet, ground plum, wood sorrel, and cat's paw all flower and produce seeds quickly, before they are overshadowed by the grasses. During the rest of the summer, these low plants grow in the subdued light of the understory; they present little competition to the summer grasses, but they are protected from being dried out by the winds and sun.

Other wildflowers, such as the hawkweed, stake out a territory by growing a tight rosette of leaves that shades a portion of the soil. But the shade cast by the rosette cannot long suppress the vigorous grasses; so as these grow taller, the hawkweed's stem grows taller along with them, keeping the rosette in the sun. Other species vary the method by developing a tall stem before their leaves or blossoms unfold, thus first assuring themselves of access to the sunlight. The autumn flowers manage to survive alongside the spring flowers by making few demands upon the prairie community until it is time for them to blossom; by then, most of the spring-flowering plants have withered away. All of these methods ensure that the grassland soil is utilized to the maximum, thus creating a greater bastion against invasion by newcomers.

Conditions for life in the grasslands differ greatly from those in a forest. A forest-dwelling animal can easily find shelter under the canopy of leaves, but the inhabitants of the grasslands require speed, strength, or the ability to burrow into the ground. To gather the food of the forest, an animal must either be agile like the squirrels, have wings like the birds, or remain small like the insects. The grassland mammals, on the other hand, find an abundance of food, rich in nutrients, only by bending down to nibble it; thus the grasslands are traditionally the home of large grazing mammals.

When European man arrived in the grasslands, bison were its chief inhabitants. Perhaps 60 million bison inhabited North America, living primarily in the grasslands, but in the eastern forests as well; as late as the eighteenth century they

LITTLE AND BIG BLUESTEM

roamed in Florida and nearly reached the Atlantic in Georgia, the Carolinas, and Chesapeake Bay. Early naturalists who had journeyed into the grasslands described great congregations of bison that extended, tightly packed, as far as the eye could see. The trampling of huge herds cut trails across the continent, which were followed by the pioneers heading west. Many of the railroad routes were laid along beds first leveled by the bison, and the Europeans sweeping westward followed portage paths and passages through the mountains pioneered by the bison.

The heavy tread of the bison trampled the grasses and compacted the soil, creating bare areas in which weeds could gain entrance to the sod. The herds of bison thus were potentially able to destroy the very habitat on which their lives depended. But other animals in the grassland community counteracted the damage done to the soil by the trampling hoofs. Gophers and ground squirrels dug numerous burrows, opening the soil again, allowing air and moisture to penetrate. It has been estimated that in some places the soil-inhabiting rodents of the grassland gave the soil the equivalent of a plowing every twenty years. But these little animals likewise potentially could destroy the habitat. In North Dakota and Manitoba, the heaviest consumer of grass is not the bison, or the pronghorn, or any of the insects; it is a small vole which in places is so abundant that every square foot of soil has several runways. Some species of these meadow mice may populate grasslands in excess of 50 mice per acre. The checks on their population are disease, starvation, and predators. Hawks and owls, snakes and coyotes all take a great annual toll of these little rodents.

In their intimate association with each other, the plants and animals of the grassland had woven a tight but elastic web. In years in which the supply of grasses was reduced by drought, the grazing animals were weakened and fell prey to coyotes; their decline relieved the pressure on the grass, and during the next wet year it recovered. In a year when the grass supply was ample, the rodents multiplied rapidly, whereupon the coyotes switched over to a rodent diet, relieving the pressure on the grazers. With abundant food, the grazers were free from the threat of starvation; since the coyotes were busy with the rodents, the size of the herds increased. When drought returned, the grazers once again went into decline, making more food available for the predators. The balance of life in the grassland can thus be visualized as one that swayed rhythmically, that altered from year to year, but under natural conditions never broke down.

However, as soon as any one strand in the grassland web is broken, the entire web begins to unravel. Extermination of large numbers of bison at the end of the last century caused the grasses to suffer, for the droppings of the huge beasts had served them as a natural fertilizer. Extermination campaigns against hawks and owls caused a corresponding increase in the rodents on which these birds had preyed. The reverberations of a decreased population of birds of prey echoed through the grasslands: as inroads were made on the grass by the multiplying rodents, the grazers suffered from a lessened food supply, and other kinds of predators increased. In places where the prairie grasses suffered from damage by the rodents, wind and water stripped the unprotected soil and deposited it on other areas, smothering the grass.

Driving hour after hour through the prairie today, one catches but a faint glimpse of its former splendor. By 1920, only a few score bison remained in the United States. Since then, many herds, numbering thousands of animals, have been built up at wildlife refuges. In some of these refuges, the grassland is coming back also. At the National Bison Range near Moiese, Montana, for example, there are nearly 500 bison. The original buffalo grass does not grow there, but wheat grass and other native grasses are abundant. Predators such as prairie falcons, horned owls, goshawks, coyotes, and bobcats have moved into the refuge. Gradually, helped by the hand of man, the web of grassland life is being rewoven.

The grassland has produced animals that rely on speed and endurance for safety and to find water and winter forage. Sight also is of survival value in the open spaces of the grassland, and many of the animal inhabitants accordingly possess keen vision. The herd instinct which causes animals to congregate in large groups, and which is much more noticeable in grassland species than in those of forests, is likewise believed to be an aid to survival.

Typical of the grassland dwellers of the continent is the American antelope or pronghorn. (It is not a member of the antelope family of the Old World, and is more properly called simply a pronghorn. Its horns are hollow, like those of goats, but it sheds the sheaths each year.) It lives solely in the grassland and most particularly in the western short-grass plains. It is well suited for this environment. It possesses remarkable powers of sight, and can spot danger at tremendous distances; by nature it is as wary as a deer. It is the swiftest runner of all mammals on the continent. These provisions for safety are combined with a most efficient signal system that enables it to warn other members of the herd, even when they are a great distance away. The signal is a white patch on the pronghorn's rump; when the animal becomes frightened, its muscles contract so that the white hairs rise and the patch flashes in the sun like a tin pan. In addition, the animal possesses a gland that throws off a musky warning odor at the same time that the white patch is flashed.

Prairie dogs also rely on sight and the herd instinct for protection in the grassland. The prairie dog's real nature is concealed by two inaccurate names. It is not a dog; rather, it is related to the squirrel. Nor does it usually inhabit the prairies, but rather the short-grass plains. Before the plains were settled, prairie dog towns in many places stretched as far as the eye could see. One group of Texas prairie-dog towns was estimated, probably with some exaggeration, to cover 25,000 square miles, and to have a total population of 400 million animals.

But the settlers declared war on the little rodents, and today they have largely disappeared from the Great Plains, except in the national parks and other refuges. The towns that one finds today cover only tens of acres.

The sun-baked soil and sparse grass of a prairie-dog town are dotted with mounds constructed by the animals. The plump, cinnamon-colored rodents sit on their haunches and bark at visitors and one another; they are constantly going and coming, chasing and playing games with each other. A complex pattern of social behavior has developed in these towns. Most mammals are content to live in family groups or small herds, perhaps combining into larger herds at migration time; but the prairie dogs

PRONGHORN

reach a height of sociability. There are complex rules of town government which the young prairie dogs must learn. There are rules to protect the town against attack by predators, and rules to prevent overcrowding of the population.

The landscape of the town is altered to suit the needs of the animals. Any tall grass that happens to grow within the town limits is uprooted, achieving two benefits: predators have less cover by which to infiltrate the town; and the growth of weeds, whose abundant seeds are a source of food, is encouraged. The burrows are intricate pieces of engineering, not simply holes in the ground. There may be upwards of twenty entrances to the acre; each one is in the middle of a mound of soil a foot or two high and about four or five feet across. The digging is usually undertaken immediately after a rain, when the earth is soft and can be easily worked, for the prairie dog's only tools are the long digging claws on its front feet. The elevation of the burrow usually prevents it from being flooded during cloudbursts and also serves as a lookout platform. The rodents have much to be wary about. Destruction comes from the air in the shape of hawks and eagles, on the ground from coyotes, foxes, bobcats, badgers, and ferrets.

The burrow entrance leads into a precipitous tunnel, sometimes descending to a depth of fourteen feet. Then it turns at a right angle, continues horizontally for a distance, and gradually rises. Short branches fork off from this main route. One of them is a grass-lined nest. Another is a flood hatch located at the end of the rise, within a few inches of the surface. When water overtops the mound and pours into the burrow, the prairie dog scrambles to this underground flood hatch. There it is safe, because the inrushing water produces an air pocket in this highest part of the burrow. The flood hatch is the reason why so few prairie dogs are drowned, even though their towns may be inundated completely for several hours.

Each town is divided into numerous "precincts," and animals inhabiting one precinct are unwelcome in another. Occasionally an animal is seen to jump to its hind legs and raise its forefeet into the air, so abruptly that it sometimes falls over backward. At that time it gives a loud yip, a territorial warning to another prairie dog not to trespass upon that precinct. No territorial yip goes unanswered; there are immediate replies from neighboring mounds, and one after another the animals near by jerk themselves into the air and give their loud call. The spread of territorial yips through a town is somewhat like the spread of coughing in a theater; one does not know from exactly which direction the next outburst will come.

Prairie dogs belonging to the same precinct maintain friendly relations and use each other's burrows. They groom each other's fur, and they are constantly at play. Whenever one prairie dog on a patrol along the precinct borders sees another, it will scurry alongside and rub noses. That is their means of identifying a fellow member of the precinct; if the animal is an outsider it will not rub noses, but instead run off at the approach of the other.

The imminence of danger produces a call quite unlike that of the territorial yip. One kind of call is merely a warning; upon hearing it, all the prairie dogs of the surrounding precincts immediately stop feeding and sit up alert. A higher-pitched call of alarm causes them all to plunge hurriedly into their burrows. In this way, predators are usually detected long before they reach the town limits. The eyes of prairie dogs are particularly well adapted to spotting any predators in the air; they are placed so high on the head that they are the first part of the animal's body to emerge when it crawls out of its burrow. Most predators leave the town hungry. It is only a lucky hawk that catches an ailing or slow animal far from its burrow. Black-footed ferrets, which can race through the burrows, and badgers, which can dig the prairie dogs out, are more serious threats.

Prairie dogs are comparatively slow breeders; nevertheless, they have developed a remedy for overpopulation. In late spring, after the birth of the young, the adults begin to forage in the suburbs, outside the limits of the town. At first they return every night to their precinct, but gradually they spend more and more time away from it. A few individuals become pioneers, starting new villages miles from the old towns; others find a neighboring precinct that is underpopulated, and appropriate a portion of it. It is during this temporary breakup of the precinct system that expansions and readjustments of territory are made; and thus some precincts come to resemble gerrymandered voting districts. By summer the boundaries are again fixed, and the young of the year have learned, from reprisals taken on them while wandering, just where the boundaries are.

The mounds of the prairie dogs are welcome disruptions of the monotony of the high plains. A traveler coming toward the Rockies from the east is made aware by numerous subtle changes that he has crossed into the high plains. In the vicinity of the 100th meridian—the line of longitude that passes through eastern North Dakota down to western Texas—the colors of the landscape change from muted greens to brown. East of the meridian the annual rainfall is more than twenty inches a year; to the west it is less than twenty.

At approximately the 100th meridian the border of the high plains is also marked by a low, east-facing escarpment. In some places the escarpment forms a quite definite belt of hills or ridges; elsewhere it is absent. It can be clearly seen in southern Canada. In North Dakota, if one looks to the west from a point about 50 miles east of the Missouri River, one can make out a range of low hills between 300 and 400 feet high, which form the edge of the high plains. Pronounced escarpments are found throughout almost the whole length of South Dakota. In southern Kansas they appear as the rugged Red Hills, which swing westward into Oklahoma and then southward into Texas. In many places the escarpment can be recognized as a belt a few miles wide in which considerable erosion has taken place.

PRAIRIE DOG

To the west of the escarpment, the high plains are as flat as any land surface can ever be. The origins of the high plains go back millions of years, to an uplift of the Rocky Mountains and the ensuing reduction in rainfall to the east. Before the uplift of the Rockies captured the moisture in the winds, the region was one of extensive forests. The surface of the high plains today consists of an overlying mantle of debris brought down from the Rockies by streams. A moist climate like that of the northeasern states is characterized by stream erosion, the taking away of rock materials by water; a dry climate, on the other hand, is usually characterized by stream deposits or building up of the land. A debris-laden stream rushing down from the Rockies is slowed as it reaches the

ROCKY MTS.

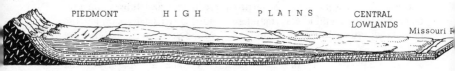

PIEDMONT H I G H P L A I N S CENTRAL LOWLANDS Missouri R

CROSS SECTION of the grasslands between the Rockies and the Missouri River shows the high plains, which were formed from sediments brought down from the Rockies, their eroded escarpment on the east, and the prairies. Note the steady rise of the land from the east to the west.

plains, and the debris is deposited as an alluvial fan. The formation of an alluvial fan is due to the dwindling of the river as it rushes out of the mountain. There is rapid evaporation on the hot plains; much water is absorbed by the dry, porous soil; there is little rainfall to keep the river flowing. As the river gradually diminishes in size and volume, it spreads its load of debris at the base of the mountains.

Such deposits gradually fill in the bed of the stream itself; the stream overflows either to the right or to the left, finds a new channel, and repeats the process of deposition there. Since all of the streams issuing from the Rockies build alluvial fans, the result has been that the fans have eventually merged and spread away from the base of the mountains. Through the course of time, the process has laid down a single gentle, sloping plain. The escarpment of the high plains at the 100th meridian marks approximately the farthest eastward extension of this apron of debris from the eroding Rockies.

There are many parts of the high plains, such as the Staked Plains of western Texas and New Mexico, that have been virtually untouched by stream erosion. Instead, they are subject to erosion by wind. The faster the wind blows, the more soil it carries away with it. The particles may be transported only a few feet, or they may travel for hundreds of miles. When the wind dies down, the load of soil is dropped. Anyone driving through the plains in the spring cannot escape the sight of the wind at work. The air is hazy and yellow with countless motes of soil; little clouds of it seem to rise out of the earth. Every year nearly four million acres of agricultural land, on an average, suffer damage from blowing. During the dust bowl years of the 1930's, a total of about eighteen million acres was turned into desert by the winds. Huge clouds of plains dust billowed over New York City and darkened the skies over the city of Washington; throughout the plains themselves, street lights had to be turned on at noon.

Great as the dust storms have been in recent decades, they do not approach in magnitude those that occurred following the retreat of the glaciers. Everywhere in the plains can be seen thick deposits of loess, the name given by geologists to wind-deposited dust. The outwash from the glaciers consisted of immeasurable quantities of powdered rock which, once they had dried, were easily picked up and carried in swirling clouds by the wind. Once aloft, the lighter particles traveled immense distances; there are even loess deposits on the slopes of the Rockies, at altitudes above 10,000 feet. Some of these deposits, more than a hundred feet deep, are revealed where the Missouri and other rivers have cut through them; around Sioux City, Iowa, are towering loess cliffs that bear testimony to the power of the winds and the abundance of dust.

The most violent of all wind phenomena, the tornado, has its greatest occurrence in the plains. Oklahoma, Kansas, Nebraska, and southern Iowa form the heart of the tornado belt; next in frequency are Arkansas, northern Texas, western Missouri, and a long, narrow belt across the deep south from Mississippi to Georgia. Tornadoes may occur practically anywhere in the eastern two thirds of the United States; they almost never occur west of the Rockies. More than 900 tornadoes strike the United States every year, the majority of them in the plains.

A tornado bears a superficial resemblance to the dust devil, a spinning funnel of soil which rarely reaches more than a few hundred feet into the air, and which is often seen on the plains. But there is a great difference between the two. A dust devil is a whirlpool of air created by the heating effects of the sun. It begins at the level of the ground, and occurs only during the day. A tornado, on the other hand, is a funnel of whirling air that begins in the atmosphere and may occur during day or night. No one knows exactly how a tornado is born; one expert asserts that at least 26 weather conditions must coincide before a tornado can develop. A major requirement is that extremely hot air must meet cold air; this condition frequently occurs in the plains and prairies, where hot air from the Gulf of Mexico collides with air that has been cooled by its passage over the Rockies. When the two air masses meet, they try to pass each other, with the result that the air begins to whirl upward, just as water does when it is stirred rapidly.

Only when the tip of the funnel reaches the ground does the tornado cut its long swath of destruction. Its color turns brown, black, or white from the soil or snow it has picked up. No tornado ever measures more than 1300 feet in width where it touches the ground; more often it is not much wider than a city street. Each tornado packs a terrifying punch as a result of the pressure at its edge and the suction in its center. An ordinary fifty-mile-an-hour windstorm can uproot trees; some tornadoes exert pressures a hundred times greater than that. So great is the force exerted by a tornado that it has been known to lift a railroad locomotive off its tracks. Its life is brief; ordinarily it breaks up suddenly and disappears less than three hours after it has first formed.

There are, however, extensive areas in the plains where erosion by water also has occurred, producing the bizarre landscape known as a "badland." This is an area where streams have dug so deeply into soft rock that only pinnacles remain. The badlands are trapped in an endless cycle: since erosion there is very rapid, plants have little chance to become established; because there are few plants to pin down the land, erosion continues to take place rapidly. Badlands originate as a high plateau through which a river flows, leaving bluffs on both sides of its channel. As the river meanders along its course, the zone of bluffs retreats farther from the stream; the tributary streams flowing to join the large mainstem keep pace by likewise cutting deeply into the plateau. The result is a landscape dissected by a maze of channels and gullies.

The most dramatic example of this type of scenery in North America exists at the Badlands National Monument in southwestern South Dakota. There the White River has cut a deep valley into the soft, easily eroded rock of what were once gently rolling hills. The cliffs of the White River have now retreated until in some places they are miles away from the channel. The flat land that today exists between the river and the cliffs was once badland also; but it has been eroded down to a plain as its materials were carried away by the river. The erosional remnants between the gullies have taken on an innumerable variety of strange shapes. There are razor-sharp ridges, complex canyons, knobs and spires.

The badlands of South Dakota are an almost barren world. It has been estimated that about 60 per cent of the land included in the Monu-

HEAVILY ETCHED BADLANDS of South Dakota lift their barren slopes out of the short-grass plains.

ment is devoid of vegetation. There are, however, a few trees that manage to survive in this tortured land, usually along the courses of streams. The deep green of scattered small groves of juniper relieves the harshness of the landscape. Peppering the ravines are other trees: cottonwood, elm, boxelder, chokecherry. A remarkable variety of birds can be seen at the Monument, feeding on the seeds of wildflowers and grasses and the fruits of trees and shrubs. From the east come the robin, the black-capped chickadee, the white-breasted nuthatch, the northern cliff swallow, and the goldfinch. In the South Dakota badlands they meet representatives of the western fauna: the western vesper sparrow, the western lark sparrow, the canyon wren, and many others.

It is the life of the past that most often intrigues visitors to the Badlands National Monument. As the sediments poured down from the Rockies, tens of millions of years ago, to form the original upland, numerous kinds of animals were buried. These overlying sediments have now been removed by erosion, uncovering extensive fossil beds. From these fossils it is possible to reconstruct a picture of what the life of the badlands was like some 40 million years ago. This land was once flat, with many swamps, shallow lakes, and sluggish streams. The vegetation was luxuriant and supported many grazing animals, such as horses, camels, and rhinoceroses, as well as rats, mice, squirrels, and rabbits. These animals provided food for predators: tigers, wild dogs, eagles, and owls. This community of the Dakota swamps was utterly obliterated by the mantle of sediments, as much as 2000 feet thick, that poured over it.

The badlands were nearly level in the past, and ultimately they will be level again. Every breeze and each raindrop dislodges additional particles of rock; the spires and pinnacles are continually being undercut and toppled; gullies are incessantly merging to produce flat land. In time, the fissured hillsides will be reduced to gentle mounds, which will become covered with grass. These mats of vegetation will retard erosion and the badlands will become stabilized, as have many other areas of the high plains. This step in the development of the badlands can already be seen in places. Grass, mostly the grama and needle-and-thread of the high plains, extends to the very wall of the badlands. Eventually the sea of grass will engulf the badlands and the landscape will again stretch unbroken to the horizon.

15 : High Plateau

T HE COLORADO PLATEAU is a vast tableland that covers nearly 150,000 square miles in northern Arizona and New Mexico, western Colorado, and eastern Utah. In this area is concentrated some of the outstanding scenery on the continent: the awesome Grand Canyon, the pinnacles of Bryce Canyon, the towering cliffs of Zion, Monument Valley, and Mesa Verde. These fantastic views are but variations on the fundamental theme of the plateau: as the weaker rocks are cut away, resistant remnants are left behind in the form of buttes, natural arches, cliffs, and pinnacles that alternate with extensive flat areas.

It is a paradox that in this thirsty land, water has been the prime creator of scenery. Water formed these sedimentary rocks under ancient seas, and water sculptured them as they rose. Water carved the buttes and mesas, chiseled Bryce Canyon into every shape known to man, and sawed the mile-deep chasm of Grand Canyon. Water has cut innumerable gullies into the weaker rocks on countless slopes. Wherever a stream finds a sufficient incline to attain speed, it picks up the silt on its bed and uses it like emery paper to deepen the channel. Major John Wesley Powell was one of the first people to understand this fact about the western rivers. When he set off in 1869 to explore the Colorado River by boat, he believed that the warnings he had been given about high waterfalls on the river were unfounded. He was convinced that such a muddy river would already have ground down most falls, leaving only rapids. He staked his life on the correctness of his understanding of erosion in the plateau.

Everywhere in the plateau country, the rocks appear to be painted with vivid, glowing colors: vermilion, lavender, flaming red, yellow, and a wide range of browns. The coloring of the plateau can best be seen in the Painted Desert of northeastern Arizona, where the sparsity of the vegetation reveals the rocks in all their brilliance. The colored rocks are largely the result of weathering, and generally the colors are only skin deep. The hues a cliff assumes depend upon the minerals that compose it. Iron compounds are particularly effective coloring agents: ferric hydrate, for example, produces tones of light red, brown, and maroon. Other iron compounds in different proportions produce an almost infinite variety of colors at the red end of the spectrum. Organic material buried with the sediments usually colors the rocks dark gray or black. Even the same layer of rock usually displays a variety of tones, for the reason that a cliff exposed to the weather for a considerable time usually is more brilliant in color than a fresh fracture.

Wherever the rivers have cut deeply into weak rocks, the horizontal structure of the plateau can be seen: the neat, precisely defined layers of sedimentary rock which were laid down one upon the other to build the plateau. These sedimentary layers of sandstone, shale, and limestone were uplifted with little distortion; only occasionally are the flat-lying beds interrupted by faults or buckling. Fossils of marine creatures embedded in the rocks reveal that most of the layers were formed under the seas that periodically washed this part of the continent. The limestones were formed under deep waters; shales originated as mud when the sea was shallow; many of the sandstones came into being when high sand dunes were buried by new layers of sediment. There are numerous gaps in the sequence of the rocks, evidence that at these times, for periods lasting millions of years, the seas had retreated and no sediments were laid down. It is estimated that the building up of the Colorado plateau, layer by layer, took at least a billion years.

During the times that the plateau was above water, forests grew. Reminders of those extensive forests are today found throughout the Painted Desert: huge petrified tree trunks strewn about the land as though the area had just been logged. Some of the trunks are more than a hundred feet long and as much as eight feet in diameter. These trees grew more than 150 million years ago. Floods carried them into shallow lakes and marshes where they were quickly buried, before decay could take place. As ground water passed through the tiny pore spaces in the wood, it dissolved the wood away, fiber by fiber. This water contained large amounts

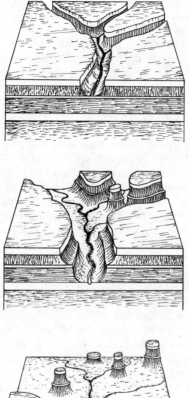

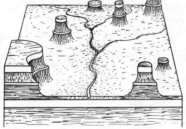

THE CYCLE OF EROSION in arid lands begins with a youthful plateau cut by a swift-flowing river. As the plateau matures (center) the canyons widen and merge, leaving resistant buttes between them. In old age (bottom), the plateau is nearly ground down to a level plain once again, as at Monument Valley.

of silica and other minerals in solution; they replaced the wood and left in its stead a mineral reproduction of the exact structure of the wood, including growth rings and cells. Iron, manganese, and other minerals in the water furnished the brilliant colors that made these petrified logs into rainbows brought to earth. They have been uncovered again by erosion, which removed an estimated 3000 feet of overlying shales and sandstones. Undoubtedly there are other stone woodpiles, hundreds of feet beneath the present surface, which will some day be brought to view by erosion.

Of the few things in this world which are beyond description by poets or painters, surely the Grand Canyon is one. There has never been a line written about it that matches its profound depths, or a painting that captures its full range of colors. One can look at the canyon, one can measure it, but it eludes comprehension. This greatest abyss on the face of the earth can be reduced to geological definitions; an array of statistics can be presented concerning it; its history can be explained and its hues described in words. Yet the canyon is always something more than the sum of these particulars. It is the most humbling scene on the continent, the greatest visual shock a human being can experience.

This 220-mile-long gash is the result of fortuitous circumstances. First, there had to be thick rock strata, crossed by a river that carried large amounts of sediment. As such a potential cutting tool, the Colorado was unexcelled. It is the second longest river in the United States; it flows at speeds up to twenty miles an hour, and averages nearly twenty feet in depth. The sand and silt carried by the turbulent, muddy Colorado past the Grand Canyon in an average day amounts to half a million tons.

Second, there had to be a gradual uplift of the land, not so rapid that it would spill the river out of its course. As the rocks rose, the river scoured out its bed at approximately the same rate, much as a cake would be sliced if one held the knife steady and raised the cake against the blade. Although the plateau has risen a mile in height, the Colorado River has held to approximately its same distance above sea level.

Finally, for the grandeur of the Canyon to come into being, the uplifted land had to be arid, since thick vegetation would have slowed the process of erosion and would have converted the steep-walled channels into rounded valleys.

The walls of Grand Canyon are nearly vertical in many places, in sharp contrast to the typical river valley of the eastern states. In the east, plentiful rain and snow erode the rim of a canyon as rapidly as the river cuts down into its bed; the valley widens at least as fast as the river deepens it, with the result that the valley has sloping sides. In drylands, on the other hand, the sides widen much more slowly than the river digs into its bed. That is why the drylands are the region of deep canyons with vertical sides, while the eastern rivers usually flow through gentle valleys. There appears to be an exception to this rule in the gorge at the bottom of Grand Canyon, through which the Colorado River now flows. Its sides form a V, and are reminiscent of a youthful eastern stream. The reason is that the gorge is being cut through rocks which are much more resistant than the overlying sedimentary layers. The Colorado excavates through these at a considerably slower rate, allowing a greater widening of the banks in proportion to the downcutting.

Not only does this gash in the earth reveal the story of canyon formation, but it also tells much about the history of life on the planet. Standing on the rim, one can clearly see twelve major layers of rock, which form distinct bands of color. The vertical cliffs are layers of limestone and sandstone; the crumbling slopes are usually shales. The step-

GRAND CANYON is a monument to the power of water erosion. Note the V-shaped canyon now being cut into ancient rocks by the Colorado River.

like layers that form the walls of the canyon are due to the alternating strata of resistant rocks and softer ones. The top layer is the one most recently formed; the layers become successively more ancient toward the bottom of the canyon. These layers are like pages in a book of earth history. Many of the pages are wrinkled and creased, and whole chapters are missing. But those that remain provide a clear picture of the succession of life on the continent, for buried in most of the layers are fossils of the kinds of life that existed when the rocks themselves were being formed.

A visit to the gorge can be made in a leisurely trip on the back of a surefooted mule. On the way down, the visitor finds himself trying to come to grips with the overpowering scenery. The return trip is slower, and a better time to read the story of the earth as told by the rocks. The first chapter begins with the black rocks of the gorge now being cut by the Colorado. These rocks bordering the muddy river are the basement upon which the layers of sediment were deposited, and they are among the most ancient rocks to be seen anywhere in the world. The careful observer will notice that these basement rocks seem to fall into two distinct groups. They are reminders of the antiquity of the continent, for each group represents a sequence of mountain building in which ramparts were uplifted and then ground down, rose again and were ground down for the second time, leaving only their roots. Thousands of feet of rock were thus twice removed, particle by particle, over hundreds of millions of years. And all of this was accomplished before even a single layer of sediment was deposited.

No fossils exist in the basement rocks. There probably was no life on the planet at that time; but if it had existed, fossils would have been obliterated by the heat and pressure these rocks have undergone. However, the first sedimentary layer, formed about 550 million years ago, contains fossils of algae, which are among the simplest forms of life. By the time one has ascended to the Tonto platform, fossils are abundant, particularly those of trilobites. These primitive arthropods flourished for about 200 million years, and during much of that time they were the dominant animals in the sea. They resemble the little pillbugs often found in moist forests, and some of them possessed the same ability to roll themselves up into a ball.

As the visitor ascends to the Redwall—a flaming red rock layer which is the most distinctive of all—the fossils reveal that life on the planet has evolved considerably since the Tonto platform rocks were laid down. The Redwall was created by a vast sea that built up these 550 feet of limestone from the bodies of dead marine animals. It was formed at a time when the seas swarmed with life—with primitive fishes, shelled animals, and corals—and when the swamp forests of the Carboniferous Period were being built on land. Anyone who chips off a piece of the brilliant Redwall will see that this rock is not red at all underneath. Rather, it is a bluish limestone that has been stained by iron oxide leached down from the rocks above.

The next extensive layer above the Redwall consists of dark shale. By the time it was formed, life had changed markedly. The great boundary between sea and land had been crossed by many forms of life that had developed organs for breathing air and moving on land. There were numerous kinds of primitive insects, amphibians, and reptiles—the advance guard of the flood of life that occupies the earth today. The most recent layer of rocks at the south rim of the canyon breaks off the story at a point more than 200 million years ago, just as the dinosaurs were making their appearance and before the arrival of mammals on the planet. There are no rocks at the south rim of the Canyon that contain fossils of more recent life; this part of the story is told in a sequel on the north rim, and at Bryce and Zion canyons.

The descent from the rim to the river is a passage not only through a succession of time, but through a succession of climates as well. The walls of the canyon can be visualized as forming an inverted, hollow mountain, a mirror image of the mountains surrounding the canyon. In the same way that there are life zones as one ascends a mountain, there are also life zones on the descent into the canyon. Standing on the south rim, one is in the Upper Sonoran Zone, the land of pinyon pine and juniper, whereas the climate at the bottom of the canyon is tropical, equivalent to that of the Yucatan Peninsula of Mexico.

It takes a human being a day or two to hike down the south rim and across the gorge and then to climb up to the north rim. Such a trip would not appear to be too strenuous for most animals, yet there are numerous kinds that do not make it. The reason is that to go from the south rim to the north rim would mean passing through unfamiliar life zones with unsuitable climate and food. Thus the canyon exists as the southern barrier for a number of northern animals, and the northern barrier for a number of southern animals. Several kinds of pocket gophers, wood mice, pocket mice, and field voles reach their northern limits at the south rim of the canyon; there are related but different species that inhabit the plateau on the other rim.

The best-known of the animals that have never crossed the life-zone barrier of the canyon are two species of squirrels, probably the handsomest of their kind on the continent. Larger than the common eastern gray squirrel, they have reddish-brown fur and huge, fluffy tails. The two species can easily be told apart. The Abert squirrel, which lives south of Grand Canyon, has a grayish tail, a white belly, and great tufted ears. The Kaibab squirrel, found only on the north rim, has a black belly and a pure white tail. The habits of both these squirrels are very much the same; both kinds obviously had a common ancestor in the distant past, before the canyon was excavated and became a barrier. But now they are completely isolated from each other, not by the distance of a mere few miles across the gorge but because of the life zones they would have to cross.

For a human being to go from the south rim to the north rim by car requires a drive of more than 150 miles across the Painted Desert to the east, as far as Navajo Bridge, where the canyon is narrow enough for a span to have been built across it, then another 85 miles of doubling back to the north rim. The road from the south rim to the bridge descends some 3000 feet into the Lower Sonoran Zone. It is a desperately arid land, whose limited vegetation consists of several kinds of short grasses, saltbush, desert thorn, prickly pear, and narrow-leafed yucca.

Crossing the Colorado River and driving toward the north rim, the traveler ascends once again, to the Kaibab Plateau. Soon after leaving the bridge, one again sees the pinyons and junipers that grew at the south rim. As the road climbs into the Transition Zone, the pinyons and junipers are replaced by the open groves of ponderosa pine. These soon give way to the forests of the Canadian Zone: Douglas fir, white fir, blue spruce. At the north rim, which stands much higher than the south rim, the climate is reminiscent of Canada, and the forests of spruce, fir, and aspen are similar to the north woods; in winter the thermometer drops lower than it does at Halifax, Nova Scotia.

The plateau-like formation of the north rim evidently bewildered the Paiute Indians, perhaps because the forests growing there were a kind usually found on mountain slopes—for Kaibab in the Paiute language means "mountain lying down." The Kaibab is a part of the Colorado Plateau that has been uplifted several thousand feet higher than its surroundings. When the Colorado Plateau was uplifted, not all parts of it were raised equally. Rather, the layers of rock were pushed up in the form of a gentle dome, whose higher elevation was cut in two by the Colorado River. Since erosion generally attacks the highest parts of the landscape, the younger rocks near the river have already been stripped away. But to the north and south, where the sides of the dome dip down, there has been less erosion, and consequently younger rocks remain. The rocks to the south of Grand Canyon have been the scene of much volcanic activity and faulting; thus, it is to the north of the canyon that one must go to find the remains of younger rocks.

The story told by the rocks at Grand Canyon was interrupted some 200 million years ago, just as the giant reptiles were about to assume leadership of the living world. The rocks at Zion Canyon to the north continue this story for another 75 million years, including the development of the great reptiles, the first birds, and some early mammals. Embedded in these rocks are the bones and tracks of land animals, among them those of dinosaurs. Like the rocks at Grand Canyon, they tell a story of vast inland seas, dry land, swamps, and sand dunes, the ceaseless changes the land has undergone. The dominant feature of Zion is the canyon of the Virgin River—deep, almost crushingly narrow, and brilliantly colored. Throughout much of its course through Zion National Park, the canyon is about a quarter of a mile wide, bordered by steep walls half a mile high. But at the Narrows, the walls close in until the river pours through a gap only twenty feet across, less than the width of most city streets.

Bryce Canyon, to the northeast of Zion, displays some of the most recent sedimentary rocks in the Colorado Plateau. Unlike the Grand Canyon, which owes its existence to the Colorado River, or Zion, which was created by the Virgin River, Bryce is not the work of any single major stream. Rather, its plateau has been crossed by myriads of smaller streams, which bit into the rock and formed a number of intersecting amphitheaters or semicircular basins. As the streams cut downward, they followed the numerous faults and joints in the rocks, leaving ridges standing between them. The streams, however, did not actually create the thousands of weirdly eroded features—the skyscrapers, columns, pinnacles, and spires that bristle from the amphitheaters; they merely exposed expanses of rock wall to other forces of erosion. Alternate freezing and thawing for as many as 275 days a year drove wedges of ice into rock crevices; raindrops dissolved the natural cement that held the rock particles together; water from rain and melting snow formed steep gullies, similar to those of the badlands.

At Bryce, one stands on the rims of the plateaus and gazes into amphitheaters filled with clusters of these fantastic erosional remnants. Perhaps the best description of these formations is the translation of the original Indian name for them: "red rock standing like men in a bowl." Just as apt in its own way is the remark attributed to Ebenezer Bryce, who pastured his cattle on the plateau and after whom the canyon was named. Concerning the rainbow-hued amphitheater with its astonishing formations, he said simply, "It's a hell of a place to lose a cow."

ROCK FORMATIONS at Bryce Canyon are the result of erosion by myriads of small streams, followed by the decomposition and disintegration of the rocks.

Many places in the Colorado Plateau exhibit a type of erosion that appears to be one of the wonders of nature. It produces the natural bridges and arches, great hoops of rock that seem to defy gravity as they soar against the sky. The greatest of these natural spans is Rainbow Bridge, slightly north of the Arizona-Utah border and inaccessible except on horseback. It remains the most perfect formation of its kind, not only because of the symmetry of the inside arch, but also because the upper surface of the arch is parallel to it, so that the whole resembles a rainbow. Its graceful 278-foot span, which at its highest point rises 309 feet into the air, is the largest natural bridge known, large enough to straddle the Capitol Building in Washington, D.C.

Rainbow Bridge was formed from a neck of resistant rock in the loop of a meandering river. The river had been forced to loop because it could not penetrate the resistant sandstone. However, the resistant neck rested upon a foundation of softer rock, and as the river cut more deeply into its bed, it reached this softer layer. Thus it was able to undercut the resistant neck, converting it into a thick bridge; whereupon the river abandoned the loop of its ancient channel and followed the new route under the bridge. In times of flood, the river's swollen waters tore at the buttresses of the bridge, widening the arch and causing blocks of sandstone to fall from the underside, and thus gradually making the arch higher and more slender.

Rainbow is but one of the many spectacular natural bridges formed in the sandstones of the plateau country. Its main rivals are the three spans at Natural Bridges National Monument in the southeast corner of Utah, which together illustrate remarkably well the stages through which a typical bridge passes. Kachina Bridge, 210 feet high with a span of 206 feet, is the youngest of these three bridges. It is huge and bulky, and its opening is comparatively small; the White River is still actively enlarging it. Sipapu, the largest of the three, is mature. It is both graceful and symmetrical, and its buttresses lie far enough from the river that they are being little cut at the present time. Old age is represented by Owachomo, the smallest of the three bridges. It is no longer being eroded by the river; but its delicate arch is continually under attack by frost, rain, and windblown sand, and the crack that will eventually cause its collapse may already have started. Its fate may be seen a short distance up

A NATURAL BRIDGE is formed when a river undercuts the neck of a loop, finding a direct route through the neck and abandoning its horseshoe channel. Continuing erosion enlarges the opening and deepens the gorge.

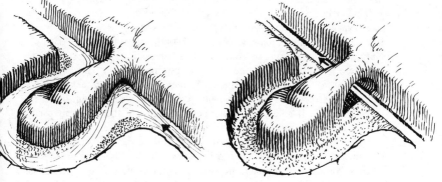

A NATURAL BRIDGE at Bridges National Monument, Utah, was gouged out by an ancient river. Its thin span reveals its advanced age; eventually it will topple, leaving only the buttresses on both sides as a reminder.

the canyon from Sipapu; there, all that remain of a fourth bridge, which once spanned the canyon, are buttresses on the canyon wall.

Smaller but no less graceful bridges are found throughout the plateau country. There are magnificent examples at Capitol Reef in Utah, at Bryce Canyon, and at Navaho National Monument in northern Arizona. Natural bridges are not so common in other sections of the continent, but there is a well-known one in southwestern Virginia. This bridge is about 100 feet long and rises some 150 feet above Cedar Creek. At one time Cedar Creek was a subterranean river that flowed through joints in limestone rock. It enlarged its channel until most of the roof collapsed, leaving the natural bridge as a remnant.

When a span is formed by the disintegration of the weaker parts of a rock mass, rather than by erosion by a river, it is called a natural arch. Arches National Monument in eastern Utah contains more than 80 arches carved through huge vertical slabs, known as "fins," in a layer of sandstone 300 feet thick. At one time these gaping holes in the

THE DOUBLE ARCH at Arches National Monument, Utah, was carved out of the rock by seeping ground water rather than by the force of a river.

AT MONUMENT VALLEY a remnant of the original plateau soars above the surrounding land, which has been partially worn down to form a level plain.

rock were credited to the wind, but it is now known that they are largely the product of disintegration by ground water.

The original block of sandstone had been subjected to a series of fractures, about twenty feet apart, that ran through the entire block. Running water entered these parallel cracks, wearing away the rock until the thin cracks developed into deep fissures. Continued weathering broke the mass of sandstone into a series of fins less than twenty feet thick and more than a hundred feet high. It is through these fins that the arches have been formed. The upper part of each fin is porous, and rainwater can enter; once inside the fin, the water dissolves the natural cement in the rock, crumbling it into its original sand grains. This percolating water, combined with freezing and the pull of gravity, breaks away small chunks of rock from the center of the fin. At first only gaping holes or windows are formed, but later these enlarge to form arches. Arches in all stages of development and decay can be seen at the Monument. Delicate Arch and Landscape Arch, for example, are both exceptionally thin; most of the fins out of which they were carved have already weathered away.

The Colorado Plateau generally is a youthful area in which water has only recently, geologically speaking, begun to cut. Its future will be one of continued widening of the canyons and the carrying away of the eroded material. The tributaries of the Colorado River still have much downcutting to do, and in the next several million years it is predicted that they will have carved the plateau into a network of numerous ridges and buttes. The landscape will then resemble present-day Monument Valley, on the Arizona-Utah border, where remnants of the original plateau stand boldly above a level plain. These scattered monuments are only the resistant remnants of what was once a continuous plateau. Even farther along than Monument Valley in the cycle of destruction of the plateau is the Painted Desert. Eventually even these remnants will disappear; the fate of the Colorado Plateau is to be worn down once again to a level plain, several thousand feet lower than when it was originally uplifted. Canyons and angular cliffs will have disappeared, and the streams will flow sluggishly through a monotonous landscape. But judging by the past history of this land, mountain-building forces will again uplift it and begin the cycle of canyon-cutting anew.

16 : The Great American Desert

T HE DESERT is the battleground of the primeval elements of fire and water, and their effects on the land can everywhere be seen. The fires of the sun have baked the bare rocks and sands, sucked the moisture out of plants and left them shriveled. It has created dry washes, where streambeds fill with water only following a rain and then disappear abruptly. It has cast upon the land a pitiless heat, and at noonday the desert appears barren. Water, on the rare occasions when it comes, brings the desert suddenly to life. The plants grow quickly and burst into bloom; many kinds of animals produce young during the fleeting periods of abundant water. Fire and water occasionally battle to a draw, as can be seen on those summer days when black clouds roll across the desert, bringing promise of rain. But no water reaches the desert surface; the heat of the sun evaporates it before it can moisten the dry sands.

Deserts are the result primarily of a low annual rainfall, usually of less than ten inches. In addition, a high temperature is necessary to create a desert; otherwise, the moisture would be retained as snow or ice, as it is in the polar regions. The high temperature results in the rapid evaporation of the scant rainfall, making only a very small proportion of the total actually available to plants. As if these conditions were not sufficiently harsh, the rainfall is not distributed evenly throughout the year. From a third to a half of the annual precipitation may occur during a single cloudburst, and most of this moisture will be lost to the plants because of the rapid runoff.

Yet a typical desert landscape reveals many kinds of perennial and annual herbs, grasses, and shrubs all living together and coping in their own way with the shortage of water. All have developed modifications to survive the cycle of scarcity and plenty, and to ensure the continuation of their species. The desert plants can be divided roughly into two groups, the drought-evaders and the drought-resisters. The drought-resisters put up a fight against the paradoxical threat of death from the life-giving sun. Many kinds of perennials maintain life during dry periods in their roots and underground stems, so that when the rains come, they are able to leaf out in a very few days. With the return of dryness the leaves are promptly shed, thus reducing evaporation, and the plants become dormant once again. The ocotillo is unusually sensitive to varying water conditions. It promptly grows a set of leaves in response to a shower, and it casts them off just as promptly. It may grow and lose more than half a dozen sets of leaves in a single year.

Other kinds of desert plants actively resist the drought by storing water within their stems, leaves, or roots. While all is withered around them, the succulents, as these water-storers are called, continue to grow. The cacti, one group of succulents, are noted for their large size and longevity. After a rain a giant saguaro 50 feet tall might have a weight of ten tons, nine tons of which might consist of stored water. Many of the succulents develop extensive root systems that lie near the surface and form a network so closely meshed that it functions as a bowl, catching all the water that falls in the immediate vicinity; whereupon the remarkably efficient roots transport this moisture to the storage tank of the stem. The squat, cylindrical shape of the cactus's water-storing stem exposes a minimum of evaporating surface to the air, thus sharply decreasing the water loss.

Many of the drought-resisters have developed other methods of hoarding moisture once they have captured it. The cactus has developed a way of living that dispenses with leaves entirely, except as spines. The spines probably evolved as protection against thirsty animals, but they give other benefits also. They break up air currents moving over the cactus, thus decreasing the wind's ability to suck moisture from the stems; the spines also afford some shade, in much the same way that the slats a nurseryman puts over his seedlings protect them against the sun. The cactus is green all over because the chlorophyll, used in manufacturing food by the process of photosynthesis, is distributed throughout its stem.

The paloverde is not a close relative of the cactus, but it has independently evolved the same solution to the problem of dispensing with leaves prodigal of water. During the wetter periods of the year the paloverde, obeying some ancient law of treedom, puts out leaves. But they are thin and only about an eighth of an inch in length; and as the water supply fails, they are promptly shed, exposing to the sunlight the twisted green branches that contain chlorophyll.

Numerous drought-resisting plants do have leaves, but these are notably adapted to desert conditions. Many plants twist their leaves during the warmest part of the day, with the result that only the thin edges are exposed to the sun's rays. Others have leaves that curl up like cigars, likewise preserving moisture. The breathing pores of the leaves are usually very small and are also often sunken in hair-lined cavities. Some plants, such as the creosote bush, have leaves covered with a waxy coating that resists evaporation.

Even in the driest deserts, plants are abundant along the dry washes, and that is where most of the trees grow. Instead of developing ways to store water, these plants have evolved a single adaptation, an extraordinarily long taproot that enables them to search for it underground. The mesquite, a plant so abundant on the dry washes that it is almost an indicator of them, resembles a small, springy apple tree; its taproot has been traced to a depth of more than 40 feet, giving it access to a deep source of water long after the stream bed has dried out. That explains why the mesquite often remains a bright green while all the vegetation around it is parched. One wonders how the seedling mesquite ever stayed alive long enough to reach this deep source. The answer is that the mesquite germinated during the wet season. It put out virtually no top

ADAPTATIONS OF DESERT PLANTS are typified (left to right) by the deep roots of the mesquite; the storage roots of the night-blooming cereus; the drought-evading desert dandelion; the leaf-dropping habit of the ocotillo; and the collecting roots and storage tank of the saguaro cactus.

growth, but instead used the dowry of food contained in the seed to grow downward. Only when it had finally tapped a water source did it begin to develop above ground.

Anyone who has visited the desert both before and after the wet season will have observed the sudden change that sweeps over it. Arriving just before the onset of the rains, one may encounter light sprinkles that do not markedly change the desert's face. A few of the more responsive shrubs may have put out leaves, and some plants may appear a little greener, but the widely spaced plants still leave chasms of bare soil between them. Then, after the first heavy rains, the entire desert suddenly becomes carpeted with hosts of brilliant flowers. These are the drought-evaders coming to life. The evaders make no battle against the harsh climate, as the drought-resisters do; bowing before it, they find victory in apparent defeat. They are usually small plants that have modest water requirements. Most of them are annuals whose seeds lie dormant in the soil until a rainfall of sufficient intensity awakens them to life; then they grow rapidly, blossom, and put out a new crop of seeds which will lie dormant until the next heavy rainfall.

These little ephemerals display none of the adaptations of the drought-resisters. They have no need to do so. Since they grow from seeds to mature seed-producing plants in hardly more than six weeks, they avoid many of the problems connected with a limited water supply. They need no taproot, no extensive root system, no water-storing parts, no specially adapted leaves. But there is one thing they do require: a regulator to ensure that the seeds will not germinate during periods of merely light rain, with the inevitable result that the plants would wither before they could produce a new seed crop. Most of the desert annuals possess such a regulator. They seem to "know" when the rainfall is sufficient for them to germinate, leaf, flower, and produce seeds.

A shower of less than an inch does not awaken these plants, nor does a tremendous cloudburst. This discrimination on the part of the seed about when to germinate is due to a growth-inhibiting chemical in the seed coats. So long as there is little or no moisture, the chemical prevents the seed from germinating. Some seeds are also equipped with growth-promoting chemicals; a too-heavy cloudburst washes these away, with the result that germination does not occur. A rainfall of suitable intensity, however, dissolves the inhibitor but not the growth-promoter, and germination is the result. Even so, not all seeds of a particular species germinate when conditions are favorable. Some of them always remain dormant, an insurance that the species will not be annihilated should the rains fail before seeds for the following year can be produced. Some of these dormant seeds can lie in dry soil for years without losing their ability to sprout.

Each of the major deserts of North America has its own typical community of plants. The Great Basin Desert is the largest desert on the continent; it includes much of the land beween the Sierra and the Rocky mountains, and it extends as far north as northern Oregon. In this most desolate of American deserts, the characteristic plant is the sagebrush. The Great Basin gradually merges into the Mohave of southeastern California, whose indicator plant is the grotesque Joshua tree. The Mohave is actually a transition between the Great Basin Desert and the Sonoran Desert to the south. The Sonoran is North America's best-known desert. It stretches from southern California to western Arizona, and is typified by the saguaro cactus. To the southeast of the Sonoran is Mexico's Chihuahuan Desert, which lies between the mountain ranges of the Sierra Madre Occidental and Sierra Madre Oriental. The Chihuahuan sends prongs jutting into southeastern Arizona, New Mexico, and western Texas.

The Great Basin is the bleakest of American deserts; the landscape is monotonous and almost completely devoid of trees, except along the occasional watercourses where willows and cottonwoods manage to grow. It is an arid upland of plateaus and broad basins, all shut off from the moist Pacific winds by the lofty Sierra, which borders it on the west. The low fault-block ranges that thrust out of the desert are about the only places hospitable to trees, and there grow sparse pinyon pine and juniper. Cacti are practically nonexistent in the Great Basin, except for a few low-growing clumps scattered in places protected against the cold winters and dry summers. The green of many other common desert plants likewise is absent. In their place is the abundant sagebrush, whose low, clumpy form is seen everywhere.

During the time of the retreat of the glaciers, much of the Great Basin consisted of inland streams and vast lakes that received tremendous amounts of water from melting snow and ice. A remnant of one of these glacial lake systems is the Great Salt Lake of Utah. The ancient Lake Bonneville, at its greatest extent after the glacial melt, was an enormous inland sea that covered most of western Utah, eastern Nevada, and southern Idaho; it was almost as large as the present Lake Michigan, and much deeper. The surface level of Lake Bonneville was at least 1000 feet above that of the present Great Salt Lake. As the glacial waters receded, Bonneville shrank steadily, until only a string of lakes remained in the deeper basins: Great Salt, Little Salt, Sevier, and Utah. These are all salt lakes except for Lake Utah, which has remained fresh because it has

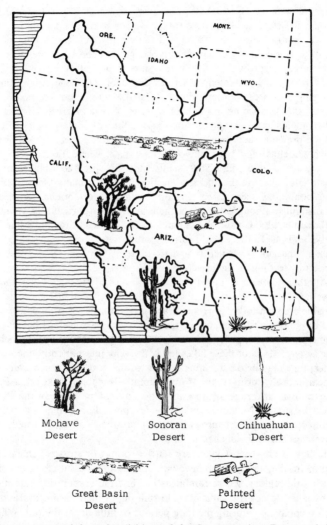

Mohave
Desert

Sonoran
Desert

Chihuahuan
Desert

Great Basin
Desert

Painted
Desert

THE BOUNDARIES of the major divisions of the Great American Desert and their indicator plants: the Joshua tree of the Mohave, the saguaro cactus of the Sonoran, the agave of the Chihuahuan, and the sagebrush of the Great Basin. The Painted Desert is very barren, but petrified trees are relatively abundant.

an outlet into the Great Salt. The evaporation of the water of Lake Bonneville left a vast level desert, with a floor so solidly packed that the automobile race track could be laid out on it. And it also left behind the most sterile of American deserts, because of the large quantities of mineral salts deposited by the evaporation of the waters.

As Bonneville retreated, it left evidence of its former high stages. Traveling along the borders of Great Salt Lake, one can see, marching off into the distance upon the hills, a series of seven terraces. These are not remnants of an earlier Mormon agriculture, as some people believe, but the previous shorelines cut by Lake Bonneville. There are sandbars, beaches, deltas, and wave-cut cliffs that mark where Bonneville once lapped against the hills. These cliffs, and likewise the islands in the Great Salt Lake, are the ancestral nesting places for many kinds of birds more commonly seen at the seashore: pelicans, cormorants, terns, and various gulls, among others. The gulls have been particularly valuable to the settlers. Kit Carson shot a batch in 1843 to feed Frémont's starving party, and in 1848, when Mormon crops were being devastated by crickets, the gulls swarmed inland from Great Salt Lake and prevented disaster by feeding on the insects.

Another prehistoric lake of the Great Basin Desert, Lake Lahontan of Nevada, at its maximum was about the size of the present Lake Erie; its remains are seen today at Honey Lake in California, as well as at Pyramid Lake, Walker Lake, and the Humboldt and Carson sinks in Nevada. Numerous scattered pools in Nevada at one time belonged to this ancient lake system. Many of these lakes today are only intermittently filled with water; they may be dry for nine months of the year, and some even disappear entirely during years of low rainfall. Temporary lakes that form after rains in arid regions are known as playas. One playa in the Black Rock Desert of Nevada contains water only during the wet winter months; it sometimes covers an area of more than 450 square miles, yet it averages only a few inches in depth.

In humid areas most lakes are fed by springs or streams which flow into them; they usually also have an outlet at a low point along the rim. But in arid regions, where rainfall is low and the evaporation rate high, many lakes do not rise sufficiently to spill out of their basins. Still others dry up completely during the long periods of little or no rainfall. Whenever there is a high rate of evaporation and no outflow, substances in the lake water become more and more concentrated, and eventually precipitate out as salts. Some desert lakes are "salt lakes"; their waters leave behind large amounts of sodium chloride, common table salt, as they evaporate. Others, known as "bitter lakes," contain sulphates; the "borax lakes" precipitate out various borate minerals. Owens Lake in California contains rich deposits of bicarbonate of soda. Great Salt Lake is a combination of bitter lake and salt lake. Pint for pint, Great Salt is occasionally seven times as salty as the oceans; during low water, its salinity exceeds that of the Dead Sea. The lakes of the western deserts thus appear to be one of nature's jokes perpetrated upon a thirsty land. For in a country where water is life, these lakes are more sterile even than the desert sands.

When the traveler approaching the southwestern borders of the Great Basin Desert encounters his first Joshua tree, he can be as sure as though there had been a boundary marker that he has reached the Mohave. This yucca, which grows as high as 40 feet and appears to be holding handfuls of daggers at the ends of its armlike branches, is found nowhere outside of the Mohave; if a line were drawn about this tree's range, that line would closely follow the borders of the Mohave Desert.

John C. Frémont, in 1844, during a search for a mythical river that watered the desert, was probably the first European to see a Joshua tree. He immediately labeled it "the most repulsive tree in the vegetable kingdom." The wildly waving arms of the Joshua tree grow that way because of its method of flowering. Flowering is a relatively rare event in the life of the Joshua tree; but after it has occurred, the plant puts forth a branch at a right angle beneath the flower cluster. Thus is formed a kind of shoulder with an upper arm attached. After years of slow growth, this branch also flowers at the tip, and another branch arises just below the flowers, producing what looks like a forearm. As the tree matures, more beckoning arms are added. To the Mormon colony of California, setting out across the Mohave to join the main group in Utah, these branches appeared to be arms urging them across the searing desert to a promised land; to their eyes the tufts of shaggy leaves somewhat resembled the beard of an Old Testament patriarch. So they named this strange, gesticulating plant after Joshua, the leader of the children of Israel into the land of Canaan.

At one time, the Mohave was a region of numerous rivers and lakes, which supported an abundance of plants and animals. Even as recently as 10,000 years ago, a number of animals now extinct—mammoths, ground sloths, camels, and three-toed horses—roamed this land. As the climate became more arid, the waterways that supported this life gradually dwindled. The only reminders today of the abundance of water are the old shorelines and wave-cut terraces on the mountainsides, and the numerous playa lakes that dot the desert. The Panamint, Searles, Silver, Soda, and Manix basins at one time were filled with lakes.

BECKONING ARMS of the Joshua tree are indicators of the Mohave Desert.

In this sere desert, the visitor from the humid east might be surprised to find a number of animals usually associated with moister areas. Crackling sounds, almost like those of a fire, are made by adult cicadas, incorrectly called "locusts." There are several species of beautifully colored snails that inhabit the desert; in the dry season they can be found under rocks, where they await the rains that will produce an exuberant new growth of plants for them to feed upon. Even at those seasons they emerge from their hiding places only during the night and on overcast days. During the rest of the time, they secrete a seal of mucus across the openings of their shells and are thus immured against heat and drying winds. Another abundant species is a desert tortoise; it resembles a turtle, but possesses clawed toes for walking rather than the turtle's swimming flippers.

The primary attraction of the Mohave for many visitors is Death Valley, which consists of two shallow basins surrounded by ranges of low hills. The southern basin contains vast, shimmering salt beds and the lowest spot on the continent: Badwater, 279.6 feet below sea level. The highest point on the mainland United States—Mount Whitney, 14,495 feet above sea level—is only 80 miles away. The Panamint Range, rising to heights between 6000 and 11,000 feet, forms the western wall of Death Valley. The precipitous slopes of the Amargosa Range, with elevations ranging between 4000 and 8000 feet, make up the eastern rim. The northern end of the valley is blocked by the Last Chance Range, and the southern end by the Avawatz and Owlshead mountains.

The curved trough lying between these mountains varies from four to sixteen miles in width. Thus, the walls of the naked ranges are always on the horizon, barricades of red, tan, pink, and gray towering out of the white pit. The heavy rains that occasionally fall on these mountains run swiftly down the steep slopes and into the valley, where they almost immediately evaporate. The average annual precipitation in the valley is only about two inches; in one year there were 351 clear days. Its maximum air temperature of 134 degrees stood as a world record until a temperature two degrees higher was recorded in the Libyan desert. At one time the valley was occupied by an extensive lake, whose shores have created terraces on the mountain slopes; these are most clearly visible at Shoreline Butte in the Death Valley National Monument. The remnant of that ancient body of water, Lake Manley, which was once as much as a hundred miles long and 600 feet deep, is today only a temporary pond. The evaporation of this ancient lake concentrated the salts contained in the waters, laying down salt beds mixed with gravel that are a thousand feet thick. In the fantastic section called the Devil's Golf Course, the salt beds cracked into blocks, which have been eroded by water and wind into a landscape reminiscent of Bryce Canyon.

Despite the apparent bleakness of Death Valley, animals and plants are remarkably abundant. A survey of the vegetation in Death Valley National Monument revealed 608 different kinds of plants; they grow everywhere except on the salt flats, the only totally barren portion of the Monument. As in other deserts, much of this plant life lies dormant and invisible until one of the rare rains occurs. Then, desert sunflowers deck the sands with gold; primroses carpet the alluvial fans; poppy fields shine against the backdrop of cacti, which also put out their colorful large blossoms. Many unusual plants grow here, for example the bear-poppy, whose striking bluish foliage is covered with long white hairs, and the wetleaf spiderling, whose leaves are always moist, even in the searing summer sun. Birds are the animals most commonly seen, and about 160 species have been recorded in the 550 square miles that lie below sea level; a total of 230 species have been observed in the entire Monument. Many kinds are only migrants or winter visitors, but at least fourteen species nest on the valley floor.

South of the Joshua Tree National Monument is the third major division of the Great American Desert, the Sonoran. Its western extension into California surrounds the lower reaches of the Colorado River and is known as the Colorado River Desert. As in the Mohave, at its heart is a vast basin—the Salton Sink, a depression about 200 miles long and nearly 50 miles wide, which a Spanish explorer called "the valley of torture." About a quarter of its 8000 square miles are below sea level. But unlike Death Valley, Salton Sink actually contains a lake, a salty one about 35 miles long and nearly 20 miles wide, whose surface is more than 200 feet below sea level. At one time this entire desert lay submerged under the Gulf of California, which extended northward to the San Bernardino Mountains. But this arm of the gulf was cut off by silt deposited at the mouth of the Colorado River. The delta formed from this silt stretched from mainland Mexico to the peninsula of Lower California, forming a dam behind which the ancient lake known to geologists as Cahuilla was trapped. The Colorado River is believed to have replenished this lake periodically by pouring its overflow into it through a presently-dry channel known as New River.

Lake Cahuilla existed until approximately 200 years ago; by 1900 it had become reduced to a tiny saline lake. The present Salton Sea, which is much larger, was formed in 1906 when the Colorado River broke out of its channel and flooded the sink. At times water poured in at the rate of 100,000 cubic feet a second; it was not until about 1920 that the Salton Sea subsided to approximately its present size. But the Colorado River Desert is still an unstable region. A subsidence of the land less than 50 feet in places would allow not only the Colorado River to pour in, but also the Gulf of California to reclaim once again this land that it has lost.

Like all bodies of water in desert country, the Salton Sea has become a magnet for birds. Each year hundreds of thousands of birds are drawn to it; how these gulls, terns, and pelicans have managed to find it is something of a mystery, for they have had to cross hundreds of miles of inhospitable desert to reach it. The first pelicans arrived at Salton Sea only a year after the lake was formed. The closest known breeding place for laughing gulls was about a thousand miles away, in Texas, yet within twenty years these birds had found the new lake also. Hordes of ducks, primarily widgeons, have descended on the lake and stripped, almost overnight, whole fields of alfalfa growing around the shore. The U.S. Fish and Wildlife Service has made diversionary plantings to keep the ducks within the sixty-mile-long refuge on the lake. Another stratagem, which startles many visitors when they first see it, is the use of "duck cowboys" who use helicopters to round up the waterfowl and herd them from agricultural land to the refuge.

The Sonoran Desert, of which the Colorado River Desert is but a part, lies mainly in the Mexican state of Sonora. It is the most magnificent of all American deserts, and the only one in which sizable trees and treelike cacti are able to grow. It also contains numerous evergreen and deciduous shrubs, a great variety of succulents, and unequaled wildflower displays. And the saguaro or giant cactus, the symbol of this desert, grows nowhere else.

The saguaro was once described as "a tree designed by someone who had never seen a tree." Its bizarre shape gives a cactus forest an appearance of unreality. Although it so little resembles a tree, it is one nevertheless—a tree turned inside out. Its woody skeleton is actually underneath the pulpy tissue. When the massive stem and branches are filled with water, the saguaro's arms are uplifted as though in praise of the desert; at other times, when dryness has been upon the land, the arms sag forlornly, sometimes even falling so low that they touch the ground.

The saguaro displays numerous adaptations for coping with a restricted rainfall. Its gigantic fluted column, which may rise to a height of 50 feet, is in fact an adjustable storage reservoir: as water is taken in, the pleats expand like those of an accordion. As much as a ton of water may be absorbed by the plant after a rain; sometimes 95 per cent of its total weight is water. Even after years of virtually no rain, this water hoard is enough to permit the saguaro to flower. The tough outer hide of the reservoir is practically impervious to sun and wind, which would otherwise soon deplete the store of moisture. This vast storage tank de-

SAGUARO CACTI typify the Sonoran Desert.

pends for its efficiency upon the saguaro's unusual root system, which consists of an anchoring taproot and a maze of surface feeding roots. These shallow roots form a basin, sometimes as much as 90 feet in diameter, which gathers in the moisture falling within its boundaries. The taproot stabilizes the immense tank; it does not probe for water, for where the saguaro grows there is usually little beneath the surface.

In the saguaro forest, the giant cacti and their lesser associates dot the desert with no sign of crowding, as if they had been planted by a gardener. Each plant stakes out a territory in which its roots establish full claim to the soil, and all water rights; it is almost impossible for an intruder to find living space in this mesh of roots. A number of desert plants keep down competition by a kind of chemical warfare. Among these is the common desert brittlebush, which invariably flourishes in solitude, without another plant very close to it. Experiments have revealed that the brittlebush's fallen leaves possess toxic properties, which retard the growth of many other plants, and even kill them outright.

Another, the desert guayule or rubber plant also possesses toxic substances that suppress the seedlings of its own kind.

In the Sonoran life centers around the saguaro. Spiders, silverfish, moth larvae, and lizards inhabit the pleats in the trunk. The fruit is eaten by birds and rodents. White-winged doves build their nests on the branches; and the great trunks are also the home of two woodpeckers, the gila woodpecker and the golden flicker. With what seems to be impressive foresight, these birds drill their nesting holes in the soft pulp not at the beginning but at the *end* of the nesting season. During the months that follow, scar tissue develops, transforming the gash in the pulp into a dry hole. Here, in the following season, the woodpeckers lay their eggs and rear their young. They use a particular hole for only one nesting, drilling a new one in another part of the saguaro when the season is over; thus an aged cactus may be peppered with dozens of these holes. As soon as a hole is vacated by a pair of woodpeckers, it is taken over as living quarters by one or another of a multitude of other desert birds: pygmy and elf owls, flycatchers, purple martins. Later, as these holes age, the birds abandon them and they become the homes of rats, mice, lizards, and snakes.

The Chihuahuan Desert, which takes its name from the Mexican state in which it mainly lies, is nearly as extensive as the Great Basin. It includes a large portion of the Mexican plateau south of the Rio Grande River, as well as portions of southern Arizona and New Mexico and of western Texas. Like the other divisions of the Great American Desert, it has its omnipresent indicator plants. These are a little yellow-flowered agave known as the lechuguilla, and the narrow-leafed sotol.

Among the attractions of this desert's extension into New Mexico are widespread lava flows, lost rivers, beaches formed by an ancient lake—and extensive dunes of dazzling white sand. The white sands are almost pure gypsum—the mineral from which plaster of Paris is made. Despite constant loss to the winds, the supply of gypsum is continually being renewed. At the southwest end of the dunes is the ephemeral Lake Lucero, into which flow gypsum-bearing waters from the nearby mountains. During the summer the water evaporates, leaving behind the gypsum particles, which are picked up by the prevailing southwesterly winds and deposited in the dune area. At least an equal quantity of gypsum is derived from the beds under the dunes. Water rising to the surface as a result of capillary attraction—the blotting-paper principle—brings up the dissolved mineral, which is likewise left behind after the water evaporates.

At the White Sands National Monument one can see gypsum deposited in rounded hills up to 50 feet high, which cover an area of nearly 500 square miles. Breezes continually sweep over the dunes, forming varied ripple patterns which are rarely duplicated. It seems impossible that any living thing could endure in the white sands, yet, as in other inhospitable environments, plants somehow manage to gain a foothold and to attract animal life. At least 60 species of plants frequent the dunes, but only a few pioneers are able to colonize a fresh dune. One of the most abundant dune plants is the little yucca or soapweed. As the sands pile up, threatening to smother the yucca, the plant's crown rides the crest of the dune by increasing in height. Occasionally the yuccas are buried by the sands, but often they win the race by keeping their heads above the billowing sands. In places where dunes have blown away, some yuccas have been found with stems nearly 40 feet long.

The yucca is one of seven pioneer shrubs at White Sands National Monument that are able to lift their heads above the dunes. They pin down many of the dunes with their roots, and their decaying parts may supply enough organic matter to the soil for other plants to take hold. The problem encountered by plants living in this white desert is not dryness, for gypsum readily absorbs the water that falls upon it, and retains it for long periods. What must be endured are the instability of the dunes and the high proportion of salts they contain.

The tracks across these dunes, observable every morning before they are erased by the wind, are testimony that this desert supports animal life also. The pad marks of coyotes, the thin paths of lizards' tails, the deep hollows left by jack rabbits, the delicate tracery of rodent footprints can all be seen. The animals of the gypsum dunes have become adapted to life on a sheet of glistening whiteness, where dark animals are easily seen and captured by predators, but where light-colored animals receive protection from their background. As a result of uncounted ages during which the darker individuals were the first to be caught, the only animals to survive and reproduce are those that have inherited a light color. For example, a little pocket mouse which is usually black when it lives on the laval rocks only a few miles from the dunes, is the color of light straw in the dunes. Also found in the dunes are white lizards and white spiders.

The theme the desert sets forth to the visitor is the same as in all other landscapes on the continent. It is a theme of constant alteration in the basic stuff of the landscape, whose result is change in the living inhabitants as well. It is but one more variation of the theme of the endless interplay of valley with hillside, of mountain with lowland, and of the continental margins with the sea.

VII

THE CHANGING FACE OF THE LAND

Man's Imprint

ODAY THE GREEN WILDERNESS that greeted the explorers has been
vastly altered. The great tide of forest that swept from the Atlantic
shore westward to the Mississippi and beyond, survives only in isolated
remnants, green patches between the ribbons of concrete. Instead of immense herds of bison trampling the plains, there are now herds of cattle.
The arteries of rivers and streams that once flowed pure are now clotted
with refuse.

But there are also many features of the continent that have scarcely
changed. The Grand Canyon is still very much the same, and probably
will remain so for centuries to come. The Rockies, the Cascades, and the
Sierra still thrust out of the western land; the virgin forests high on their
flanks still set back the clock of time to an age before the white man's
discovery of the New World. Only along the fringes and watercourses
of the desert has man made a very deep imprint. Many of the animals
the Indians hunted still abound, despite all attempts to extirpate them.
For example, within a few miles of the city limits of New York there are
bears, coyotes, and rattlesnakes; in winter, when the Hudson River is
frozen over, deer occasionally come to Manhattan Island; falcons nest
on the man-created cliffs of midtown Manhattan skyscrapers.

The earth changes taking place all around us—the filling in of lakes,
the downcutting of streams, the uplift of mountains, the submergence
and emergence of shores—were going on before man appeared on the

continent, and there is very little he can do to modify them. Man may be able to clear forests and break the soil of plains, but still the ancient cycles go on: trees in wet years advance into the plains, and in dry years are pushed back.

The poets who sang of the everlasting hills were totally mistaken. In no place on the continent is there anything permanent or unchanging. Indeed, no square foot of the continent is exactly the same from one day to the next. Geological erosion has been in progress since the first land rose above a lifeless sea. The coming of life to the planet speeded up many geological processes. The lichens, among the earliest plants to grow on land, formed a crusty growth on rocks and decomposed them; tree roots have entered cracks in rocks and pried them apart. Nor is man the only animal who alters his environment. An alligator in an Everglades slough changes living conditions, both for itself and for its neighbors, when it digs a hole which even during droughts remains filled with water. By their burrowing and uprooting of plants, prairie dogs have accelerated erosion in many places. Beavers have destroyed sections of forest by drowning them, replacing the forest with the meadows of silt that accumulated behind their dams.

But these have all been minor earth-movers compared to man; in his brief tenancy on the continent, he has altered its face more than all the other animals combined. He has shaved off the forests and skinned the grass from the prairies, created bleeding gullies, converted rivers into open sewers. In this speeding up of the process of geological erosion, fertile soil has been washed and blown off farmlands by the carload.

A foreshadowing of what European man would do to the face of the continent was given by the Indians. Although there were probably less than a million Indians in all of North America at the time European man arrived, they had left a deep imprint on the land. Long before Plymouth was settled, fires had periodically swept over the grasslands and through the forests. Many were no doubt set by lightning, but many others were the work of Indians. The American Indian was not the conservationist and husbandman we like to think him today. He obliterated huge forests with fire, simply to drive out game or to clear a path. The typical Indian settlement of the east coast consisted of a village surrounded by cornfields, which had been hacked out with stone axes and cleared with fire. As the fertility of a field declined, lands farther from the village were likewise cleared of trees. Beyond the cultivated fields, the forests were worked over for fuel and set on fire to keep down the undergrowth. Many of the early voyagers sailing along the Atlantic coast commented on the large numbers of fires they saw. When the Pilgrims arrived at Plymouth, the clearing they found was an abandoned Indian village cut out of forest; and they survived their first year largely because they were immediately able to plant crops in the clearing.

Burning by Indians was practiced throughout the continent; as recently as the 1830's, for example, Indians around Chicago were still burning the land every year. Indians of the southern and midwestern states often made extensive clearings and built high ceremonial mounds, many of which survive today as conspicuous features of the landscape. The Effigy Mounds on the river bluffs near McGregor, Iowa, typify those

DUST STORMS, produced by a combination of natural events and human neglect, have buried this Great Plains farm under tons of soil.

found throughout the upper Mississippi Valley; shaped to resemble animals and birds, they are like huge sphinxes fashioned out of mud. The Indians of the southwest changed the face of the land by developing remarkable irrigation systems; in the Salt River Valley of Arizona, for example, it is estimated that a quarter of a million acres were under irrigation before European man arrived. Even the non-agricultural Indians of the plains altered the land by setting repeated fires so as to stampede the bison herds. Repeated fires and the trampling by bison herds are believed to have suppressed forests in some grassland areas where the soil and climate were suitable for the growth of trees.

When European man arrived, forests were leveled and the plains were broken at an accelerated rate. The Indians, as a part of the native fauna, were brushed aside no less ruthlessly than were the herds of bison. "Our lands were originally very good; but use and abuse have made them quite otherwise," complained George Washington. "We ruin the lands that are already cleared, and either cut down more wood, if we have it, or emigrate into the Western country." In the early days of settlement, the frontier began just beyond the borders of the farmland that was losing its fertility. Year by year, the frontier was pushed westward; ahead of the frontier, the barrier of a virgin forest was thrown back; behind it was left a wasteland.

The pushing back of the frontier by European man was at first very slow. As late as 1700, settlements were confined to a swath less than a hundred miles wide along the coast from Massachusetts to Virginia. But once the Appalachians were breached, the westward movement was very rapid; the Mississippi River was reached by settlers within another 50 years, and the whole of the 2000 miles to the Pacific Ocean within 50 more. The scramble to clear the wilderness was intensified by giving land at a low cost or entirely free to railroads, land companies, retired soldiers, and new states. Entire forests of walnut, oak, maple, and other huge trees went up in smoke; teams of horses and oxen broke the thick sod of the grasslands; swamps were ditched to drain away water.

And wherever the Europeans traveled on the land, they carried with them weeds from the Old World, vigorous plants that found new living space and flourished. These were the very plants that had taken over disturbed soils in Europe centuries before. They did the same thing in the New World, hitchhiking across the grasslands in prairie schooners, following the routes of stagecoaches and railroads. Hundreds of plants that are now familiar parts of the landscape—such as dandelion, plantain, mullein, daisy, chicory, Queen Anne's lace, black mustard, and butter-and-eggs—had their origins in Europe.

The pressure to cross the Appalachian Mountains to the virgin lands of the west increased; by 1830, a third of the American population lived beyond the mountains. Within a few more years, all the lands east of the Mississippi River were taken. It was only a few successive steps across the Mississippi to the heart of the grasslands, and from there to the high plains; the Rockies were breached, and the searing deserts were crossed in the drive toward the Pacific. In 1890 the U.S. Census Bureau noted that there was no more free land left; the frontier had disappeared. The wilderness, even as it was being destroyed, had placed its stamp on the American character and spirit, dominated its literature and painting, and shaped its social values. The loss of wilderness, however, was a great price to pay for culture.

The muscle and bone of the land today are much as they were before European man arrived. But the skin is everywhere scarred by abuses, defaced by the open sores of polluted waterways, and marked by the lesions of highways. The toll taken of the American land was summarized in 1909 by a report to President Theodore Roosevelt. In the previous 40 years, the report noted, forest fires had destroyed some $50 million worth of timber. Sheer wastefulness had destroyed a quarter of the standing timber wherever logging had been carried on. Merely extracting turpentine from longleaf pine in the southern states had killed a fifth of the trees. About two thirds of the United States' original endowment of timber had been consumed.

The report catalogued the economic damage, but not what had been done to the structure of the land itself. For example, the primeval forests of the northeastern states had been made up of mixed deciduous trees and conifers. The deciduous trees had largely been either left or cut out slowly, with the result that the vigorous sugar maple had become dominant in many places. The pine and hemlock forests had been completely destroyed. After these valued conifers had been logged out, the woods often were burned; and in many areas, since no seed trees were left standing, white pine disappeared completely, to be replaced by weed species such as aspen, birch, oak, and hazelnut. Excessive burning destroyed all woody growth and produced the barrens of Wisconsin and Michigan. In the place of the original forest with its occasional clearings, the land in many parts of the midwest became what is known as savanna: a man-created grassland with scattered clumps of trees. The savannas provided routes through which birds of the western grasslands could move east. The meadowlark and the prairie horned lark, to name only two species, extended their range across the once-forested region to the eastern seaboard. Prairie plants such as ragweed and black-eyed

Susan advanced eastward from the plains, and are today familiar weeds along eastern roadsides.

The changes wrought by European man, although they differed only in degree from the lesser changes made by native animals and Indians, disrupted the intricate relations among living things to such an extent that they can never be restored. One might consult pioneer histories that tell exactly what trees were present, and in what proportions, in the eastern forests; one might plant an exact replica of that virgin forest; one might restore the mammals and birds that formerly inhabited it. But the original wilderness can never be re-created. The whole web of inter-relations developed in that wilderness over millions of years has been irretrievably lost.

Once destroyed, a wilderness is gone forever, without any hope of complete restoration. The best that modern man can do is to halt any further thoughtless destruction. Gifford Pinchot once described modern forestry as "the art of using the forest without destroying it." Today's forester carries a textbook instead of an ax. He understands the relationship between living things and the health of the forest; he has learned that a forest is more than a collection of trees to be converted into lumber; he no longer "cuts out and gets out." As a result of forest conservation measures, new forests are in the making, and approximately as much timber is now being grown every year as is harvested.

The greatest rebirth of forests has taken place in the southern states. At one time, pine forests spread in a curving arc from the Atlantic to the western coast of the Gulf of Mexico. Then trees were cleared, and the land was planted with tobacco and cotton. Now there are new pine forests, planted by man, growing on these lands. One can drive for a hundred miles across the south today and see pine forests broken only now and then by villages and occasional patches of corn, tobacco, and cotton. The new forests of the south are rebuilding the soil, once again providing living space for wildlife. It is true that these are not the same piny woods that greeted European man; they are man-created, and there is something mechanically tidy in their appearance. To the lover of wilderness, it is somewhat dismaying to find the trunks of pines lined up in neat rows as far as the eye can see. On the other hand, they are an environment created by one species, man, according to his own way of doing things. From that point of view they are no less "natural" than a pond created by another species, the beaver, or a town built by prairie dogs.

Aldo Leopold, a lover of the American land, once wrote: "Everybody knows that the autumn landscape in the north woods is the land, plus

SENTINEL COLUMNS of longleaf pine, rebuilding the forests of the south, stretch as far as the eye can see.

a red maple, plus a ruffed grouse. In terms of conventional physics, the grouse represents only a millionth of either the mass or the energy of an acre. Yet subtract the grouse and the whole thing is dead." Great efforts are being made by the modern tenants of the American land to keep wildlife—the element represented by the grouse—in the picture. There are today more deer, more moose, and more songbirds than when Columbus arrived. In the past half century, no animal with a chance of surviving has been denied the help that the hand of man could offer. Largely through the impetus given by the National Audubon Society, the American egret, roseate spoonbill, whooping crane, flamingo, and half a dozen other notable species have made the long flight back from near-extinction. Several decades ago the bison, the elk, the pronghorn, the beaver, the sea otter, and many other mammals appeared doomed as species; they are no longer in deep peril today.

Conservationists are likewise working to heal the wounds in the soil. Traveling over the continent today, one can see that the bleeding gullies have become fewer than even a few decades ago, that black, muddy rivers are lightening in color as man-caused erosion is reduced. The boundaries of farms are still rectangular, but a new pattern is being imprinted upon them. In place of the old patchwork of little checkerboard squares, there are now sweeping curves, where the crops follow the contours of the land. Fields are plowed on the contour, rather than up and downhill, thus preventing the runoff of water and the erosion that follows. Terraces and farm ponds have been built; grass strips have been planted between crop rows to reduce the loss of water. It is a phenomenal fact that in no more than 30 years the damage done to farmlands by generations of misuse has been about a third repaired.

These are the new, man-made changes on the face of the land. They can never restore the old completely; at best, they can only seek to work constructively *with* the natural forces that have produced the landscape, rather than against them. The most that a rational conservationist asks today is that man behave like a member of the living community of plants and animals.

But before our eyes, there are other changes taking place that man

SNAKELIKE furrows, terraces, and crops planted in alternating strips typify the new conservation that is changing the face of the land.

is powerless to prevent. A bluebird's nest is usurped by a starling, and there is the possibility that bluebirds will not be able to meet the steady pressure from more aggressive birds. In every stream the pebbles, tools of abrasion, are further carving the land. In the New England forests, the trunks of many maples, oaks, and birches are gaunt, leafless skeletons, victims of unexplained diebacks. Some authorities believe that it is the result of a steady warming in climate during this century. A warming trend has, in large part, been responsible for the march of many mammals and birds across the continent. Moose have penetrated northern Canada; coyotes have made the long trek from the western plains to Massachusetts and Connecticut; northern United States and Canada have been invaded by at least fifteen species of southern birds. Down the long stretches of time, the only dependable thing on the continent has been change.

Appendix

Outstanding Natural Areas of North America, by State and Province

The establishment of Yellowstone National Park in 1872 was the first attempt in history by a national government to preserve some of its natural beauty for future generations. Since then, hundreds of additional national parks and monuments, wilderness areas, and wildlife refuges have been added to the public holdings. The settlers of the North American nations have despoiled much of the wilderness they found here, but they have preserved much of it, too—a greater proportion of the total area than in any other region on earth.

The national parks and monuments are administered by the National Park Service, a division of the U.S. Department of the Interior. The parks were established with the intent of preserving notable scenic regions in their pristine state and of protecting all plants and animals (except fishes) within their confines. A national monument preserves a specific object of scientific or historic interest.

The national forests administered by the Forest Service, a division of the U.S. Department of Agriculture, are not sanctuaries. They are areas in which many uses are served: lumbering, cattle grazing, mining, protection of headwater streams, and recreation. In many of the forests, however, extensive areas of primeval land have been set aside where no roads may be built and no lumbering carried on. These are respectively designated as Wilderness Areas (those containing more than 100,000 acres), Wild Areas (those containing 5000 to 100,000 acres), and Natural Areas (those under 5000 acres).

National wildlife refuges, under the administration of the Fish and Wildlife Service of the U.S. Department of the Interior, were in most instances established to protect particular species of wildlife. To further this end, unnatural conditions have often been encouraged: impoundment of water, artificial plantings, and the introduction (or, more frequently, re-introduction) of birds and mammals. These steps have served wildlife well, but not always those who seek a natural landscape. However, a number of the refuges are kept in their natural condition, and others have concentrations of native wildlife that make a visit worth while.

Canada has eleven scenic national parks and a giant's share of wilderness remaining on the continent. A study made some years ago by the Ecological Society of America and the Nature Conservancy revealed that, of the total acreage regarded by these organizations as worthy of being designated sanctuaries, about sixty million acres were in the United States and more than ten times that many in Canada. A number of the provinces also have set aside outstanding natural areas, just as have many of the states.

In addition to such public holdings, patches of wild land have been preserved through the efforts of private organizations, including the National Audubon Society, the Nature Conservancy, and local groups. A complete list of all the natural areas on the continent is obviously impossible within the limitations of this book. The approximately 750 natural areas listed here are those I believe will be most rewarding to the visitor. A certain degree of personal preference has inevitably entered into the selection. A number of wild areas have not been listed for the reason that similar places of greater interest exist near by. A number of places listed are not truly natural areas, but have been included either because they have outstanding features or because they are the nearest to the real thing in wilderness-poor parts of the continent.

ALABAMA

WILLIAM B. BANKHEAD NATIONAL FOREST, Montgomery. Limestone gorges, two natural bridges.

CHEWACLA STATE PARK, Auburn. Rugged southern Appalachian scenery.

DE SOTO STATE PARK, Fort Payne. Partly virgin forest. Canyon nearly 30 miles long, 500 feet deep. Falls more than 100 feet high.

GULF STATE PARK, Foley. Hammocks, dunes.

MONTE SANO STATE PARK, Huntsville. Partly virgin forest.

OAK MOUNTAIN STATE PARK, Birmingham. Rugged mountain country, falls.

WEOGUFKA STATE FOREST, Weogufka. Virgin forest.

CATHEDRAL CAVERNS, Guntersville. Unusual formations.

NOCCALULA FALLS, Gadsden. Attractive falls.

ALASKA

MT. MCKINLEY NATIONAL PARK, McKinley Park. Highest mountain in North America, and peaks of the great Alaska Range. Numerous large glaciers. Greatest concentration on the continent of spectacular large mammals: grizzlies, wolves, moose, Dall sheep, caribou, etc.

GLACIER BAY NATIONAL MONUMENT, Juneau. A living textbook of glaciers, past and present. The Muir Glacier is a prime attraction, but all of the glaciers are worthy of interest.

KATMAI NATIONAL MONUMENT, McKinley Park. The Valley of Ten Thousand Smokes, scene of a violent eruption in 1912, is one of the world's foremost volcanic regions. Virgin tundra and many large mammals.

CHUGASH NATIONAL FOREST, Juneau. Large glaciers, fjords. *National Moose Range* adjoins.

TONGASS NATIONAL FOREST, Juneau. Glaciers, fjords, salmon runs. Great stands of virgin spruce.

ARCTIC NATIONAL WILDLIFE RANGE, Fairbanks. Nearly nine million acres of arctic wilderness, preserving unique wildlife.

CLARENCE RHODE NATIONAL WILDLIFE RANGE, Bethel. Vast tundra breeding ground for numerous waterfowl: cackling geese, black brant, emperor geese, whistling swans, numerous ducks. One of the best places on the continent to see birds in their wilderness setting.

IZEMBEK NATIONAL WILDLIFE RANGE, Cold Bay. Spectacular scenic features combined with extensive tundra and eelgrass beds. The continent's entire black brant population summers in the lagoons.

KODIAK NATIONAL WILDLIFE REFUGE, Kodiak Island. Rugged mountains, Kodiak bear, salmon runs.

NUNIVAK NATIONAL WILDLIFE REFUGE, Kenai. Tundra-covered volcanic island. Large musk ox herd. Vast seabird rookeries on the sea cliffs.

ARIZONA

GRAND CANYON NATIONAL PARK, Grand Canyon. The biggest hole in the earth, 217 miles long and between 4 and 18 miles wide. Four life zones represented. *Grand Canyon National Monument,* adjoining to the west, preserves the beauty and ruggedness of the canyon, without the hordes of sightseers; it is, however, considerably rougher going.

CANYON DE CHELLY NATIONAL MONUMENT, Chinle. Sheer red cliffs and caves eroded into the canyon walls. Prehistoric Indian cliff dwellings. Adjoining *Canyon del Muerto* is a precipitous wall 1000 feet high.

CHIRICAHUA NATIONAL MONUMENT, Wilcox. Pillars of volcanic rock have been eroded into many grotesque forms: balanced rocks, hammers, mushrooms, etc. Less accessible is adjoining *Chiricahua Wild Area* with similar rock formations and pinyon-juniper forest.

ORGAN PIPE CACTUS NATIONAL MONUMENT, Ajo. Many Sonoran Desert plants, most spectacular of which is the organ pipe cactus.

PETRIFIED FOREST NATIONAL MONUMENT, Holbrook. Large fields of strikingly colored petrified logs. In midst of the *Painted Desert,* a stark land in which the colors are those of rocks rather than the plants. Numerous buttes.

SAGUARO NATIONAL MONUMENT, Tucson. Giant cactus forest. A beautiful cross section of the plants of the Sonoran Desert.

SUNSET CRATER NATIONAL MONUMENT, Flagstaff. Considered one of the most beautiful volcanic cones on the continent. The color of its rocks gives the upper part the appearance of being bathed in perpetual sunset. About 400 other volcanic cones are in the vicinity.

KOFA GAME REFUGE, Yuma. About 400 bighorns found in rugged mountains that rise sharply from desert.

CABEZA PRIETA GAME RANGE, Yuma County. Forested mountains and deserts. Pronghorn, bighorn, peccary.

BLUE RANGE WILDERNESS AREA, Apache and Gila national forests. Largest remaining wilderness in the state. Traversed by *Mogollon Rim,* a cliff about 2000 feet high that extends for 200 miles. Subalpine and montane forests.

MAZATZAL WILDERNESS AREA, Tonto National Forest. Precipitous mountains, pinyon-juniper forests.

SUPERSTITION WILDERNESS AREA, Tonto National Forest. Sculptured peaks and oak-pinyon forests.

GALIURO WILD AREA, Coronado National Forest. Knifelike mountains jutting out of the desert.

MOUNT BALDY WILD AREA, Apache National Forest. Montane and subalpine forests at the head of the West Fork of the Little Colorado River.

PINE MOUNTAIN WILD AREA, Prescott and Tonto national forests. Rough terrain along the Verde Rim.

SIERRA ANCHA WILD AREA, Tonto. Precipitous mountains, pinyon-juniper forests.

SYCAMORE CANYON WILD AREA, Coconino and Kaibab national forests. Cross section of canyons and associated plants and animals of northern Arizona.

BUTTERFLY PEAK NATURAL AREA, Coronado National Forest. Virgin desert and forest.

OAK CREEK CANYON NATURAL AREA, Coconino National Forest. One of the most beautiful smaller canyons, with brilliant cliffs. Virgin montane forest.

SAN FRANCISCO PEAKS, Coconino National Forest. Highest peaks in Arizona, of volcanic origin.

KAIBAB NATIONAL FOREST, Williams. Includes *Grand Canyon National Game Preserve* with famous Kaibab deer herd. North rim of the Canyon.

TONTO NATURAL BRIDGE, Payson. Natural bridge 150 feet high. A number of caves near by.

SOUTH MOUNTAIN PARK, Phoenix. Compact cross section of the Arizona desert. Many interesting rock formations.

FISH CREEK CANYON, Roosevelt. Towering and brilliantly colored walls.

MOUNTAIN PARK, Tucson. Game refuge, mountains, mesa, large saguaro forest.

COLOSSAL CAVE, Tucson. Vast caverns, with beautiful formations.

METEOR CRATER, Winslow. Crater nearly a mile in diameter, produced by impact of meteor from outer space.

ARKANSAS

OZARK NATIONAL FOREST, Russellville. Oak forests.

BIG LAKE NATIONAL WILDLIFE REFUGE, Blytheville. Lake formed by earthquake of 1811. Swamp is paradise for birds.

BUFFALO RIVER STATE PARK, Marion County. Caves and waterfalls.

DEVIL'S DEN STATE PARK, Fayetteville. Rugged section of Boston Mountains.

PETIT JEAN MOUNTAIN, Morrilton. Largely virgin hardwood forest.

CALIFORNIA

KINGS CANYON and SEQUOIA NATIONAL PARKS, Three Rivers. Incomparable High Sierra scenery. Two magnificent canyons of the Kings River, one of them the deepest canyon on the continent. Mount Whitney, highest peak on mainland United States, and huge groves of giant sequoias.

LASSEN VOLCANIC NATIONAL PARK, Mineral. Only active volcano in mainland United States, it last erupted in 1921. Effects of vulcanism can be seen around the peak.

YOSEMITE NATIONAL PARK, Yosemite. Glacier-cut gorge is one of the continent's leading attractions. Profusion of hanging waterfalls includes Yosemite Falls, highest on the continent (2425-foot plunge). Three groves of giant sequoias. Nearby *Devil's Postpile* is remnant of a basaltic flow, fractured into tall columns.

CHANNEL ISLANDS NATIONAL MONUMENT, Santa Barbara. Large sea-lion rookeries and colonies of sea birds on Santa Barbara and Anacapa Islands.

DEATH VALLEY NATIONAL MONUMENT, Death Valley. Vast salt and borax desert, the lowest point on the continent. About 550 square miles lie below sea level. Despite the impression of being a total wasteland, 600 different kinds of plants have adapted to conditions here.

JOSHUA TREE NATIONAL MONUMENT, Twentynine Palms. Cross section of the Mohave Desert.

LAVA BEDS NATIONAL MONUMENT, Tulelake. Bleak volcanic landscape. Many caves lined with ice formations.

MUIR WOODS NATIONAL MONUMENT, Mill Valley. Virgin stands of redwood. Other notable redwood groves are at: ARMSTRONG REDWOODS STATE PARK, Guernerville; BIG BASIN REDWOODS STATE PARK, Santa Cruz; DYERVILLE FLATS, Scotia; HUMBOLDT REDWOODS STATE PARK, Eureka; PFEIFFER–BIG SUR STATE PARK, Monterey; PRAIRIE CREEK REDWOODS STATE PARK, Orick; RICHARDSON GROVE STATE PARK, Benbow; COWELL REDWOODS STATE PARK, Santa Cruz; MILL CREEK REDWOODS STATE PARK, Del Norte.

PINNACLES NATIONAL MONUMENT, Paicines. Landscape molded by vulcanism and erosion. Many colorful spires and crags; deep caverns cut by streams.

HIGH SIERRA WILDERNESS AREA, Inyo, Sierra and Sequoia national forests. Magnificent Sierra wilderness, with alpine meadows and immense stands of Jeffrey pine.

MARBLE MOUNTAIN WILDERNESS AREA, Klamath National Forest. Northern California forests, including rare Brewer's spruce.

SALMON TRINITY ALPS WILDERNESS AREA, Klamath and Shasta national forests. Granite peaks and alpine lakes.

YOLLA BOLLY–MIDDLE EEL WILDERNESS AREA, Mendocino and Shasta-Trinity national forests. Numerous high peaks and rugged terrain.

AGUA TIBIA WILD AREA, Cleveland National Forest. Scenic country in southern California.

CARIBOU PEAK WILD AREA, Lassen National Forest. Forested plateau adjoining Silver Lake.

CUCAMONGA WILD AREA, San Bernardino National Forest. Rugged portion of Coast Range.

DESOLATION VALLEY WILD AREA, Eldorado National Forest. Very rugged alpine scenery.

DEVIL CANYON–BEAR CANYON WILD AREA, Angeles National Forest. Deep canyons, chaparral forest.

EMIGRANT BASIN WILD AREA, Stanislaus National Forest. Heavily forested; many deep canyons and lakes.

HOOVER WILD AREA, Toiyabe and Inyo national forests. High granite peaks, glaciers. Near by is *Palisade Glacier,* most southerly on the continent.

MOUNT DANA–MINARETS WILD AREA, Inyo National Forest. Spectacular peaks, including many of the highest in southern California.

SAN GORGONIO WILD AREA, San Bernardino National Forest. Habitats range from desert to alpine.

SAN JACINTO WILD AREA, San Bernardino National Forest. Chaparral and alpine vegetation.

SAN RAFAEL WILD AREA, Los Padres National Forest. Includes the main San Rafael Mountains.

SOUTH WARNER WILD AREA, Modoc National Forest. Numerous peaks and lava flows. Magnificent 15-mile ridge more than 9000 feet high.

THOUSAND LAKES WILD AREA, Lassen National Forest. Lava flows and craters, ice caves, caverns, numerous lakes.

VENTANA WILD AREA, Los Padres National Forest. Primeval redwood forests, desert scrub.

PLUMAS NATIONAL FOREST, Quincy. Feather Falls is one of the highest and most picturesque cataracts in the United States. Limestone caves, deep valleys.

ANZA DESERT STATE PARK, Julian. Canyons, plants of Colorado desert.

BOREGO DESERT STATE PARK, Julian. Outstanding desert preserve.

CALAVERAS BIG TREES STATE PARK, Angels Camp. Giant sequoias.

CASTLE CRAGS STATE PARK, Dunsmuir. Granite domes and spires tower above Sacramento River.

DRY LAGOON BEACH STATE PARK, Orick. Rocky headlands and lagoon.

FREMONT PEAK STATE PARK, San Juan Bautista. Chaparral-clothed mountain.

MCARTHUR–BURNEY FALLS STATE PARK, Burney. Underground creek and unusual falls.

NATURAL BRIDGES STATE PARK, Santa Cruz. Wave-carved arches.

POINT LOBOS RESERVE STATE PARK, Carmel. Groves of Monterey cypress, sea lions, rugged coast.

SALTON SEA STATE PARK, Mecca. Two hundred feet below sea level. Preserves ancient beach line from a time when the sea was part of the Gulf of California.

TORREY PINES STATE PARK, Del Mar. Rare trees.

VAN DAMME and RUSSIAN GULCH STATE PARKS, Mendocino. Two impressive canyons.

BUENA VISTA LAGOON, San Diego. Series of fresh-water lagoons formed behind sandbars. Outstanding refuge for migrating waterfowl.

LA JOLLA CAVES, La Jolla. Ocean-carved caves.

NORTHERN CALIFORNIA COAST RANGE PRESERVE, Branscomb. Small wilderness with last substantial stand of coastal Douglas fir still in primeval condition.

PALM CANYON, Palm Springs. A 15-mile canyon in which grow thousands of aged palms.

COLORADO

MESA VERDE NATIONAL PARK, Cortez. Extensive tableland with thick pinyon-juniper forests. Hundreds of caves in the cliffs hold some of the best prehistoric Indian dwellings on the continent. Large mammals.

ROCKY MOUNTAIN NATIONAL PARK, Estes Park. A slice of the most delectable portion of the Rockies, containing 65 peaks over 10,000 feet high. The alpine meadows are vibrant with the display of nearly 700 wildflower species. Many moraines left by valley glaciers.

BLACK CANYON OF THE GUNNISON NATIONAL MONUMENT, Fruita. Dark ancient granite and inky depths; one of the great canyons of the continent.

COLORADO NATIONAL MONUMENT, Fruita. Erosion of sandstone rocks has created sheer canyons and towering monoliths.

GREAT SAND DUNES NATIONAL MONUMENT, Alamosa. Highest dunes in the United States, deposited over thousands of years by winds halted at the barrier of the Sangre de Cristo Mountains. Lost rivers.

FLAT TOPS WILDERESS AREA, White River National Forest. Spectacular canyons, falls, caves, springs, and alpine lakes.

SAN JUAN WILDERNESS AREA, San Juan National Forest. Virgin forests, cataracts, unusual rock formations.

GORE RANGE–EAGLE NEST WILD AREA, Arapaho and White River national forests. Among the most rugged and picturesque ranges in the state.

LA GARITA–SHEEP MOUNTAIN WILD AREA, Gunnison, Rio Grande, and San Isabel national forests. Considerable portions above timberline. Mountain sheep and elk.

MAROON–SNOWMASS WILD AREA, White River National Forest. Alpine lakes and rugged peaks.

MOUNT ZIRKEL–DOME PEAK WILD AREA, Routt National Forest. Virgin stands of lodgepole pine and Engelmann spruce. Continental Divide. Alpine lakes.

RAWAH WILD AREA, Roosevelt National Forest. Small glacier and numerous glacial lakes.

UNCOMPAHGRE WILD AREA, Uncompahgre National Forest. Extremely rugged mountains, falls, lakes, subalpine forest.

UPPER RIO GRANDE WILD AREA, Rio Grande National Forest. Mountainous watershed of the Rio Grande River.

WEST ELK WILD AREA, Gunnison National Forest. Alpine meadows, lakes.

WILSON MOUNTAIN WILD AREA, San Juan National Forest. Includes two major peaks of the Wilson Range.

GOTHIC NATURAL AREA, Gunnison National Forest. Virgin spruce-fir forest.

MOUNT GOLIATH NATURAL AREA, Arapaho National Forest. Alpine meadows.

BLACK FOREST, Colorado Springs. Beautiful stand of ponderosa pine.

GARDEN OF THE GODS, Colorado Springs. Red sandstone eroded into remarkable formations.

GRAND MESA, Grand Junction. Largest flat-topped mountain on the continent.

NORTH CHEYENNE CANYON, Colorado Springs. Numerous waterfalls and unusual rock formations.

RED ROCKS PARK, Denver. Brilliantly colored rocks, ponderosa pine forest.

ROYAL GORGE, Canon City. Narrow canyon of the Arkansas River.

CONNECTICUT

DEVIL'S HOPYARD STATE PARK, Middlesex County. Unique rock formations.

HURD STATE PARK, Middlesex County. Rocky ridge with unusual formations.

KENT FALLS STATE PARK, Litchfield County. Heavily wooded area with series of cataracts.

CATHEDRAL PINES, GOLD PINES, KENT NORTHERN HARDWOOD FOREST, Cornwall Bridge. Three small patches of unspoiled forest.

STEEP ROCK PARK, Washington. Primeval forest.

AUDUBON NATURE CENTER, Greenwich. Typical native plants, wildflower displays.

FLORIDA

EVERGLADES NATIONAL PARK, Homestead. A large portion of the Everglades in virtually unspoiled condition. Contains examples of many habitats: mangrove forests, hammocks, sawgrass, fresh-water sloughs. North America's only crocodiles found here, with numerous alligators, many unusual and rare birds.

FORT JEFFERSON NATIONAL MONUMENT, Dry Tortugas Islands. Reached by charter boat from Key West, 70 miles away. Coral reefs, subtropical vegetation, mangroves.

APALACHICOLA NATIONAL FOREST, Tallahassee. Bottomland swamps, rare yews and cedars.

OCALA NATIONAL FOREST, Tallahassee. Subtropical palms, scrub pines, hardwoods. Juniper Springs have a flow of eight million gallons of water a day.

OSCEOLA NATIONAL FOREST, Tallahassee. Cypress swamps.

GREAT WHITE HERON NATIONAL WILDLIFE REFUGE, Monroe County. Virgin mangrove islands, Key deer.

ANASTASIA STATE PARK, St. Augustine. Coquina rock.

COLLIER-SEMINOLE STATE PARK, Naples. Nearly virgin mangrove, cypress, pine. Palm hammocks.

CORAL REEF STATE PARK, Key Largo. The continent's only underwater park. A fabulous coral reef that can be seen either by skindiving or from glass-bottom boats.

FLORIDA CAVERNS STATE PARK, Marianna. Extensive caves surrounded by virgin forest.

HIGHLANDS HAMMOCK STATE PARK, Sebring. Extensive hammocks and lagoons.

HILLSBOROUGH RIVER STATE PARK, Tampa. Nearly virgin hardwood forest.

MYAKKA RIVER STATE PARK, Sarasota. Prairie interspersed with hammocks and marshes.

SUWANNEE RIVER STATE PARK, Madison. Nearly virgin stands of hardwoods and pines.

TORREYA STATE PARK, Blountstown. Virgin forest of magnolia, beech, rare trees.

CORKSCREW SWAMP, Collier County. Preserves a characteristic Florida landscape, including sawgrass marsh, virgin cypress swamp, and pine woods.

MATHESON HAMMOCK, Coral Gables. Extensive hammock with many West Indian trees, mangrove shore.

OBSERVATION ISLAND, Clewiston. In relatively untouched part of Lake Okeechobee. Spectacular birds, including the rare Everglades kite.

WAKULLA SPRINGS, Wakulla Springs. One of the world's largest springs, surrounded by cypress forest.

GEORGIA

OCMULGEE NATIONAL MONUMENT, Macon. Large Indian mounds.

CHATTAHOOCHEE NATIONAL FOREST, Gainesville. Blue Ridge Mountains, extensive bald. Contains *Tallulah Gorge,* 1000 feet deep, waterfalls.

BLACKBEARD ISLAND NATIONAL WILDLIFE REFUGE, McIntosh County. Partly virgin coastal marsh.

OKEFENOKEE WILDLIFE REFUGE, Waycross. One of the most primitive swamps on the continent. A typical cross section can be seen at *Okefenokee Swamp State Park,* where there are a boardwalk and an observation tower.

AMICALOLA FALLS STATE PARK, Dawson County. Cascades more than 700 feet high.

LITTLE OCMULGEE STATE PARK, McRae. Sand hills and swamps.

VOGEL STATE PARK, Blairsville. Unspoiled wilderness, falls.

CLOUDLAND CANYON, Dade County. Georgia's little Grand Canyon.

FERNBANK FOREST, Atlanta. Undisturbed for more than a hundred years.

STONE MOUNTAIN, Atlanta. Granite dome, one of the largest areas of exposed granite in the world.

IDAHO

CRATERS OF THE MOON NATIONAL MONUMENT, Arco. Volcanic area displaying craters, caves, lava flows. The closest thing to a moonscape on the continent.

IDAHO WILDERNESS AREA, Challis, Salmon, and Payette national forests. Rough mountainous country, heavily burned in the past but now making a comeback. Middle Fork of the Salmon River is a turbulent sight. Wide variety of large mammals.

SAWTOOTH WILDERNESS AREA, Boise, Challis, and Sawtooth national forests. Numerous glacial lakes, rough terrain.

SELWAY-BITTERROOT WILDERNESS AREA, Clearwater, Nezperce, Lolo, and Bitterroot national forests. Nearly two million superb acres of mountains, forests. Many large mammals.

CANYON CREEK NATURAL AREA, Kaniksu National Forest. Nearly virgin forests.

MONTFORD CREEK NATURAL AREA, Coeur d'Alene National Forest. Virgin forest.

BOISE NATIONAL FOREST, Boise. Virgin stands of ponderosa pine.

CHALLIS NATIONAL FOREST, Challis. Headwaters of the Salmon River, lost rivers, hot springs, Sawtooth Mountains. Big Lost River vanishes in lava rocks, re-appears at *Thousand Springs,* near Buhl, where water cascades from the side of a canyon.

KANIKSU NATIONAL FOREST, Sandpoint. Rugged back country, large lakes, ancient grove of cedars, Chimney Rock.

MINIDOKA NATIONAL FOREST, Burley. Fantastic display of rocks eroded by wind and water; alpine lakes.

PAYETTE NATIONAL FOREST, McCall. Rugged mountains with nearly a hundred high lakes. Grand Canyon of the Snake River.

SAINT JOE NATIONAL FOREST, Saint Maries. Canyons in Bitterroot Range, virgin pine stands.

SALMON NATIONAL FOREST, Salmon. Boat trips down one of the most turbulent rivers on the continent, through gorges and rapids, canyons with precipitous walls.

TARGHEE NATIONAL FOREST, Saint Anthony. Many falls, views of the Grand Tetons.

HELL'S CANYON, Nezperce National Forest. The construction of three dams has tamed the deepest and wildest canyon on the continent, but it is still mag-nificent in places. Boats from Lewiston and Homestead, Oregon, take visitors up the *Grand Canyon of the Snake River.*

BIG SPRINGS, Ashton. Large springs at the base of a plateau, from which gushes Henry's Fork of the Snake River.

ILLINOIS

SHAWNEE NATIONAL FOREST, Harrisburg. Confluence of Ohio and Mississippi rivers. Interesting rock formations, bluffs, Indian mounds.

APPLE RIVER CANYON STATE PARK, Stockton. High limestone bluffs.

BEAVER DAM STATE PARK, Carlinville. Small lake originally formed by beavers.

BUFFALO ROCK STATE PARK, Ottawa. Scenic rock formations, bison herd.

CAVE-IN-ROCK STATE PARK, Kenton. Bluffs of Ohio River, Indian mounds, cave.

DIXON SPRINGS STATE PARK, Grantsburg. Upwards of a thousand small waterfalls.

FERN CLYFFE STATE PARK, Goreville. Two large sandstone caves.

GIANT CITY STATE PARK, Carbondale. Huge blocks of stone that resemble city buildings.

KICKAPOO STATE PARK, Danville. Ravines, stone ledges, lakes.

MATTHIESSEN STATE PARK, La Salle. Falls, caves, cliffs.

MISSISSIPPI PALISADES STATE PARK, Savanna. Rugged wooded cliffs of the Missis-sippi.

STARVED ROCK STATE PARK, Ottawa. Wooded bluffland on Illinois River; 20 gorges, sandstone cliffs, unusual vegetation.

WHITE PINES FOREST STATE PARK, Oregon. Virgin stand of pine.

ALLERTON PARK, Monticello. Partly virgin oak-hickory forest.

BROWNFIELD WOODS, Urbana. Nearly virgin oak-maple stand.

PORTAGE ISLAND WILDLIFE SANCTUARY, Elsah. Almost virgin bottomlands of the Mississippi.

VOLO and WAUCONDA BOGS, Lake County. Two outstanding bogs that demonstrate succession from bog to forest. Only a little pond about 200 feet across remains in Volo, the rest having become dry land. Wauconda is even further advanced; the pond has disappeared entirely.

WILLIAM TRELEASE WOODS, Urbana. Nearly virgin oak-maple forest.

INDIANA

HOOSIER NATIONAL FOREST PURCHASE UNITS, Bedford. Outlet of Lost River, bison trail.

CLIFTY FALLS STATE PARK, Madison. Unspoiled beech-oak-hickory forest. Falls.

INDIANA DUNES STATE PARK, Michigan City. Dunes fronting on Lake Michigan. Partly undisturbed beech-maple forest.

KANKAKEE RIVER STATE PARK, Schneider. Vast swamp.

MCCORMICK'S CREEK STATE PARK, Spencer. Limestone canyon.

MOUNDS STATE PARK, Anderson. Outstanding Indian mounds.

MUSCATATUCK STATE PARK, Jennings County. Heavily timbered hills, rocky gorges.

SHADES STATE PARK, Waveland. Virgin patches of beech-hemlock forest. Unusual geological formations.

SPRING MILL STATE PARK, Mitchell. Partly virgin poplar-beech-oak forest; underground rivers, caverns.

TURKEY RUN STATE PARK, Kingman. Deep canyons and gorges; one of the most picturesque spots in the state. Partly virgin beech-maple and oak-hickory forests.

VERSAILLES STATE PARK, Versailles. Virgin patches of oak, hickory, beech, sweet gum, red maple.

WYANDOTTE CAVE, Wyandotte. One of the larger caves on the continent, with outstanding formations.

IOWA

EFFIGY MOUNDS NATIONAL MONUMENT, Marquette. Indian mounds in shapes of birds and animals.

GEODE STATE PARK, Danville. Unusual rock formations.

LACEY-KEOSAUQUA STATE PARK, Van Buren County. Massive sandstone outcroppings.

LAKE MANAWA STATE PARK, Council Bluffs. An oxbow of the Missouri River.

LEDGES STATE PARK, Boone. Dense hardwood forest, sandstone cliffs.

MAQUOKETA CAVES STATE PARK, Maquoketa. Limestone caves, 50-foot natural bridge, large balanced rock.

WILD CAT DEN STATE PARK, Muscatine County. Rock formations.

These state parks, in particular, contain primeval forest: AMBROSE CALL RECREATIONAL RESERVE, Algona; LEDGES STATE PARK, Boone; MCGREGOR HEIGHTS STATE PARK, McGregor; SPRINGBROOK STATE PARK, Guthrie Center; WANATA FOREST RESERVE STATE PARK, Peterson; WILD CAT DEN STATE PARK, Muscatine; WOODTHRUSH WAYSIDE, Fairfield; WOODMAN HOLLOW, Fort Dodge.

True prairie remnants are at: GITCHIE MANITO, Larchwood; LAKESIDE PRAIRIE, Milford; SILVER LAKE FEN, Lake Park; LIME SPRINGS PRAIRIE, Howard County; KALSOW PRAIRIE, Manson.

KANSAS

WASHINGTON MARLAT MEMORIAL PARK, Manhattan. Virgin prairie.

MEADE COUNTY STATE PARK, Meade. Springs; bison and elk.

PYRAMID ROCKS, Oakley. Strangely eroded rocks that loom above the prairie. Other striking formations near by are *Castle Rock, Monument Rock,* and *Sphinx Rock.*

PAWNEE ROCK, Pawnee Rock. Projecting red sandstone cliff, a landmark for pioneers traveling the Santa Fe Trail.

KENTUCKY

MAMMOTH CAVE NATIONAL PARK, Cave City. About 150 miles of underground passages explored to date. Rock formations of onyx, gypsum, and limestone are exceptional. Underground river. Do not overlook the patches of primeval forest in the park.

CUMBERLAND GAP NATIONAL HISTORICAL PARK, Middlesboro. Water gap through Allegheny Mountains. One of the best views is from Pinnacle Mountain, which has a road to the summit.

CUMBERLAND NATIONAL FOREST, Winchester. Sandstone cliffs, Red River gorge, numerous limestone caves and springs. Near by are *Cumberland Falls,* with a remnant of the original forest, and *Natural Bridge State Park. Rock Creek Natural Area* is a largely virgin northern hardwood forest.

AUDUBON MEMORIAL STATE PARK, Henderson. Here John James Audubon made many of his observations and paintings. A virgin stand of beech remains.

CARTER CAVES STATE PARK, Olive Hill. Cliffs, caves, natural bridges.

PINE MOUNTAIN STATE PARK, Pineville. Primeval oak-chestnut and hemlock stands.

LOUISIANA

KISATCHIE NATIONAL FOREST, Alexandria. Stands of virgin pine. Many bayous and lakes.

DELTA NATIONAL WILDLIFE REFUGE, Pilottown. Delta country with salt and fresh-water marshes.

SABINE NATIONAL WILDLIFE REFUGE, Sulphur. Immense stretch of bayous, numerous virgin islands. Muskrat, mink, water birds.

RAINEY WILDLIFE SANCTUARY, Abbeville. Coastal marshes, lakes, bayous. Concentrations of wintering blue geese and numerous other birds.

MAINE

ACADIA NATIONAL PARK, Bar Harbor. Rugged coastal area on Mount Desert Island typifies much of wave-battered Maine coast. Has the highest elevation on the eastern seaboard. Sea caves.

MOOSEHORN NATIONAL WILDLIFE REFUGE, Calais and Dennysville counties. Representative cross section of northeastern tip of the state has birch-beech-maple and spruce-fir-pine associations.

KATAHDIN WILDLIFE STATE SANCTUARY, Piscataquis County. Partly virgin spruce-fir forest. Moose, bear, pine marten, fisher.

BAXTER STATE PARK, Millinocket. Extensive areas of northern wilderness, dominated by Mount Katahdin (5267 feet).

CAMDEN HILLS STATE PARK, Camden. Shore views, extensive forests.

TODD WILDLIFE SANCTUARY, Hog Island. Shore features, spruce forest.

APPALACHIAN TRAIL. The longest marked foot trail in the world has its northern terminus on Mount Katahdin. It stretches more than 2000 miles to Fort Oglethorpe, Georgia, traversing 14 states.

MARYLAND

GREAT FALLS PARK, Washington. The Potomac River cuts through rocks, creating wild cliffs and breaking up into small watercourses.

ROCKS STATE PARK, Bel Air. Rugged rock formations.

SWALLOW FALLS STATE PARK, Oakland. Virgin hemlock forest, falls.

BATTLE CREEK CYPRESS SWAMP, Prince Frederick. Vigorous stand of bald cypress, highest more than 100 feet tall.

PLUMMERS ISLAND PRESERVE, Washington. Partly virgin woods.

Maryland has within its borders a large number of record-size trees. Among them are the largest white oak, at WYE OAK STATE PARK in Talbot County; bigtooth aspen, at Rocks; flowering dogwood, near Oriole; honey locust, near Queenstown; sugar maple, in Garrett County; eastern red cedar, at Cumberstone; tulip tree, at Annapolis; and black walnut, in Ann Arundel County.

MASSACHUSETTS

MONOMOY NATIONAL WILDLIFE REFUGE, Chatham. A spit projecting southward from Cape Cod's elbow. Waterfowl converge on the island during migrations; in some years a million eiders and scoters may be in the area.

PARKER RIVER NATIONAL WILDLIFE REFUGE, Newburyport. Salt marshes, dunes.

CAPE COD NATIONAL SEASHORE. Preserves patches of undeveloped sand dunes, scrub pine forests, extensive beaches.

BEARTOWN STATE FOREST and MOUNT EVERETT STATE RESERVATION, Great Barrington. Representative landscapes of the Berkshires.

CARLISLE PINES STATE FOREST, Carlisle. Small patch of primeval white pine.

GRANVILLE STATE FOREST, West Granville. Small gorge, laurels.

MARTHA'S VINEYARD STATE RESERVATION, Martha's Vineyard. Scrub oak and pitch pine woods.

MOUNT GREYLOCK STATE RESERVATION, North Adams. Some primeval forest on highest mountain in the state (3491 feet).

MOUNT SUGARLOAF STATE RESERVATION, South Deerfield. Unusual red sandstone formation.

MOUNT TOM STATE RESERVATION, Holyoke. Precipitous ridge, heavily forested.

SKINNER STATE PARK, South Hadley. Volcanic formation. Views of Connecticut River valley from top of Mount Holyoke.

WILLARD BROOK STATE FOREST, Ashby. Spruce-pine forest, falls.

CHESTERFIELD GORGE, West Chesterfield. Narrow gorge, hemlock forest.

PLEASANT VALLEY WILDLIFE SANCTUARY, Lenox. Native plants and animals of the Berkshires.

MICHIGAN

ISLE ROYAL NATIONAL PARK, Houghton. Largest island in Lake Superior, it has preserved its wilderness aspect. Rugged coastline, picturesque crags and ridges. Large moose herd, small population of wolves, coyotes, and mink.

HIAWATHA and MARQUETTE NATIONAL FORESTS, Escanaba. Bordering on Lakes Huron, Michigan, and Superior. Waterfalls.

OTTAWA NATIONAL FOREST, Ironwood. Beautiful forest with some virgin patches. *Ottawa Natural Area* has virgin cedar swamp.

SENEY NATIONAL WILDLIFE REFUGE, Germfask. Extensive forests and marshes. Large numbers of breeding water birds. Sandhill cranes, bald eagles, Canada geese and 200 other species have been recorded here.

BALD MOUNTAIN STATE PARK, Oakland County. Rolling hills, glacial lakes.

FLETCHER STATE PARK, Posen. Partly virgin forest.

GRAND MARAIS STATE PARK, Grand Marais. Partly virgin northern hardwoods.

HARTWICK PINES STATE PARK, Grayling. Some virgin stands of white and jack pine, hemlock, balsam fir, spruce.

HIGHLAND STATE PARK, Oakland County. Extensive forests; lakes.

INTERLOCHEN STATE PARK, Traverse City. Partly virgin forest.

LUDINGTON STATE PARK, Ludington. Sand dunes, extensive forest.

MCLAIN STATE PARK, Houghton. Lake Superior shore, dense forests.

MUSKEGON STATE FOREST, Muskegon. Sand dunes, pine and hardwood forest.

PORCUPINE MOUNTAIN STATE PARK, Ontonagon. One of the finest remaining forests of northern hardwoods and hemlock.

TAHQUAMENON FALLS STATE PARK, Luce and Chippewa counties. Falls.

WARREN DUNES STATE PARK, Bridgman. Nearly virgin stands of maple, oak, hemlock, white pine. Sand dunes.

PICTURED ROCKS, Munising. Rugged cliffs and grottoes along Superior shore.

REESE'S BOG, Tip o' the Mitten County. Spruce bog.

SLEEPING BEAR DUNE, Glen Haven. Unusual sand formations. Buried forest.

TOUMEY VIRGIN FOREST, Lansing. Virgin beech-maple forest.

WARREN WOODS, Three Oaks. Nearly virgin beech-maple and flood-plain forests.

MINNESOTA

CHIPPEWA NATIONAL FOREST, Cass Lake. Headwaters of the Mississippi; hundreds of other large lakes. Remnants of the great forest that once covered the state.

SUPERIOR NATIONAL FOREST, Duluth. Largest wilderness area east of the Rockies. Adjoins Canada's *Quetico Provincial Park,* with which it forms the largest and finest expanse of canoe country on the continent.

PIPESTONE NATIONAL MONUMENT, Pipestone. Quarries of red rock where Indians mined stone for their pipes; other geological points of interest. Virgin prairie.

Remnants of the "Big Woods" of Minnesota can be seen at: NERSTRAND WOOD STATE PARK, Northfield; KILEN WOODS STATE PARK, Jackson; SCENIC STATE PARK, Bigfork; PRIMEVAL PINE GROVE PARK, Little Falls; SIBLEY STATE PARK, New London.

BAPTISM RIVER STATE PARK, Two Harbors. Highest waterfall in state.

GOOSEBERRY FALLS STATE PARK, Two Harbors. Two high falls. Little-disturbed north woods.

INTERSTATE STATE PARK, Taylors Falls. Lava cliffs of the St. Croix River.

ITASCA STATE PARK, Park Rapids. Source of the Mississippi. Nearly 160 other lakes, surrounded by stands of virgin pine.

JAY COOKE STATE PARK, Duluth. Gorge of St. Louis River.

LAKE CARLOS STATE PARK, Alexandria. Dense tamarack swamp.

LATSCH STATE PARK, Winona County. Limestone bluffs along Mississippi.

MINNEOPA STATE PARK, Mankato. Deep gorge and falls.

WATERLOO STATE RESERVATION, Waterloo. Outstanding marshes.

WHITEWATER STATE PARK, Rochester. Wide ravine.

WILDERNESS STATE PARK, Carp Lake. Coniferous and deciduous forests. Lake Michigan shore.

BERNARD BAKER SANCTUARY, Battle Creek. Exceptionally fine marsh. Breeding sandhill cranes.

NIAGARA CAVE, Harmony. Interesting cave formations, underground waterfall.

MISSISSIPPI

BIENVILLE NATIONAL FOREST, Jackson. Virgin loblolly pine.

DELTA NATIONAL FOREST, Jackson. Virgin hardwood forest.

TISHOMINGO STATE PARK, Iuka. Outstanding highland forest.

TOMBIGBEE STATE PARK, Tupelo. Ridges, pine forest.

MISSOURI

CLARK NATIONAL FOREST, Rolla. Ozark Mountains, oak and pine forests.

MARK TWAIN NATIONAL FOREST, Springfield. Numerous coves, rock cairns, springs.

BIG OAK STATE PARK, Charleston. Primeval hardwood forest.

ROUND SPRING STATE PARK, Eminence. Limestone cliff and large spring.

SAM BAKER STATE PARK, Patterson. Gorge and Mudlick Mountain.

TRAIL OF TEARS STATE PARK, Cape Girardeau County. Excellent views of Mississippi River bluffs.

Exceptional springs and remnants of the original Missouri forest are found at: ALLEY SPRINGS STATE PARK, Eminence; BIG SPRINGS STATE PARK, Van Buren; BABLER STATE PARK, St. Louis; MONTAUK STATE PARK (springs that form the headwaters of the Current), Salem; MARAMEC SPRING STATE PARK, St. James.

BRIDAL CAVE, Camdenton. Finest cave in the Missouri Ozarks, with extensive onyx formations.

EAST ASHLAND CONSERVATION AREA, Columbia. Virgin sugar maples.

HYER WOODS, Dent County. Remnant of the Missouri hardwood forest.

ROCKWOODS RESERVATION, St. Louis. Rugged oak-hickory forest.

TUCKER PRAIRIE, Columbia. Tall-grass prairie never broken by the plow.

MONTANA

GLACIER NATIONAL PARK, West Glacier. Part of the Waterton-Glacier International Peace Park, which straddles the U.S.–Canadian border. About 60 glaciers, 200 mountain lakes, superb views of glacier-carved scenery. Almost every large mammal of the United States mainland is resident in the park. More than 1000 species of wildflowers; vegetation ranging from prairie to pine forests. Spectacular *Going-to-the-Sun Highway* crosses the Continental Divide.

NATIONAL BISON RANGE, Moiese. Large herd of bison, as well as mountain bighorns and elk. Virgin prairie and coniferous forest.

RED ROCK LAKES NATIONAL WILDLIFE REFUGE, Beaverhead County. High valley rimmed by mountains. Trumpeter swans.

ANACONDA-PINTLAR WILDERNESS AREA, Beaverhead, Bitterroot, and Deerlodge national forests. Chain of barren, precipitous peaks; subalpine forest, large mammals. *Lost Creek Canyon,* near by, has walls 2000 feet high.

BEARTOOTH WILDERNESS AREA, Custer and Gallatin national forests. High mountainous area; includes loftiest peak in the state and *Grasshopper Glacier.* Hordes of grasshoppers frozen into this glacier have left black lines across its face.

BOB MARSHALL WILDERNESS AREA, Flathead, and Lewis and Clark national forests. Largely virgin montane and subalpine forests. Outstanding population of large mammals.

ABSAROKA WILD AREA, Gallatin National Forest. High mountain area, subalpine forest.

CABINET MOUNTAINS WILD AREA, Kootenai National Forest. Mostly virgin forest in grand mountain setting.

GATES OF THE MOUNTAINS WILD AREA, Helena National Forest. Spectacular limestone cliffs.

MISSION MOUNTAINS WILD AREA, Flathead National Forest. Glaciers and large mammals.

SPANISH PEAKS WILD AREA, Gallatin National Forest. Wild terrain; subalpine forest and mountain meadows.

HELL CREEK STATE PARK, Jordan. Badland formations.

LEWIS AND CLARK CAVERNS STATE PARK, Whitehall. Colorful limestone caverns, among the most beautiful on the continent.

MAKOSHIKA STATE PARK, Glendive. Vividly colored buttes.

RED LODGE–YELLOWSTONE PARK SCENIC HIGHWAY, Red Lodge. Auto route to top of plateau and northeastern entrance to Yellowstone. Road flanked by rugged terrain and numerous lakes.

NEBRASKA

SCOTTS BLUFF NATIONAL MONUMENT, Scottsbluff. Great cliff rises 800 feet above North Platte River.

CHIMNEY ROCK NATIONAL HISTORIC SITE, Bayard. This eroded sandstone monolith was a landmark for pioneers on the Oregon Trail.

NEBRASKA NATIONAL FOREST, Halsey. Some virgin prairie, sand hills. Game refuge: largest mule deer herd in the state, prairie chickens, nesting grounds of great blue heron.

FORT NIOBRARA NATIONAL WILDLIFE REFUGE, Valentine. One of the outstanding wild areas in the state, with native prairies, dunes, swamps, lakes. Large mammal population includes bison, elk, longhorn cattle.

FONNETELLE FOREST, Omaha. Virgin hardwood forest.

NEVADA

NEVADA NATIONAL FOREST, Ely. Highest peak wholly in Nevada. Towering pines. *Lehman Caves National Monument,* in the forest, has winding tunnels and galleries cut in white limestone, superlative stalagmites and stalactites.

TOIYABE NATIONAL FOREST, Reno. East slope of Sierra Nevada. *Sweetwater Natural Area* has virgin pinyon-juniper forest.

JARBRIDGE WILD AREA, Humboldt National Forest. Rugged mountainous terrain, with eight peaks over 10,000 feet.

DESERT GAME REFUGE, Las Vegas. Striking Great Basin Desert scenery and plants. Red Rock area rivals views at Bryce Canyon. Largest desert bighorn population in existence.

SHELDON NATIONAL ANTELOPE REFUGE, Washoe County. High Great Basin Desert country. Large pronghorn population.

CATHEDRAL GORGE STATE PARK, Caliente. Eroded cliffs of this long valley resemble pillars and vaults of a cathedral.

KERSHAW CANYON STATE PARK, Caliente. Scenic cliffs.

VALLEY OF FIRE STATE PARK, Crystal. A large basin filled with eroded sandstone formations.

PYRAMID LAKE, Reno. Deep blue lake set among deserts and mountains. Anahoe Island is breeding ground for large pelican colony.

NEW HAMPSHIRE

WHITE MOUNTAIN NATIONAL FOREST, Laconia. A major portion of the White Mountains. *Mount Washington* is the highest peak in northeastern United States. *Tuckerman's Ravine* on Mount Washington is an outstanding glacial cirque. *Great Gulf Wild Area* has virgin spruce and fir forests. *Gulf of Slides* displays unusual granite formations.

CRAWFORD NOTCH STATE PARK, Bartlett. Glacial trough, falls.

FRANCONIA NOTCH STATE PARK, Echo Lake. One of the most spectacular mountain gaps in the northeast. Glacier-formed *Old Man of the Mountain,* a profile composed of five ledges jutting from the side of a mountain. Gorges, falls.

MONADNOCK STATE PARK, Jaffrey. A mountain that rises above the surrounding country aloof from other peaks.

WINSLOW STATE PARK, Merrimack County. Mount Kearsarge forests.

RHODODENDRON STATE RESERVATION, Fitzwilliam. Hemlock forest. Excellent views of Mount Monadnock.

PAWTUCKAWAY STATE RESERVATION, Deerfield. Extensive oak-hickory forest, hemlock ravine.

PISGAH MOUNTAIN TRACT, Hinsdale. Small patch of virgin white pine.

CATHEDRAL LEDGE, North Conway. Views of structure of White Mountains from granite outcrop.

DIXVILLE NOTCH, Colebrook. Wildest of the notches, densely forested.

KINSMAN NOTCH, North Woodstock. Deep gorge. A lost river winds through caverns and emerges in falls. Glacier-formed caves.

THATCHER FOREST, Hancock. Primeval white pine.

NEW JERSEY

BARNEGAT LIGHTHOUSE STATE PARK, Barnegat. Unspoiled stretch of beach.

HACKLEBARNEY STATE PARK, Morris County. Gorge on Black River.

HIGH POINT STATE PARK, Sussex County. Kittatinny ridge.

ISLAND BEACH STATE PARK, Seaside. Dunes.

PALISADES INTERSTATE PARK. Strip of land extending along Hudson River preserves volcanic cliffs.

STOKES STATE FOREST, Branchville. Mountain Woodland.

AUDUBON SANCTUARY, Stone Harbor. Famed bird sanctuary, with numerous herons.

METTLER'S WOODS, New Brunswick. One of the finest primeval forests in the east.

WITMER STONE SANCTUARY, Cape May. One of the major places in the east to observe bird migrations.

NEW MEXICO

BANDELIER NATIONAL MONUMENT, Frijoles. Unique cliff and cave dwellings.

CARLSBAD CAVERNS NATIONAL PARK, Carlsbad. Most spectacular caverns on the continent, with an endless variety of formations hollowed out of a limestone layer 1600 feet thick. *Bat Cave* has largest known concentration of bats on view.

CAPULIN MOUNTAIN NATIONAL MONUMENT, Capulin. Symmetrical cinder cone formed about 7000 years ago.

WHITE SANDS NATIONAL MONUMENT, Alamogordo. Dunes of unbelievable whiteness formed of wind-blown gypsum.

BITTER LAKE NATIONAL WILDLIFE REFUGE, Roswell. A lost river, numerous "bottomless" lakes (actually water-filled caverns). Twenty species of ducks and geese.

BLACK RANGE WILDERNESS AREA, Gila National Forest. Rugged montane and subalpine forests.

GILA WILDERNESS AREA, Gila National Forest. Forests and prairie.

PECOS DIVISION WILDERNESS AREA, Santa Fe and Carson national forests. Montane and subalpine forests.

SAN PEDRO PARKS WILD AREA, Santa Fe National Forest. Extensive plateau about 10,000 feet high, with open meadows and dense stands of spruce.

WHEELER PEAK WILD AREA, Carson National Forest. Outstanding scenery, including Mount Wheeler, highest peak in the state (13,160 feet).

WHITE MOUNTAIN WILD AREA, Lincoln National Forest. Pinyon-juniper forest.

NEW YORK

ADIRONDACK FOREST PRESERVE. More than two million acres in northern New York, covering about half of the Adirondack Mountains. Numerous lakes, rivers, and thick forests.

ALLEGANY STATE PARK, Salamanca. Largely undisturbed northern hardwoods-hemlock forest.

BUCKTHORN STATE PARK, Grand Island. Fronts on Niagara River.

CATSKILL FOREST PRESERVE. Large area in southeastern New York. Many gorges and falls; partly virgin forest.

GILBERT LAKE STATE PARK, Oneonta. Heavily wooded.

LETCHWORTH STATE PARK, Portageville. Waterfalls of the Genesee.

PALISADES INTERSTATE PARK. Continuation of the New Jersey park along the west shore of the Hudson River, extending northward to the Ramapo Mountains. Includes *Bear Mountain–Harriman State Park,* which has extensive forests undisturbed since 1910.

ROBERT TREMAN STATE PARK, Ithaca. Gorge with a dozen waterfalls.

TAUGHANNOCK FALLS STATE PARK, Ithaca. Gorge and extremely high falls.

THOUSAND ISLANDS STATE PARKS, Waterton. Fourteen separate parks in the St. Lawrence River region, some of them in relatively unspoiled condition.

WATKINS GLEN STATE PARK, Watkins Glen. Nearly twenty waterfalls; cliffs, outstanding gorge.

WHIRLPOOL STATE PARK, Niagara Falls. Bluffs adjacent to the famous whirlpool.

AUSABLE CHASM, Keeseville. Deep gorge with vertical walls, rapids, and falls.

DOME ISLAND PRESERVE, Lake George. Drumlin clothed by mature hardwood-coniferous forest.

HOWE CAVERNS, Howes Cave. Very large formations, underground lake and river.

HUYCK PRESERVE, Rensselaerville. Extensive forest.

JOHN BOYD THACHER PARK, Albany. Heavily forested escarpment of the Allegheny Plateau.

KARNER PINE BARRENS, Schenectady. Unusual scrub forest.

LAKE MINNEWASKA and LAKE MOHONK, New Paltz. Primeval forest in Shawangunk Mountains.

MIANUS RIVER GORGE, Bedford. Magnificent primeval forest of hemlock and beech on rugged terrain.

MOSS LAKE NATURE SANCTUARY, Allegany County. Kettle lake with northern bog vegetation.

SASSAFRAS BIRD SANCTUARY, Amsterdam. Outstanding primeval forest.

SUNKEN FOREST, Fire Island. Barrier-beech forest formed behind long sand dune. Predominant tree is holly, but there are also tupelo, sassafras, oak, and pitch pine.

THOMPSON POND, Pine Plains. Glacial lake; one of the best locations in the Hudson Valley for watching birds.

UNIVERSITY OF BUFFALO AREA, Buffalo. Virgin tamarack swamp.

WARD POUNDRIDGE RESERVATION, Poundridge. Ridges with partly virgin forest.

NORTH CAROLINA

CAPE HATTERAS NATIONAL SEASHORE RECREATIONAL AREA, Manteo. Barrier beach typical of the unspoiled south Atlantic seaboard. Immense concentrations of migratory waterfowl.

PEA ISLAND NATIONAL WILDLIFE REFUGE, Manteo. Narrow barrier island on the Outer Banks. One of the winter homes of the greater snow goose; only large concentration of nesting gadwalls on the Atlantic seaboard. With two nearby refuges—*Mattamuskeet* and *Swanquarter*—it provides wintering grounds for upwards of 100,000 waterfowl. Mattamuskeet has virgin stands of loblolly pine.

LINVILLE GORGE WILD AREA, Pisgah National Forest. Rugged gorge, falls.

BLACK MOUNTAIN NATURAL AREA, Pisgah National Forest. Virgin spruce and balsam.

CROATAN NATIONAL FOREST, New Bern. Large lakes; pine, swamp hardwoods.

NANTAHALA NATIONAL FOREST, Franklin. Lakes, falls.

CLIFFS STATE PARK, Goldsboro. Cliffs along Neuse River.

HANGING ROCK STATE PARK, Danbury. Geological formations.

MURROW MOUNTAIN STATE PARK, Albemarle. Heavily forested mountains.

MOUNT MITCHELL STATE PARK, Asheville. Summit of the highest mountain east of the Mississippi River. Virgin spruce forest.

UMSTEAD STATE PARK, Raleigh. Typical Piedmont area.

BLOWING ROCK, Blowing Rock. Interesting rock formations and gorge.

CHIMNEY ROCK PARK, Chimney Rock. Granite monolith over 300 feet high. Falls and rock formations.

CULLASAJA RIVER GORGE, Highlands. Three waterfalls.

GREAT DISMAL SWAMP. In northeastern North Carolina and southeastern Virginia. Great peat bog surrounding shallow Lake Drummond. Dense forests.

LOOKING GLASS ROCK, Brevard. Tremendous monolith, waterfalls.

NORTH DAKOTA

THEODORE ROOSEVELT NATIONAL MEMORIAL PARK, Medora. Part of TR's Elkhorn Ranch and surrounding badlands. Many brilliantly colored buttes and table-lands. Petrified forest. Bison and pronghorns.

UPPER SOURIS NATIONAL WILDLIFE REFUGE, Bottineau and McHenry counties. Thousands of acres of prairie. Sandhill cranes, prairie chickens, grouse, whistling swans, numerous ducks and geese.

MORTON COUNTY REFUGE, Mandan. Virgin prairie.

ROOSEVELT WILDLIFE REFUGE, McKenzie County. Virgin prairie.

OHIO

HOCKING HILLS STATE FOREST, Logan. Outstanding forest. Near by are numerous caves, falls, gorges.

MIAMISBURG MOUND STATE MEMORIAL, Miamisburg. Outstanding Indian remains.

NELSON LEDGES STATE RESERVE, Garrettsville. Unusual rock formations.

ROCK HOUSE STATE FOREST, Laurelville. Partly virgin hemlock forest.

AKRON RESERVATIONS, Akron. Heavily wooded flood-plain forest, gorges.

BLACKLICK WOODS RESERVATION, Columbus. Undisturbed forest.

CLIFTON FALLS, Yellow Springs. Falls and gorge surrounded by picturesque woodland glens.

GLEN HELEN, Yellow Springs. Wooded ravine.

LYNX PRAIRIE, Adams County. About 50 acres of unplowed tall-grass prairie.

MILL CREEK PARK, Youngstown. Patches of virgin forest; gorges.

OHIO CAVERNS, West Liberty. Striking and colorful formations.

SEVEN CAVES, Bainbridge. Impressive caverns.

OKLAHOMA

WICHITA MOUNTAINS WILDLIFE REFUGE, Comanche County. An ancient mountain range, now heavily eroded and worn down. One of the largest bison herds on the continent; largest herd of longhorn cattle.

ALABASTER CAVES STATE PARK, Woodward County. Largest known gypsum caves in the world.

OSAGE HILLS STATE PARK, Bartlesville. Rugged sandstone area with limestone outcrops. Forests, prairies.

QUARTZ MOUNTAIN STATE PARK, Altus. Rugged hills with colorful outcroppings of quartz.

ROBBERS CAVE STATE PARK, Wilburton. True prairie, pine-oak forest.

OREGON

CRATER LAKE NATIONAL PARK, Crater Lake. Originated by the collapse of a volcano, the lake is the most beautiful to occupy a crater on the continent. Surrounded by virgin montane forest. Nearby *Oregon Caves National Monument* has great variety of formations.

THREE ARCHES NATIONAL WILDLIFE REFUGE, Oceanside. Exciting shore scenery; astonishing numbers of sea birds.

HART MOUNTAIN REFUGE, Lakeview. Pronghorn and sage grouse are the main attractions.

EAGLE CAP WILDERNESS AREA, Wallowa National Forest. High peaks, glaciers; 60 lakes. Virgin subalpine and montane forests.

THREE SISTERS WILDERNESS AREA, Deschutes and Willamette national forests. One of the most overpowering wilderness areas in the west. Virgin forests; numerous peaks and glaciers.

DIAMOND PEAK WILD AREA, Deschutes and Willamette national forests. High Cascades scenery; 33 lakes surrounded by mountain meadows.

GEARHART MOUNTAIN WILD AREA, Fremont National Forest. Virgin subalpine and montane forests.

KALMIOPSIS WILD AREA, Siskiyou National Forest. Montane forest, including many rare species of trees.

MOUNT HOOD WILD AREA, Mount Hood National Forest. Magnificent volcanic scenery, virgin forest, outstanding mountain meadows.

MOUNT JEFFERSON WILD AREA, Deschutes, Mount Hood, and Willamette national forests. Glaciers, high Cascades scenery.

MOUNT WASHINGTON WILD AREA, Deschutes and Willamette national forests. Straddles summits of the Cascades. Vast fields of recent lava formations, varied alpine forests.

MOUNTAIN LAKES WILD AREA, Rogue River National Forest. Virgin subalpine and montane forests.

STRAWBERRY MOUNTAIN WILD AREA, Malheur National Forest. Virgin montane forest.

ABBOTT CREEK NATURAL AREA, Tiller. Virgin montane forest.

COQUILLE RIVER FALLS NATURAL AREA, Powers. Virgin forest.

GOODLOW MOUNTAIN NATURAL AREA, Bly. Virgin montane and juniper forests.

NESKOWIN NATURAL AREA, Neskowin. Coastal forest.

PRINGLE FALLS NATURAL AREA, Lapine. Virgin montane forest.

FREMONT NATIONAL FOREST, Lakeview. Second largest vertical fault in the world. Oregon desert.

OCHOCO NATIONAL FOREST, Prineville. Ponderosa pine forests, many beavers.

SIUSLAW NATIONAL FOREST, Corvallis. Heavily forested Pacific shore, dunes.

UMPQUA NATIONAL FOREST, Roseburg. Spectacular cataracts.

WILLAMETTE NATIONAL FOREST, Eugene. One of the most heavily timbered of the national forests. Lakes, falls, hot springs.

PACIFIC CREST TRAIL. When completed, it will follow the backbone of the Cascades and the Sierra for 2150 miles, from the Canadian to the Mexican border. Several sections—notably Cascade Crest and Oregon Skyline—are already marked. Travel is by foot, horse, or mule only.

BATTLE MOUNTAIN STATE PARK, Ukiah. Outstanding pine forest.

BATTLE ROCK STATE PARK, Port Orford. One of the most magnificent seascapes in the Pacific northwest.

BOOTH STATE PARK, Lakeview. Virgin forest of ponderosa pine.

CAPE ARAGO STATE PARK, Coos Bay. Promontory jutting half a mile into the Pacific.

CAPE LOOKOUT STATE PARK, Tillamook. Sea birds, sea lions on wave-cut coast. Virgin Sitka spruce.

CAPE SEBASTIAN STATE PARK, Gold Beach. Largely virgin area, with tremendous variety of trees and shrubs. Headlands rise steeply to more than 700 feet above the beach.

CROWN POINT STATE PARK, Portland. Superb view of Columbia gorge.

COVE-PALISADES STATE PARK, Culver. Canyons formed at the juncture of three rivers.

DEVIL'S PUNCH BOWL STATE PARK, Newport. Ocean enters and fills unusual bowl-shaped rock.

ECOLA STATE PARK, Cannon Beach. Offshore rocks that serve as rookeries for sea lions and birds.

HUMBUG MOUNTAIN STATE PARK, Port Orford. Largely virgin coast forest, with many unusual trees.

LAVA RIVER CAVES STATE PARK, Bend. Caves formed by lava from *Newberry Crater,* in Deschutes National Forest. One lava tunnel is nearly a mile long and 50 feet wide. A wall of cinder and pumice divides the crater itself into two parts, each of which contains a lake.

NEPTUNE STATE PARK, Yachats. Spectacular wave-cut shore.

PAINTED HILLS STATE PARK, Mitchell. Colorful domes and ridges.

OSWALD WEST STATE PARK, Manzanita. Perpendicular sea cliffs.

OTTER CREST STATE PARK, Otter Rock. Bold rock with view of eroded shore, occupied by sea lions and shore birds.

PILOT BUTTE STATE PARK, Bend. Cinder cone rises to 500 feet.

ROGUE RIVER FOREST, Ashland. The Loop Drive travels the crest of the Siskiyou.

SHORE ACRES STATE PARK, North Bend. Spectacular Pacific shore views.

SILVER FALLS STATE PARK, Salem. Fourteen waterfalls up to 180 feet high.

UKIAH-DALE FOREST WAYSIDE, Pendleton. Heavily forested canyon of the North Fork of the John Day River.

UMPQUA LIGHTHOUSE STATE PARK, Winchester Bay. Sand dunes up to 500 feet high.

LAVA FIELDS, McKenzie. Largest lava field of recent origin in the mainland United States.

MALHEUR CAVE, Burns. Lava cone with large underground lake.

SEA LION CAVES, Florence. Underground cavern cut by waves and inhabited by hundreds of sea lions.

PENNSYLVANIA

ALLEGHENY NATIONAL FOREST, Warren. Virgin forests.

ALAN SEEGER STATE FOREST, State College. Outstanding hemlock-pine-hardwoods forest.

COOK FOREST STATE PARK, Clarion, Forest, and Jefferson counties. Largest stand of virgin timber in the state.

GEORGE W. CHILDS STATE FOREST, Dingmans Ferry. Forest, waterfalls.

HEMLOCK STATE FOREST, New Germantown. Beautiful forest, with stand of virgin hemlock.

JOYCE KILMER STATE FOREST and MCCONNEL NARROWS STATE FOREST, Mifflinburg. Nearly virgin hardwoods.

LEONARD HARRISON STATE FOREST, Wellsboro. Gorge 1000 feet deep.

MOUNT LOGAN STATE FOREST, Lock Haven. Nearly virgin forest.

PRESQUE ISLE STATE PARK, Erie. Forest on Lake Erie shore.

SNYDER–MIDDLESWORTH STATE FOREST, Snyder County. Partly virgin forest.

WORLD'S END STATE FOREST, Forksville. Precipitous mountains.

BEAR MEADOWS NATURAL MONUMENT, Boalsburg. Balsam bog.

BUSHKILL FALLS, Bushkill. Gorge and cascades.

CRANBERRY BOG PRESERVE, Tannersville. Typical northern bog.

DELAWARE WATER GAP, Stroudsburg. Imposing break in the Kittatinny ridge, one of the best-known water gaps in the east.

HAWK MOUNTAIN SANCTUARY, Drehersville. Immense concentrations of hawks and eagles during fall migration.

PENN'S CAVE, Centre Hall. Fascinating underground lake.

RICKETTS GLEN, Luzerne County. Twenty-eight waterfalls.

WOODBOURNE FOREST, Dimock. Remnant of a northern hardwoods-hemlock forest, about 200 acres of it in primeval condition.

RHODE ISLAND

BURLINGAME STATE PARK, Charlestown. Extensive second-growth woods, ponds.

LINCOLN WOODS STATE PARK, Lincoln. Heavily forested.

GREAT SWAMP, West Kingston. Nearly eight square miles of diverse habitat: quaking bogs, cedar bogs, sandy islands, dense forests.

SOUTH CAROLINA

CAPE ROMAIN NATIONAL WILDLIFE REFUGE, McClellanville. One of the outstanding wildlife refuges in the east. Salt marshes, sandy beaches, sea islands. Large wintering populations of shore birds and waterfowl, in addition to many unusual land birds.

SUMTER NATIONAL FOREST, Columbia. Piedmont and Blue Ridge Mountains. Spectacular displays of flowering shrubs.

CHERAW STATE PARK, Cheraw. Sand hills covered with pine.

EDISTO STATE PARK, Edisto Island. Sandy beach, semitropical plants.

HUNTING ISLAND STATE PARK, Beaufort. Nearly virgin forest.

PARIS MOUNTAIN STATE PARK, Greenville. Rugged mountains, heavily forested.

SOUTH DAKOTA

BADLANDS NATIONAL MONUMENT, Interior. Sedimentary rocks have been eroded into one of the bleakest landscapes on the continent. The whole area serves as an outdoor textbook on erosion.

WIND CAVE NATIONAL MONUMENT, Hot Springs. The limestone caverns have a small opening through which a draft of air blows, causing a whistling sound. The main attractions are the bison herds and prairie dog towns.

BLACK HILLS NATIONAL FOREST, Deadwood. Spectacular canyons and falls; caves. Virgin montane zone forest. Harney Peak (7242 feet) is the highest point east of the Rockies. *The Needles,* near Custer, is a granite spire, the overlying rocks having been removed by erosion. A *Petrified Forest* is near Piedmont.

CUSTER STATE PARK, Hermosa. Scenic section of the Black Hills. Virgin coniferous forest. Large bison herd, Rocky Mountain sheep and goats.

TENNESSEE

GREAT SMOKY MOUNTAINS NATIONAL PARK, Gatlinburg. Highest range east of the Black Hills. Great diversity of plants, more tree species than in all of western Europe. Many virgin forests. *Blue Ridge Parkway,* between Great Smoky and Shenandoah national parks, stretches 469 miles through the heart of the Appalachians.

CHEROKEE NATIONAL FOREST, Cleveland. Rugged mountains cut by gorges. *Copper Basin* at Ducktown is a man-created desert, comparable to the western badlands. Deforestation and fumes from smelters destroyed the protective cover on the land, leading to severe erosion.

REELFOOT NATIONAL WILDLIFE REFUGE, Tiptonville. Lake formed by an earthquake 150 years ago. Submerged forest, swamp.

CEDARS OF LEBANON STATE PARK, Lebanon. Large stands of red cedar. Sinks and caverns.

FALL CREEK FALLS STATE PARK, Pikeville. Three large waterfalls; stands of hemlock.

PICKETT STATE PARK, Jamestown. Caves and unusual rock formations.

ROCK CITY, Chattanooga. Rock mountain, canyons.

TUCKALEECHEE CAVERNS, Townsend. Recently discovered cave with outstanding formations.

TEXAS

BIG BEND NATIONAL PARK, Big Bend. Desert and mountain scenery along a sweeping bend of the Rio Grande River. One of the wildest areas in mainland

United States, parts of which are still unexplored. Many life zones, ranging from desert cacti to Douglas fir in the mountains. Three large canyons, volcanic rock formations.

ARANSAS NATIONAL WILDLIFE REFUGE, Austwell. Wintering ground of the rare whooping crane, which can be observed from a high tower. One of the nation's leading localities for bird watching.

SANTA ANA NATIONAL WILDLIFE REFUGE, Hidalgo County. Semitropical flora, partly virgin.

ANGELINA NATIONAL FOREST and SABINE NATIONAL FOREST, Lufkin. Sand hills with longleaf pine; hardwood forest along river bottoms. Many overflow lakes.

SAM HOUSTON NATIONAL FOREST, Huntsville. Part of the "Big Thicket" area of Texas.

BASTROP STATE PARK, Bastrop. Unusual pine forest, isolated in the western part of the state.

BIG SPRING STATE PARK, Big Spring. High mesa.

LONGHORN CAVERN STATE PARK, Burnet. One of the largest caves in the world.

MACKENZIE STATE PARK, Lubbock. Prairie-dog towns.

PALMETTO STATE PARK, Gonzales. Palmetto swamps, springs.

PALO DURO CANYON STATE PARK, Canyon. Outstanding eroded rocks.

UTAH

BRYCE CANYON NATIONAL PARK, Bryce Canyon. Highly colored pinnacles, walls, turrets, and spires make this one of the unique eroded areas in the world. All the formations were carved out of an uplifted plateau. Brilliant coloring comes from iron and manganese compounds in the rocks. Virgin pinyon-juniper forest.

ZION NATIONAL PARK, Springdale. Another outstanding landscape created by erosion. *Cedar Breaks National Monument,* near by, is a huge natural amphitheater eroded into the cliffs.

ARCHES NATIONAL MONUMENT, Moab. Huge arches, pinnacles, pedestals. The holes in the rocks were not gouged out by streams, as at many other localities, but by trickling ground water.

CAPITOL REEF NATIONAL MONUMENT, Torrey. Twenty-mile uplift of sandstone cliffs dissected by narrow gorges. Layers of contorted rocks demonstrate how strata were buckled and tilted.

DINOSAUR NATIONAL MONUMENT, Vernal. Awesome canyons of the Green and Yampa rivers. Dinosaur remains and other large fossils are common. New museum has one wall opening directly into a quarry.

NATURAL BRIDGES NATIONAL MONUMENT, Blanding. Three huge bridges, hewn from sandstone by water. Sipapu, the largest, is 222 feet high and has a 268-foot span.

RAINBOW BRIDGE NATIONAL MONUMENT, Navajo Mountain Trading Post. The world's greatest known natural bridge, an arch of pink sandstone that rises 309 feet above the bottom of a gorge. Accessible only on horseback.

BEAR RIVER MIGRATORY BIRD REFUGE, Brigham. One of the most impressive wildlife areas in the west. Immense autumn concentrations of birds, many nesters in the spring.

HIGH UINTAS WILDERNESS AREA, Ashley and Wasatch national forests. Wild region in the Uinta Range, highest in Utah. Numerous gorges. More than 1000 lakes in the vicinity.

CACHE NATIONAL FOREST, Logan. Rugged mountains; canyons, cave.

DIXIE NATIONAL FOREST, Cedar City. Spectacular colored cliffs, numerous lakes.

FISHLAKE NATIONAL FOREST, Richfield. Exceptional lake scenery, petrified forests.

MANTI NATIONAL FOREST, Ephraim. Alpine meadows, colorful canyons, unusual rock formations.

WASATCH NATIONAL FOREST, Salt Lake City. Rugged mountain terrain, magnificent lakes. At American Fork is *Timpanogas Cave National Monument,* where an outstanding cave lies in the shadow of a 12,000-foot peak.

GOBLIN VALLEY, Fruita. Fantastic rock formations.

LOGAN CANYON, Logan. Beautiful hardwood forest, ancient junipers.

MONUMENT VALLEY, Gouldings. Towering sandstone buttes and spires, some 1000 feet high.

MOUNT NEBO RECREATIONAL AREA, Nephi. Eroded rocks, large elk herd.

VERMONT

GREEN MOUNTAIN NATIONAL FOREST, Rutland. Rugged granite mountains, heavily wooded, their entire length traversed by the *Long Trail.*

CAMEL'S HUMP STATE FOREST, North Duxbury. Unusual granite formations on most impressive peak in the state.

MOUNT MANSFIELD STATE FOREST, Stowe. The mountain (4393 feet) is highest in the state. *Smuggler's Notch* is a scenic gorge.

BATTELL PARK, Middlebury. Virgin spruce.

OWL'S HEAD, Newport. Gorges and ravines.

VIRGINIA

SHENANDOAH NATIONAL PARK, Luray. Most spectacular part of the Blue Ridge Mountains. Near the cave belt. Brilliant wildflower displays. *Skyline Drive* runs the length of the park.

GEORGE WASHINGTON NATIONAL FOREST, Harrisonburg. Rugged country of the Blue Ridge, Shenandoah, and Allegheny ranges. Limestone caverns. *Little Laurel Run Natural Area* is a nearly virgin oak-chestnut forest.

JEFFERSON NATIONAL FOREST, Roanoke. In the Blue Ridge Mountains; contains highest point in the state, Mount Rogers (5719 feet).

CHINCOTEAGUE NATIONAL WILDLIFE REFUGE, Assateague Island. Long barrier island, with marshes and dunes. Numerous shore birds and waterfowl.

BREAKS INTERSTATE PARK, Breaks. Straddles the Kentucky border; one of the most magnificent gorges in the east.

DOUTHAT STATE PARK, Clifton Forge. Outstanding example of Appalachian scenery.

FAIRY STONE STATE PARK, Bassett. Partly virgin hardwood forest, curious rock formations.

SEASHORE STATE PARK, Cape Henry. Sand dunes, cypress, live oak.

BRISTOL CAVERNS, Bristol. Interesting formations.

ENDLESS CAVERNS, New Market. Vividly colored, with fantastic formations.

GRAND CAVERNS, Grottoes. A notable cavern.

GREAT DISMAL SWAMP, Wallaceton. Extensive peat bog and shallow lake.

LURAY CAVERNS, Luray. One of the world's most beautiful caverns.

NATURAL BRIDGE, Natural Bridge. Very large limestone arch, 215 feet high.

NATURAL CHIMNEYS, Mount Solon. High rock towers pierced by natural tunnels.

NATURAL TUNNEL, Gate City. Wide tunnel 900 feet long leads to natural amphitheater with colorful walls.

SHENANDOAH CAVERNS, New Market. A major Great Valley cave.

SKYLINE CAVERNS, Front Royal. Exceptionally fine cavern with rare formations, underground streams and cascades.

WASHINGTON

MOUNT RAINIER NATIONAL PARK, Longmire. Regarded by many as the most beautiful mountain on the continent. It wears a white cap of perpetual snow; its radiating glacier system is the most extensive upon a single mountain in the mainland United States. The forests and wildflowers are perhaps unequaled anywhere.

OLYMPIC NATIONAL PARK, Port Angeles. Everything in one concentrated package: mountain wilderness, glaciers, rain forest, alpine wildflowers, wave-sculptured beaches, herds of rare Roosevelt elk.

GLACIER PEAK WILDERNESS AREA, Mount Baker and Wenatchee national forests. Nearly 35 mountains above 8000 feet; many glaciers and lakes.

NORTH CASCADE WILDERNESS AREA, Chelan and Mount Baker national forests. Tremendous slice of northern Cascades with coast, montane, and subalpine forests. Most of the big mammals of the continent are represented.

GOAT ROCKS WILD AREA, Gifford Pinchot and Snoqualmie national forests. Precipitous peaks, glaciers, large lakes; profusion of alpine flowers.

MOUNT ADAMS WILD AREA, Gifford Pinchot National Forest. Spectacular scenery, largely above timberline.

LONG CREEK NATURAL AREA and LAKE 22 NATURAL AREA, Granite Falls. Two small patches of virgin timber.

NORTH FORK NOOKSACK NATURAL AREA, Glacier. Virgin coast forest.

WIND RIVER NATURAL AREA, Carson. Virgin forest.

CHELAN NATIONAL FOREST, Okanogan. Lake Chelan between precipitous ranges, snow peaks.

SNOQUALMIE NATIONAL FOREST, Seattle. Rock pillars of *The Dalles,* extensive Douglas fir forests, falls.

WENATCHEE NATIONAL FOREST, Wenatchee. Alpine meadows, lakes.

WILLAPA NATIONAL WILDLIFE REFUGE, Pacific. Virgin forest, shore birds.

DECEPTION PASS STATE PARK, Mount Vernon. Cliffs, beaches, and forest.

LARRABEE STATE PARK, Bellingham. Views of Puget Sound and San Juan Islands. Mostly virgin coastal forest.

LEWIS AND CLARK STATE PARK, Toledo. Towering stands of virgin timber.

MORAN STATE PARK, Bellingham. Primeval Douglas fir forest.

GINKGO PETRIFIED FOREST, Ellensburg. Greatest number of petrified species found anywhere.

GRAND COULEE, Grand Coulee. A dry canyon once occupied by the Columbia River. It is several miles wide, with steep walls 1000 feet high. Dry falls once used by the river.

WEST VIRGINIA

MONONGAHELA NATIONAL FOREST, Elkins. Southern Appalachian and Allegheny mountains, canyons, and falls. Spectacular rock formations, unexplored limestone caves.

BLACKWATER FALLS STATE PARK, Davis. Scenic gorge and falls.

CACAPON STATE PARK, Berkeley Springs. Extensive forests along ridges of Cacapon Mountains.

CATHEDRAL STATE PARK, Preston County. Virgin hemlock-hardwoods forest.

GRANDVIEW STATE PARK, Beckley. View of horseshoe bend of the New River.

PINNACLE ROCK STATE PARK, Bluefield. Unusual rock formations.

CRANESVILLE SWAMP, Preston County. Outstanding northern bog.

LOST RIVER, Wardensville. Places where the river vanishes and then reappears are accessible.

PETERSBURG GAP, Petersburg. Picturesque water gap, with unusual cliffs.

SENECA ROCKS, Mouth of Seneca. Intricately eroded rock mass nearly 1000 feet high.

SMOKE HOLE, Upper Tract. Steep, wooded gorge of the Potomac, with spectacular rock formations.

VALLEY FALLS, Fairmont. Falls and rapids.

WISCONSIN

CHEQUAMEGON NATIONAL FOREST, Park Falls. Hundreds of lakes, extensive pine-spruce-fir forests. *Moquah Natural Area* is a remnant.

NICOLET NATIONAL FOREST, Rhinelander. Cedar-spruce swamp forests.

BLACK RIVER STATE FOREST, Black River Falls. Bed of glacial lake.

COPPER FALLS STATE PARK, Ashland. Largely virgin forest; river gorge and falls.

DEVIL'S LAKE STATE PARK, Baraboo. Beautiful spring-fed lake enclosed by cliffs. Indian mounds.

FLAMBEAU RIVER STATE PARK, Winter. Partly virgin forest.

INTERSTATE STATE PARK, St. Croix Falls. Scenic gorge, rock formations.

KETTLE MORAINE STATE FOREST AND PARK, West Bend. One of the best places to see numerous glacial formations, including kettle lakes and moraines.

LIZARD MOUND STATE PARK, West Bend. Indian mounds in animal shapes.

NORTHERN HIGHLAND STATE FOREST, Vilas and Iron counties. Tremendous wilderness area.

PATTISON STATE PARK, Superior. Highest falls in the state.

PERROT STATE PARK, Trempealeau. Bluffs.

TERRY ANDRAE STATE PARK, Sheboygan. Lake Michigan dunes.

WYALUSING STATE PARK, Prairie du Chien. Partly virgin oak-hickory forest and tall-grass prairie. Junction of Wisconsin and Mississippi rivers. High ridge with important Indian mounds.

APOSTLE ISLANDS, Bayfield. Twenty-two rugged islands.

CAVE OF THE MOUNDS, Blue Mounds. Brilliantly colored formations.

DELLS, Wisconsin Dells. Sandstone carved into fantastic shapes by the Wisconsin River.

WYOMING

GRAND TETON NATIONAL PARK, Moose. Towering Teton Range, magnificent example of fault-block formation. *National Elk Refuge* at Jackson Hole contains about 10,000 elk, plus moose, bison, trumpeter swans, sage grouse, sandhill cranes.

YELLOWSTONE NATIONAL PARK, Yellowstone. About 3000 geysers, making this the greatest geyser area in the world. Spectacular falls and canyon of the Yellowstone River. Outstanding display of petrified trees. Example of alterations caused in the face of the land by recent earthquake. Elk, bison, grizzly, pronghorn, and bighorn.

DEVILS TOWER NATIONAL MONUMENT, Devils Tower Junction. Remains of a volcanic intrusion into overlying rocks, which are now eroded away. Falcons nest at the top of the Tower, prairie dogs have a town at the base.

BRIDGER WILDERNESS AREA, Bridger National Forest. Deep gorges, falls. Summit of Gannett Peak (13,785 feet), highest in state.

GLACIER WILDERNESS AREA, Shoshone National Forest. Rugged mountain country, innumerable alpine lakes, some of the largest glaciers in mainland United States.

NORTH ABSAROKA, SOUTH ABSAROKA, and STRATIFIED WILDERNESS AREAS, Shoshone National Forest. Glaciers, natural bridges, standing petrified trees.

TETON WILDERNESS AREA, Teton National Forest. High plateaus, wide valleys, alpine meadows.

CLOUD PEAK WILD AREA, Bighorn National Forest. Rugged mountain country, large mammals, subalpine forest.

POPO AGIE WILD AREA, Shoshone National Forest. Extremely rough terrain along Continental Divide; subalpine and montane forests.

HOT SPRINGS STATE PARK, Thermopolis. Four large springs and hundreds of lesser ones. Herds of elk and bison.

CANADA

ALBERTA

BANFF and JASPER NATIONAL PARKS, Banff. Breathtaking glacial scenery; great forests; more than 500 kinds of wildflowers; large mammals. Great diversity of landscapes, from the foothills of the Rockies to the Continental Divide. Examples of several mountain-building processes. The *Banff-Jasper Highway* follows the Bow River Valley from Lake Louise to the river's source, along a route bordered by waterfalls, lakes, and glaciers. Road passes within a few hundred yards of *Athabasca Glacier*.

ELK ISLAND NATIONAL PARK, Lamont. Bison, elk; prairie vegetation.

WOOD BUFFALO NATIONAL PARK, Fort Vermilion. Home of woodland bison, larger and darker than the plains bison. Nesting ground of whooping crane. Immense wilderness of muskegs, dark forests, torrential streams.

BRITISH COLUMBIA

GLACIER NATIONAL PARK, Field. One of Canada's leading parks, a world of snow and alpine flowers. Selkirk peaks, rich woods, falls, glaciers. Nearby *Yoho National Park* is best described by its Indian name, which means "It is wonderful."

KOOTENAY NATIONAL PARK, Radium Hot Springs. Consists of the land around the Banff-Windermere Highway, one of the outstanding scenic roads on the continent. Many notable features are close to the road: a gorge, hot springs, a natural bridge, two sheer rock towers, and several glaciers.

MOUNT REVELSTOKE NATIONAL PARK, Revelstoke. A great plateau on the western slope of the Selkirk Mountains, offering wide views of glacial features. Forests range from coastal to subalpine.

GARIBALDI PROVINCIAL PARK, Vancouver. Coast range; volcanic mountains, half a dozen glaciers.

HAMBER PROVINCIAL PARK, Mount Robson. Peaks of Selkirks and Rockies, virgin forests from coastal to subalpine; glaciers, large mammals.

KOKANEE GLACIER PROVINCIAL PARK, Kootenay Lake. Nearly virgin subalpine forest.

MANITOBA

RIDING MOUNTAIN NATIONAL PARK, Wasagaming. Summit of an escarpment, luxuriantly forested; glacial lakes.

WHITESHELL FOREST RESERVE, Winnipeg. More than 200 lakes; rivers wind through steep volcanic cliffs covered with dense forest.

NEW BRUNSWICK

FUNDY NATIONAL PARK, Moncton. Sanctuary for small furbearers: mink, otter, weasels.

THE BORE, Moncton. Tremendous tides of Bay of Fundy.

NOVA SCOTIA

CAPE BRETON HIGHLANDS NATIONAL PARK, Ingonish Beach. Spans the island from the Atlantic Ocean to the Gulf of St. Lawrence, with rugged mountains between. Includes rocky headlands and beaches, mountains and valleys. The highlands are covered with dense coniferous forest, broken by muskegs.

WAVERLY GAME SANCTUARY, Halifax. Many beautiful lakes.

ONTARIO

GEORGIAN BAY ISLANDS NATIONAL PARK, Tobermory. Unusual erosion of rocks, including 300 foot cliffs and two flowerpot-like rock columns. Many caves.

POINT PELEE NATIONAL PARK, Essex County. An outstanding place to observe birds on migration. Sand dunes, marshes, forests of southern hardwoods.

ST. LAWRENCE ISLANDS NATIONAL PARK, Kingston. Thirteen of the Thousand Islands (actually there are 1700 of them). Huge cliffs topped by big oaks and maples.

ALGONQUIN PROVINCIAL PARK, Pembroke. Immense area of lakes, islands, and forests. Large mammals. To the west are the extensive *Muskoka Lakes*.

KAKABEKA FALLS PROVINCIAL PARK, Fort William. Falls and gorges.

NIPIGON PROVINCIAL FOREST, Port Arthur. Wilderness lakes.

PRESQU'ILE PROVINCIAL PARK, Brighton. Lake Ontario shore.

QUETICO PROVINCIAL PARK, Rainy River. Adjoins Minnesota's Superior Wilderness Area. Meshwork of lakes and rivers through unspoiled forest.

RONDEAU PROVINCIAL PARK, Chatham. Lake Erie peninsula, with some virgin hardwoods.

TEMAGAMI PROVINCIAL FOREST, North Bay. Extensive pine forests, lakes.

CHAPLEAU CROWN GAME PRESERVE, Chapleau. Maze of lakes, virgin forests.

ESKER LAKES PARK, Kirkland Lake. Water wilderness.

PRINCE EDWARD ISLAND

PRINCE EDWARD ISLAND NATIONAL PARK, New London. Strip along the Gulf of St. Lawrence, with magnificent beach and eroded sandstone headlands.

QUEBEC

BONAVENTURE ISLAND–PERCÉ ROCK, Gaspé. One of the continent's outstanding bird sanctuaries. Gannets, guillemots, murres, cormorants, puffins, and other species can be seen.

LAURENTIDES PROVINCIAL PARK, Quebec. Unspoiled wilderness in the Laurentian Mountains, the oldest range on the continent, now eroded down to stumps. More than 1500 lakes.

GASPESIAN PARK, Gaspé. Includes a large part of the mountainous areas of the Gaspé Peninsula. Virgin forests.

MONTMORENCY FALLS, QUEBEC. Higher than Niagara.

SASKATCHEWAN

PRINCE ALBERT NATIONAL PARK, Waskesiu. Gateway to the north country. Primeval forests, woodland caribou, bison. Innumerable waterways.

CYPRESS HILLS PROVINCIAL PARK, Cypress Hills. Abundant mammals on the highlands of the province. Virgin prairies.

Readings

GENERAL BOOKS

The American Land by William R. Van Dersal. New York: Oxford University Press, 1943

America's Wonderlands. Washington: National Geographic Society, 1959

Autumn Across America by Edwin Way Teale. New York: Dodd, Mead & Company, 1956

The Continent We Live On by Ivan T. Sanderson. New York: Random House, 1961

The Eyes of Discovery by John Bakeless. Philadelphia: Lippincott, 1950

The Forest and the Sea by Marston Bates. New York: Random House, 1960

Journey into Summer by Edwin Way Teale. New York: Dodd, Mead & Company, 1960

The National Forests by Arthur H. Carhart. New York: Alfred A. Knopf, 1959

The National Parks by Freeman Tilden. New York: Alfred A. Knopf, 1951

North with the Spring by Edwin Way Teale. New York: Dodd, Mead & Company, 1951

Pelican in the Wilderness by F. Fraser Darling. New York: Random House, 1956

Reading the Landscape by May T. Watts. New York: Macmillan, 1957

Wild America by Roger Tory Peterson and James Fisher. Boston: Houghton Mifflin Company, 1955

SPECIFIC AREAS

Arctic Wild by Lois Crisler. New York: Harper & Brothers, 1958 (Alaska)

The Bay by Gilbert C. Klingel. New York: Dodd, Mead & Company, 1951 (Chesapeake Bay)

The Changing Face of New England by Betty F. Thomson. New York: Macmillan, 1958

Crater Lake by Howel Williams. Berkeley: University of California Press, 1941

Estes Park, Resort in the Rockies by Edwin J. Foscue and Louis O. Quam. Dallas: Southern Methodist University Press, 1949

The Everglades by Marjory Stonemar Douglas. New York: Rinehart & Company, 1947

Exploring Death Valley by Ruth Kirk. Stanford: Stanford University Press, 1956

Grand Canyon by Joseph Wood Krutch. New York: William Sloane, 1958

The Great Salt Lake by Dale L. Morgan. Indianapolis: Bobbs-Merrill Company, 1947

Inagua by Gilbert C. Klingel. New York: Dodd, Mead & Company, 1940 (Bahamas)

The Incomparable Valley by François E. Matthes. Berkeley: University of California Press, 1956 (Yosemite)

Land of the Snowshoe Hare by Virginia Eifert. New York: Dodd, Mead & Company, 1960 (north woods)

Mangrove Coast by Karl A. Bickel. New York: Coward-McCann, 1942 (Florida)

A Natural History of New York City by John Kieran. Boston: Houghton Mifflin Company, 1959

River World by Virginia Eifert. New York: Dodd, Mead & Company, 1959 (the Mississippi)

Sequoia National Park by François E. Matthes. Berkeley: University of California Press, 1956

Stars Upstream by Leonard Hall. Chicago: University of Chicago Press, 1959 (Ozarks)

That Vanishing Eden by Thomas Barbour. Boston: Little, Brown & Company, 1944 (Florida)

A Year in Paradise by Floyd Schmoe. New York: Harper & Brothers, 1959 (Pacific Northwest)

Yellowstone National Park by H. M. Chittenden. Stanford: Stanford University Press, 1949

WILDLIFE

American Mammals by William J. Hamilton. New York: McGraw-Hill, 1939

Amphibians and Reptiles of Western North America by Robert C. Stebbins. New York: McGraw-Hill, 1954

The Book of Bird Life by Arthur A. Allen. Princeton: D. Van Nostrand, 1961

Complete Field Guide to American Wildlife by Henry H. Collins. New York: Harper & Brothers, 1959

Ecological Animal Geography by W. C. Allee and Karl P. Schmidt. New York: John Wiley & Sons, 1951

Familiar Animals of America by Will Barker. New York: Harper & Brothers, 1956

A Field Guide to the Birds by Roger Tory Peterson. Boston: Houghton Mifflin Company, 1947

A Field Guide to Western Birds by Roger Tory Peterson. Boston: Houghton Mifflin Company, 1961

A Guide to Bird Finding East of the Mississippi by O. Sewall Pettingill, Jr. New York: Oxford University Press, 1951

A Guide to Bird Finding West of the Mississippi by O. Sewall Pettingill, Jr. New York: Oxford University Press, 1953

An Introduction to Ornithology by George J. Wallace. New York: Macmillan, 1955

Land Birds of America by Robert C. Murphy and Dean Amadon. New York: McGraw-Hill, 1953

Mammals of North America by Victor H. Cahalane. New York: Macmillan, 1947

The Mammal Guide by R. S. Palmer. New York: Doubleday & Company, 1954

Of Men and Marshes by Paul L. Errington. New York: Macmillan, 1957

A Natural History of American Birds by Edward H. Forbush and John B. May. Boston: Houghton Mifflin Company, 1939

The Natural History of Mammals by François Bourlière. New York: Alfred A. Knopf, 1954

The Natural History of North American Amphibians and Reptiles by James A. Oliver. Princeton: D. Van Nostrand Company, 1955

The North American Buffalo by Frank G. Roe. Toronto: University of Toronto Press, 1951

Our Wildlife Legacy by Durwood Allen. New York: Funk & Wagnalls Company, 1962

Paths Across the Earth by Lorus J. Milne and Margery J. Milne. New York: Harper & Brothers, 1958

Principles of Animal Ecology by W. C. Allee et al. Philadelphia: W. B. Saunders Company, 1949

The Web of Life by John H. Storer. New York: Devin-Adair, 1956

Wildlife in America by Peter Matthiessen. New York: Viking, 1959

THE SHAPING OF THE CONTINENT

Adventure Is Underground by William R. Halliday. New York: Harper & Brothers, 1959

Down to Earth by Carey Croneis and William C. Krumbein. Chicago: University of Chicago Press, 1936

The Earth by Arthur Beiser and the editors of Life. New York: Time, Inc., 1962

The Earth We Live On by Ruth Moore. New York: Alfred A. Knopf, 1956

The Evolution of North America by Philip B. King. Princeton: Princeton University Press, 1959

The Face of the Earth by G. H. Dury. London: Penguin Books, 1959

Field Book of Common Rocks and Minerals by Frederick B. Loomis. New York: G. P. Putnam's Sons, 1948

Geology of the Great Lakes by Jack L. Hough. Urbana: University of Illinois Press, 1958

Historical Geology by Carl O. Dunbar. New York: John Wiley & Sons, 1960

Introduction to Physical Geology by Chester R. Longwell and Richard F. Flint. New York: John Wiley & Sons, 1962

Landscapes of Alaska by Howel Williams. Berkeley: University of California Press, 1958

Larousse Encyclopedia of the Earth. New York: Prometheus Press, 1961

Living Earth by Peter Farb. New York: Harper & Brothers, 1959

The Physiographic Provinces of North America by Wallace W. Atwood. Boston: Ginn & Company, 1940

Physiography of Eastern United States by Nevin M. Fenneman. New York: McGraw-Hill, 1938

Physiography of Western United States by Nevin M. Fenneman. New York: McGraw-Hill, 1931

The Rock Hunter's Range Guide by Jay Ellis Ransom. New York: Harper & Brothers, 1962

This Sculptured Earth by John H. Shimer. New York: Columbia University Press, 1959

The World of Ice by James L. Dyson. New York: Alfred Knopf, 1962.

THE WATERY RIM

American Seashells by R. Tucker Abbott. Princeton: D. Van Nostrand Company, 1954

Between Pacific Tides by Edward F. Ricketts and Jack Calvin. Stanford: Stanford University Press, 1962

Ebb and Flow by Albert Defant. Ann Arbor: University of Michigan Press, 1958

The Edge of the Sea by Rachel Carson. Boston: Houghton Mifflin Company, 1955

Field Book of Seashore Life by Roy W. Miner. New York: G. P. Putnam's Sons, 1950

A Field Guide to the Shells by Percy A. Morris. Boston: Houghton Mifflin Company, 1951

The Living Tide by N. J. Berrill. New York: Dodd, Mead & Company, 1951

Molluscs by J. E. Morton. London: Hutchinson & Company, 1958

The Sea Shore by C. M. Yonge. London: Collins, 1949

THE INLAND WATERS

Rivers of America Series, Rinehart & Company. See the major rivers of North America for titles in print.

Field Book of Ponds and Streams by Ann H. Morgan. New York: G. P. Putnam's Sons, 1930

Life in Lakes and Rivers by T. T. Macan and E. B. Worthington. London: Collins, 1951

Streams, Lakes, Ponds by Robert E. Coker. Chapel Hill: University of North Carolina Press, 1954

THE MOUNTAINS

The Berkshires edited by Roderick Peattie. New York: The Vanguard Press, 1948

The Black Hills edited by Roderick Peattie. New York: The Vanguard Press, 1952

The Friendly Mountains edited by Roderick Peattie. New York: The Vanguard Press, 1942 (Green Mountains, White Mountains, Adirondacks)

The Great Smokies and the Blue Ridge edited by Roderick Peattie. New York: The Vanguard Press, 1943

The Great Smoky Mountains by Laura Thornborough. Knoxville: University of Tennessee Press, 1956

Our Greatest Mountain by F. W. Schmoe. New York: G. P. Putnam's Sons, 1925 (Rainier)

The Mountains by Lorus J. Milne and Margery J. Milne and the editors of Life. New York: Time, Inc., 1962

The Pacific Coast Ranges edited by Roderick Peattie. New York: The Vanguard Press, 1946

The Rocky Mountains by Wallace W. Atwood. New York: The 'Vanguard Press, 1945

The Tetons by Fritiof Fryxell. Berkeley: University of California Press, 1938

THE FORESTS

American Wildflowers by Harold N. Moldenke. New York: D. Van Nostrand Company, 1949

Deciduous Forests of Eastern North America by E. Lucy Braun. Philadelphia: Blakiston, 1950

The Forest by Peter Farb and the editors of Life. New York: Time, Inc., 1961

The Great Forest by Richard G. Lillard. New York: Alfred A. Knopf, 1947

Illustrated Guide to Trees and Shrubs by Arthur H. Graves. New York: Harper & Brothers, 1956

An Illustrated Manual of Pacific Coast Trees by Harold E. McMinn and Evelyn Maino. Berkeley: University of California Press, 1956

The Living Forest by Jack McCormick. New York: Harper & Brothers, 1959

Native Trees of Canada. Ottawa: Canadian Department of Northern Affairs and Natural Resources, 1956

A Natural History of Trees by Donald Culross Peattie. Boston: Houghton Mifflin Company, 1950

A Natural History of Western Trees by Donald Culross Peattie. Boston: Houghton Mifflin Company, 1953

The Plant Community by Herbert C. Hanson and Ethan D. Churchill. New York: Reinhold Publishing Company, 1961

Redwoods of Coast and Sierra by James C. Shirley. Berkeley: University of California Press, 1947

The Study of Plant Communities by Henry J. Oosting. San Francisco: W. H. Freeman & Company, 1956

Trees of Eastern and Central United States and Canada by William M. Harlow. New York: Dover Publications, 1957

THE DRYLANDS

Adventures with a Texas Naturalist by Roy Bedichek. Austin: University of Texas Press, 1961

The California Deserts by Edmund C. Jaeger. Stanford: Stanford University Press, 1955

The Desert by A. Starker Leopold and the editors of Life. New York: Time, Inc., 1961

The Desert Year by Joseph Wood Krutch. New York: William Sloane, 1952

The Giant Cactus Forest and Its World by Paul G. Howes. New York: Duell, Sloan & Pearce, 1954

The Great Plains by Walter P. Webb. Boston: Ginn & Company, 1931

The Natural History of the Southwest edited by William A. Burns. New York: Franklin Watts, Inc., 1960

The North American Deserts by Edmund C. Jaeger. Stanford: Stanford University Press, 1957

North American Prairie by J. E. Weaver. Lincoln: Johnsen Publishing Company, 1954

Trees and Shrubs of the Southwestern Deserts. University of Arizona Press, 1954

Index